CLASS, POWER AND IDEOLOGY IN GHANA: THE RAILWAYMEN OF SEKONDI

AFRICAN STUDIES SERIES

The African Studies Series is a collection of monographs and general studies which reflect the interdisciplinary interests of the African Studies Centre at Cambridge. Volumes to date have combined historical, anthropological, economic, political and other perspectives. Each contribution has assumed that such broad approaches can contribute much to our understanding of Africa, and that this may in turn be of advantage to specific disciplines.

BOOKS IN THIS SERIES

CLASS, POWER AND IDEOLOGY IN GHANA: THE RAILWAYMEN OF SEKONDI

RICHARD JEFFRIES

Lecturer in Politics, School of Oriental and African Studies
University of London

CAMBRIDGE UNIVERSITY PRESS

CAMBRIDGE
LONDON · NEW YORK · MELBOURNE

Published by the Syndics of the Cambridge University Press
The Pitt Building, Trumpington Street, Cambridge CB2 1RP
Bentley House, 200 Euston Road, London NW1 2DB
32 East 57th Street. New York, NY 10022, USA
296 Beaconsfield Parade, Middle Park, Melbourne 3206, Australia

First published 1978

Printed in Great Britain by
The Eastern Press Ltd., London and Reading

Library of Congress Cataloguing in Publication Data
Jeffries, Richard.
Class, power, and ideology in Ghana.
(African studies series; 22)
Bibliography: p. 234
Includes index.
1. Trade-unions–Railroads–Ghana–Sekondi.
2. Railroads–Ghana–Sekondi–Employees. I. Title.
II. Series.
HD6886. Z7R14   331.88′11′38509667   77–22872
ISBN 0 521 21806 3

TO MY PARENTS

Contents

Contents

Maps and tables

x *Maps and tables*

Acknowledgements

Research for this book, which is based on a doctoral dissertation for the University of London, was carried out mainly during a stay of some nine months in Ghana in 1971. I am grateful to the School of Oriental and African Studies for sponsoring the travel and fieldwork involved, and to the Central Research Fund of the University of London for providing additional finance for the employment of an interpreter. The School of Oriental and African Studies was also generous enough to finance a further trip to Ghana in the summer of 1974 which facilitated revision of the original manuscript.

I am, of course, indebted to a great number of people for their assistance, and there is room to mention only a few of them here. Before I commenced the fieldwork, David Sam kindly endeavoured to teach me basic Fante, and Richard Crook tendered me much useful advice on how to approach oral research under Ghanaian conditions. In Ghana itself, I was fortunate enough to be allowed access to important archival materials by A. E. Forson, General Secretary of the Railway and Ports Workers' Union; E. G. Williams, General Secretary of the Mineworkers' Union; and Mr F. A. Amissah, Personnel Manager of the Railway and Harbour Administration, who also gave me permission to conduct interviews with railway workers during working hours. Officials of the Railway Union were invariably extremely helpful, but K. G. Quartey, A. B. Essuman and Kofi Imbeah must receive a special expression of gratitude for the many hours they gave up to discussing union affairs with me. During my second visit to Ghana in 1974, G. A. Balogun was a particularly generous source of information on the politics of the TUC under the CPP regime. My greatest debt in Ghana, however, is to the many ordinary Sekondi railway workers whose friendliness and joviality made field research amongst them such an enjoyable as well as informative experience. Some recognition of their individual contributions is provided in the text and the notes.

Among the numerous scholars from whose knowledge and ideas I have profited during the preparation of this study I should particularly like to mention Robin Cohen, Baron Holmes, Jon Kraus, Adrian Peace and Richard Rathbone. The manuscript was read by Michael Twaddle and John Dunn, both of whom offered many helpful suggestions for its improvement. Donal Cruise O'Brien has been, successively, my teacher, supervisor and friend during the past ten years. To him more than any other individual I owe my present understanding of West African politics, and his moral support at those times of self-doubt which every young scholar must surely experience has been invaluable. Writing this book also required a certain knowledge of economic and, more particularly, Marxist theory. No one did more to further my understanding of the relevance of such theory to Third World conditions than Bill Warren, whose tragic death earlier this year deprived me of a very dear friend and robbed the academic community of one of its finest young minds. Needless to say, none of these contributions entails any responsibility for the defects which doubtless remain.

   I should like to thank Shirley Thompson and Janet Marks for their patience and skill in typing successive drafts of the manuscript. The assistance of Ruth Smith and the staff of the Cambridge University Press in preparing the work for publication is much appreciated. To my close friends, especially Julia Pursehouse, David Attoe, Ewen Henderson and Christine Pointon, my deepest gratitude for their determined, if sometimes unavailing, efforts to keep me cheerful and sane. My indebtedness to Janette is beyond description in a few words of prose.

London
January 1978   Richard Jeffries

Introduction

Of all groups of unionised workers in Ghanaian society, the railway-men of Sekondi occupy a place of quite unrivalled importance in the history of their country's political organisation and development. Among the first groups of workers to unionise in the 1920s, they alone were able to sustain their organisation on an active footing throughout the inter-war period, staging a number of effective (if only partly successful) strike actions. Other workers were to establish union organisations after the Second World War, but the railway workers continued to occupy a position of unchallenged leadership over the young trade union movement as a whole. Dominating the executive of the first Gold Coast TUC, which they had initiated in 1945, they attempted, in January 1950, to stage a general strike in support of Kwame Nkrumah's 'Positive Action' phase of the nationalist campaign. Although most other workers failed to respond, the railway workers' own strike action, solidly maintained for two weeks, undoubtedly harassed the colonial regime into speeding up the devolution of power, and strengthened Nkrumah's personal claim to national political leadership. Having helped bring Nkrumah to power, the railway workers also, however, revealed their preparedness to pit their strength against him. They led resistance against the attempt of the Convention People's Party to subordinate the trade union movement to its control, and, in September 1961, staged a seventeen-day strike which the Government recognised as the most serious challenge to its existence since Independence (1957). Again, in October 1971, in response to the TUC's call for anti-government demonstrations, the railway and harbour workers of Sekondi-Takoradi led the protest against the character and policies of Dr Busia's Progress Party regime, anticipating by just ten weeks Colonel Acheampong's successful military coup d'etat.

This book endeavours to explain the distinctive nature of the railway workers' political behaviour and, in particular, to explore the role of what might broadly be termed ideological factors in its determination.

1

Introduction

There are several reasons why a focus on rank-and-file attitudes would seem appropriate, both in this particular instance and within the more general context of studies of the politics of African labour. These should become fully apparent in the course of the following pages. It might be helpful, however, to clarify some of the more important assumptions and concepts informing this approach at the outset.

In the first place, it seems analytically useful to stipulate as a minimal criterion for the description of union behaviour as 'political' that it should involve a substantial element of choice – more, certainly, than is entailed in certain types of relationship with government. Much of the literature produced in the late 1950s and early 60s on the supposed prevalence of 'political unionism' in Africa was primarily concerned with an alleged voluntary inclination to ally with actual or potential regimes.[1] This was attributed to the perception by union members and leaders of a large, predominant measure of common interest with 'independent' governments in the struggle for national development. This must certainly be recognised as one possible type of political unionism, even if its incidence can hardly now be expected to be (or be thought ever to have been) particularly widespread in view of the rapid emergence in these societies of socio-economic inequalities quite startling even by comparison with advanced capitalist countries. The important point here, however, is that such voluntary alliances should be distinguished as clearly as possible from the forceful incorporation of unions by ruling parties and the frequently concomitant suppression of their representative functions. From this perspective, a closer examination of rank-and-file attitudes towards the development of a structure of so-called 'political unionism' under the CPP regime in Ghana promises to illuminate the more hazy but analytically critical areas of previous presentations.[2]

The more specific concern of this study is with oppositional political activity. This might, of course, take a number of different forms and express a wide variety of aims or motivations. It is arguable (and has in fact been argued) that, given the structure of wage employment in these societies – with the government itself being the largest single employer and exerting a strong determining influence on wage-levels in the private sector also – a political dimension is inevitably involved even in the most humdrum of wage disputes. Implicitly at least, these tend to bring unions into direct confrontation with the government on the most important issue of public policy – the relative distribution of national wealth. Strikes might also, if sufficiently determinedly maintained, constitute serious threats to the stability of notoriously fragile regimes. The failure of this approach to distinguish between 'intentionalist' and 'consequential' categories tends, however, to make of 'political unionism' a meaninglessly blanket des-

2

ignation, obscuring a number of important questions. It may be the case, for example, that the exceptional nature of the Ghanaian railway workers' political behaviour consists in, and is to be explained by, little more than their singular ability to elude the tentacles of government control. This enables them to stage strikes in which others would, if they could, participate, possibly out of the narrowest of economic motivations but in a context where the government construes any opposition (perhaps rightly) as potentially politically subversive. If, however, the distinctiveness of their behaviour also reflects a significant ideological divergence, involving a heightened political consciousness and assertiveness on the part of this particular section of the national labour force, quite different questions arise and quite different implications follow.

One type of motivation clearly meriting designation as 'political' (and that most frequently implied by the use of the term in government parlance) consists in support for an oppositional political party: and, at first sight, this might appear the most pertinent criterion for the student of labour politics. In the case of alliances with oppositional (as distinct from ruling) parties, there can be little doubting the operation of a substantial element of choice: a choice, indeed, which few serious gamblers would be prepared to take without the attraction of suitably large potential returns. Yet, as this formulation suggests, support for a political party is hardly likely, in itself, to provide sufficient motivation for union oppositional activity. One must seek to delve beyond to an understanding of the objectives it is hoped to further through such an alliance; and recognise that, in many cases, such an alliance might be considered by workers unnecessary, even deleterious, to their political purposes.

It is, of course, often difficult to identify these purposes at all precisely, particularly since some of the ideas and grievances which lie behind them are none too clearly articulated, and perhaps none too clearly formulated, in the minds of the actors themselves. Somewhat roughly speaking, however, the question of political motivation centres on the degree to which the propellants and aims of strike actions (or other forms of oppositional activity) extend beyond immediate occupational interests to disagreement over broad societal issues and goals – to a concern, ultimately, with the legitimacy of the prevailing political and socio-economic order. Further distinctions might be drawn between 'revolutionary objectives', more modest 'pressure for economic and political reforms' and the largely negative desire to displace a particular regime. Beyond this, though, typologies would seem to be much less useful or illuminating than the attempt to portray the attitudes of participants as delicately as possible.

3

Certainly, any adequate assessment of the degree to which labour oppositional activity represents a radical political force must take into account this subjective or ideological dimension. One cannot rest content with its all too common labelling as radical or elitist by the crude criterion of the relative socio-economic position of the participants or, alternatively, that of the ideological complexion of the regime against which it is directed. Indeed, the whole debate as to the rapidity (or even the occurrence) of a process of class-formation in African societies rests, in at least one crucial respect, on the flimsiest of evidence. There has been virtually no serious investigation into the attitudes of groups of workers in Africa, their view of the surrounding social order, or the quality of their political consciousness.[3] It is one of the main purposes of this study to contribute to the filling of this immense and critical gap in our knowledge.

The following study is divided into two parts, of which the first is primarily historical and the second analytical and comparative. This is, of course, only a rather rough distinction. The historical approach of the first section is also (necessarily) analytical, and in fact directed toward the consideration of particular theoretical questions. Whence have the railway workers derived their exceptional union militancy, solidarity and political orientation? What degree of ideological consistency or continuity have they displayed, and how significant is this in the explanation of their political behaviour? Should they be considered a radical or elitist political force, and how do other sections of the Ghanaian masses in fact perceive the relationship between their own interests and railway worker oppositional activity? Such questions are raised in somewhat cursory manner in the first instance, however, and only in Part II developed and elaborated in a comparative and theoretical framework.

The general approach adopted in the historical section represents a conscious attempt to delve deeper than the narrowly intra-elite perspective characteristic of much of the literature on trade union politics in Ghana, to an understanding of the shop-floor 'view from below'. At the same time, a knowledge of developments at the national level is clearly an essential prerequisite for an understanding of reactions at lower levels, and it is important that the former should be presented in as objective a manner as possible. Accordingly, separate chapters have been included on TUC relations with the government and internal conflicts under the CPP and successive regimes.

The account of Railway Union history is based on both documentary and interview materials. The former consist primarily of records in the Railway Union archives which were made available to me by kind permission of A. E. Forson, the General Secretary of the Railway Union in

4

1971. This information was supplemented wherever possible by interviews with Railway Union officials, past and present, and also with some ordinary members of long standing. These interviews (a total of sixty-five), together with several hundred informal conversations held with railway workers in Sekondi-Takoradi in April–November 1971, were the main sources of the quotations presented in the narrative to illuminate railway worker perceptions. In addition, a lengthy, structured, but open-ended questionnaire was administered to some ninety workers in the Railway Location workshops in Sekondi in July and August 1971 by permission of the Ghana Railways and Ports Authority. This served several purposes, the main one being to ascertain the degree of consensus in attitudes among the Sekondi railway workers, and the most important determinants of such differences as obtained. But it also provided an additional source of illuminating comments on Railway Union political history. The questionnaire employed is presented in full in the Appendix, together with an account of the manner of its administration, and an assessment of the representative status of the sample.

Nearly all of the interviews with union officials were conducted in English, since their command of the language was generally good and the presence of an interpreter might have impeded the development of that intimacy of relationship which I sought (often, I believe, successfully) to cultivate. As regards the questionnaire survey, most of the interviews were conducted in Fante, the first language of the great majority of railway workers, and the lingua franca of Sekondi-Takoradi. This was also the language normally used during informal interviews and conversations with railway workers (and some other local residents) in the bars and various leisure spots of the city. Here the special qualities of my interpreter, Jonas Kwablah, are to be emphasised. Himself a Krobo, but a fluent speaker of virtually all the main languages in Ghana, he had previously been employed on two occasions by British field researchers, and rapidly developed a fine understanding of the purposes and requirements of the research in hand. My own knowledge of Fante, which I had begun to learn in London, sufficed, as the fieldwork progressed, to understand most of the content of responses; but it remained inadequate for me to converse fluently or conduct interviews without the assistance of an interpreter. The limitations of working through an interpreter are to be admitted, but these were, I believe, reduced to a minimum in this instance by Jonas' friendly and unofficious manner toward interviewees. It is worth observing, in this regard, that every effort was made to conduct interviews in as informal a manner as possible; that Jonas and I spent virtually every evening for four months conversing with railway workers in the bars of Sekondi-Takoradi; and that some of the most illuminating oral material for this study was obtained by simply 'listening in' to conversations on these occasions.

It should be noted that the period of fieldwork in Ghana was one during which a liberal atmosphere prevailed as to the expression of political opinions. Very little difficulty was experienced, therefore, in eliciting what were apparently frank, and often certainly outspoken, opinions. It was also a period free of the intensive political party campaigning of election times, and therefore one in which attitudes were unlikely to be severely conditioned or distorted by the passion of party allegiances. It is perhaps also worth remark that, by 1971, Ghanaians were generally inclined to take a more balanced and dispassionate view of the Nkrumah regime (1951–66) than they would (or could) have done in the years immediately following its downfall. In attempting to gather the full potential harvest from such fruitful conditions for attitudinal research I made every effort to keep the restricting influences of my own preconceptions to a minimum, and to listen to what people felt it important to say. It is hoped that, notwithstanding the constraints of academic generalisation, some of the immediacy and subtlety of the railway workers' own view of their world is communicated in the following pages.

I A POLITICAL HISTORY OF GHANAIAN RAILWAY UNIONISM

I

The railway and harbour workers of Sekondi-Takoradi: a sociological profile

Ghanaian railway unionism cannot, strictly speaking, be equated with the behaviour of the union's Sekondi-Takoradi membership alone. By 1970 (as can be seen from Table 1.1), workers based in Sekondi-Takoradi accounted for slightly less than half of the total labour force of the Railway and Harbour Administration, nearly all of whom were union members. More than one quarter were employed in the railway and harbour installations at Accra-Tema. This, however, represented a major shift in the pattern of dispersal of the labour force which occurred after 1961 with the completion of a new harbour at Tema, and the redirection of a large volume of freight – particularly imported goods – through Tema instead of Takoradi. For the major part of the period under discussion, the Sekondi-Takoradi workers might properly be portrayed as the concentrated nucleus of Railway Union[1] membership. It is in any case the behaviour and attitudes of this group which, for obvious reasons of political impact, constitute the main concern of this study. The differing attitudes and behaviour of the members of other branches, though briefly discussed when they led to important political divisions within the Railway Union, are peripheral to the central focus. It seems appropriate, therefore, to provide a preliminary sketch of the historical growth and sociological characteristics of this section of the labour force and its surrounding urban environment.

Development of the railway network and the permanent way labour force

At the end of the nineteenth century, Sekondi (situated 140 miles west of Accra in the Western Province of the Gold Coast) was little more than a fishing village. Its only claim to distinction lay in the location there of both British and Dutch forts, established in the seventeenth century, but by then long disused. In the depth of its coastal waters, however, it possessed a resource of as yet unrealised value. As one of the few natural ports

9

along the coast suitable for large ships, it was chosen, in 1897, as the site for the railway terminus and workshops. In the following year construction began on a thirty-nine-mile section from Sekondi to Tarkwa, and this had been extended to Kumasi by 1903. A second line was begun from Accra and had reached Kumasi by 1927. To complete the triangular network, a third line was constructed from just north of Tarkwa stretching into the Central Province during 1923–7.[2] By 1928, the rail system of Ghana, as it now exists, was virtually complete (see Map 1).

In the early years of the construction of the railway, the principal labour requirement was a large army of unskilled and semi-skilled labourers. Southern Ghanaians proved reluctant to do such work, arguably for cultural reasons – associating unskilled labouring with slavery – as much as out of lack of interest in the low rates of remuneration. Since the Colonial Government would not openly permit the forced recruitment of labour in the southern 'Colony' area, most of the labour required was

Table 1.1. *Numerical strength of railway and harbour labour force by branches (1970)*

Branch	Established[a]	Non-established	Total
Takoradi[b]	1,931	2,425	4,356
Sekondi Location	950	1,779	2,729
Tarkwa	291	388	679
Dunkwa	140	205	345
Kumasi	424	466	890
Nkawkaw	30	125	155
Accra	574	1,750	2,324
Tema	587	1,601	2,188
Northern[c]	109	775	884
Southern	60	651	711
Overall total			15,261

Source: Personnel Department of the Ghana Railways and Harbour Administration.

[a] Includes virtually all clerical and administrative staff but, of the manua employees, only 'artisans' and the various supervisory grades: unskilled and semi-skilled workers were at this time classified as 'non-established' and 'non-pensionable'.

[b] Includes staff working at the running sheds situated between Takoradi harbour and Sekondi Location, together with those members of the permanent way labour force based in the Sekondi-Takoradi area.

[c] This and the following category refer to the permanent way labour force, subdivided according to the lines of track on which they work, but excluding those based in Sekondi-Takoradi or Accra-Tema.

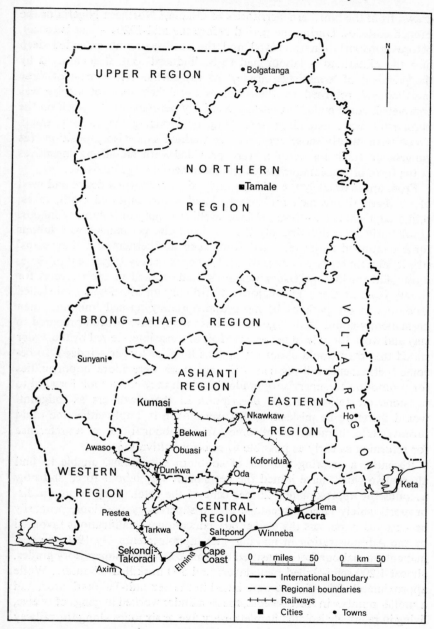

Map 1. Ghana's railway system
After a map drawn by the Survey of Ghana

11

drawn from the Northern Territories of Ghana,[3] Northern Nigeria or the French colonies. During the period before the mid-1920s – that is to say, before transportation improved and the cash economy extended deep into the hinterland – labour had to be 'induced' out of such areas by the payment of 'conscience money' to the chiefs. While most of these 'northerners' returned to their homes once their term of service was completed, some ended up settling relatively permanently to work on the permanent way, extending, rerouteing or servicing the railway track. These were mostly those who, having attained supervisory positions (as gangers or track inspectors), were provided with stabilising incentives in the form of pensionable status and incremental wage increases.

From approximately the mid-20s onwards, the growing desire and need of northern young men for cash in hand – for imported cloth, taxes, bridal payments etc. – resulted in a swelling supply of voluntary labour. Until fairly recently, virtually the whole of the permanent way labour force continued to be recruited from such northerners and 'Lagosians' (the local term for Nigerians). By 1971, approximately 10 per cent of these, most of them in supervisory positions, had worked in the railways for twenty years or more. The majority of ordinary unskilled and semi-skilled labourers might perhaps be more appropriately termed 'migrant' than permanently committed wage-earners, yet many have proved prepared to stay and work for at least ten years. Most of those interviewed by the writer stated that they would choose to stay as long, or longer – indeed, to become 'permanent' railwaymen – if only there were more opportunities for promotion to supervisory grades in which they could look forward to pensions on retirement. A description of these workers as 'migrant' would therefore be misleading if it were taken to imply either the rapid turnover rate characteristic of some African labour forces, or a preference for returning as early as possible to peasant cultivation.

Recently, a growing number of southern Ghanaians, unable to find alternative work, have joined the permanent way labour force and now account for approximately 20 per cent of the total. They occupy a disproportionately large percentage of the supervisory positions, primarily because many possess the elementary educational qualifications favoured by the Administration in making such appointments. By 1970 the permanent way labour force consisted of some 200 men in supervisory grades, almost 1,200 semi-skilled plate-layers and 500 unskilled labourers. While approximately 250 of these were based in the Sekondi-Takoradi area, and a similar number in Accra-Tema, the remainder worked in gangs of twelve, living in relatively isolated hamlets every five or six miles along the railway track. These often included both northerners and southerners; yet the evidence of interviews indicated that there was little in the way of ethnic friction at this level. The functional necessity of subsuming such potential sources of conflict in a small-group situation might be held to account for this since, at higher (union) levels, the issue of literate southerners' preferment in promotion to supervisory posts has recently been the subject of acrimonious dispute.

Composition and sociological characteristics of the labour force at Sekondi Location and Takoradi harbour

From approximately 1910 onwards, the Railway Administration employed a growing number of clerical, skilled and semi-skilled workers to man the administrative headquarters and locomotive workshops (Location) at Sekondi. The opening of a new deep-water port at Takoradi – some five miles west of Sekondi – in 1928 and, more particularly, the boom in import and export traffic during the late 30s and 40s, required still more enginemen and maintenance fitters, as well as crane drivers, signalmen and tug and launch crews, to operate the harbour installations. (In the early 1930s the Railway and Harbour Administrations were merged and provided with new headquarters at Takoradi.) By 1936 almost 6,000 Africans, the large majority manual workers, were employed by the Railway and Harbour Administration, and more than half of these in Sekondi-Takoradi (see Table 1.2). This represented the largest single concentration of manual workers in the Gold Coast at this time with the partial exception of the mineworkers.

Precise statistics on the structural composition of the Sekondi-Takoradi labour force in the 1930s are unfortunately unavailable. It is improbable, however, that any major changes have occurred during the intervening period. Accordingly, one might estimate that, then as now, between one half and two-thirds were either skilled or semi-skilled workers.[4] The majority of these were (and are) literate or semi-literate Fantis from the nearby

Table 1.2. *Railway and Harbour Administration employees in 1936*

European staff	107
African clerical grades	509
African artisans	1,688
African plate-layers	1,179
African labourers[a]	2,296

Source: *RAA*, Gold Coast Railway and Harbour Department Staff List, 1936.

[a] It would seem that the term 'labourers' was used at this time as a general category to cover many who were in reality semi-skilled workers.

Table 1.3. *Composition of the Sekondi Location labour force by tribe* (*1971*)

Tribe	%
Fanti	58
Ahanta	18
Ashanti	8
Nzima	5
Akwapim	4
Ewe	3
Others	4

Source: Sample survey conducted by the writer.

coastal towns, particularly Cape Coast and Elmina (see Table 1.3). Clerical staff constitute about 15 per cent of the Location labour force and a slightly higher proportion (25 per cent) at Takoradi harbour. This 'clerical' category comprises a wide range of sub-categories, sharply differentiated in income-levels, from 'clerical assistants' at one extreme to 'senior executive officers' at the other. The majority, however, are employed as 'clerical officers'. The clerical officers are now on the same salary scale as the 'artisans' (fully qualified skilled workers), but, prior to 1939, they enjoyed somewhat higher salaries as well as pensionable status and various accompanying privileges denied to the mass of skilled manual workers.

Within the ranks of the manual workers, three broad categories might be distinguished: skilled, semi-skilled and unskilled workers. Much of the literature on the political economy of sub-Saharan Africa emphasises the importance of the distinction between skilled workers and unskilled, portraying the former as a 'labour aristocracy' relative to the latter. While systematic consideration of this contention must be postponed to Part II of this study, it might be pointed out here that, since the majority of manual workers employed in the Railway Administration are classified as 'semi-skilled', it is difficult and arguably misleading to draw a single line of differentiation in this manner. Most of these semi-skilled workers receive rates of pay approaching the starting-rate of the artisans. For the purpose of depicting the extremes of economic differentiation, one might nevertheless compare the basic rates of pay of artisans and unskilled labourers. The differential ratio between the two appears to have maintained a fairly consistent relationship of around 2:1 since 1910, though narrowing slightly during the past two decades (see Table 1.4). Prior to 1968 the artisans' entitlement to annual incremental increases meant that their average incomes exceeded those of unskilled labourers rather more

14

substantially, but the differential accruing from this factor was lessened by the introduction of incremental scales for all railway employees in that year.

From a sociological rather than a purely economic point of view, there is something to be said for a simplified twofold classification – placing the semi-skilled workers of Sekondi Location and Takoradi harbour in one category with the skilled workers, and the permanent way plate-layers in another with the unskilled. This division tends to coincide with, and find expression in, various social dimensions of differentiation. While virtually all skilled workers, on this definition, are literate southern Ghanaians (mostly of the 'Akan' cultural group), the mass of unskilled workers are illiterate northerners. The former tend to be committed to much longer terms of wage employment than the latter. Further, many (though not all) northern railwaymen based in the city cluster with other northerners and non-Ghanaians in the 'zongo' residential areas (the 'stranger' neighbourhoods). Here, they still strongly adhere to a modified form of their traditional culture and to a political system markedly different from that of the southerner Akan.

Numerous sub-classifications might be distinguished within the ranks of the skilled and semi-skilled workers, particularly at Takoradi harbour with its proliferation of various types of semi-skilled employee, and, to a lesser degree, between the machinists, electricians, fitters, carpenters and blacksmiths employed in the Sekondi Location workshops. Cross-cutting these latter job categorisations one finds an official distinction between

Table 1.4. *Rates of pay in the Railway Administration (per day)*[a]

	1910	1930	1950	1970
Labourers	1s. 0d.	1s. 6d.	3s. 0d.	7s. 6d.
Artisans	2s. 0d. to 3s. 0d.	3s. 0d. to 5s. 0d.	6s. 0d. to 10s. 0d.	12s. 0d. to £1

Source: *RAA*.

[a] The actual figure for the 1970 labourer's wage (i.e. the government's minimum wage) was 75 pesewas. In July 1965 Ghana adopted a currency system of cedis and pesewas, with 100 pesewas to the cedi. One pesewa was equivalent to one old penny, so one cedi equalled 8s. 4d. In February 1967 the NLC Government introduced the new cedi, which was to be regarded as equivalent to 10s. This rate has been used in translating the 1970 wage into a sterling equivalent both in the interests of simplicity and because, in 1970, the Ghanaian people still commonly used this calculation (and still commonly talked about money in terms of 'shillings and pence'). In reality, however, the new cedi had been devalued by 30 per cent relative to sterling in July 1967.

'apprentices'; 'artisans', who have successfully completed the Administration's own five-year apprenticeship scheme; and 'tradesmen' (grades I and II), who have been recruited from outside to perform skilled or semi-skilled work on the basis of their training in the mines, for example, or local 'craft' industries. Such sub-classifications are always potentially divisive, given the sensitivity to status differentials customarily displayed by craftsmen, and their occasional importance in Railway Union politics will be chronicled in the following pages. Yet only one such distinction has been of any long-term historical significance. The enginemen have regarded themselves from the earliest days, and largely succeeded in being treated, as a particularly high-status group. They were the first section of the African manual labour force to be accorded 'established' status and thereby to become eligible for pensions and regular paid holidays, as well as receiving substantially higher rates of pay than other skilled workers. Geographically, too, they form a group somewhat distinct from other skilled workers, being mostly based at the running sheds situated between the Location workshops and Takoradi harbour.

With this partial exception, and in spite of the existence of several potential sources of division, it is the common characteristics and situation shared by the skilled and semi-skilled railway workers which strike the observer most forcefully. These workers display (and apparently have always displayed) an impressively high level of job commitment and stability. While no precise statistics on labour turnover are obtainable from the Railway and Harbour Administration, the more recent annual staff lists provide information on the length of service of 'established' employees (i.e. artisans and above). These show that, in 1970, 50 per cent of artisans (if one includes 'Junior foremen') had worked in the railways for fifteen years or more, and 72 per cent for over ten years. It is also possible, through an analysis of changes in the annual staff lists over time, to make an estimate of the labour turnover rate amongst artisans. Such an analysis suggests that, during the 1960s, less than 4 per cent left the railways each year voluntarily – that is, without having reached compulsory retirement age. It is possible, indeed probable, that the turnover rate for semi-skilled workers has been rather higher. The impressions of union officials and Personnel Department staff nevertheless confirm this picture of a relatively committed skilled and semi-skilled work force.

This is not to suggest that most skilled railway workers wish, or intend, to spend the whole of their working life in the railways or alternative wage employment. The most commonly expressed aspiration is rather to become 'independent' through accumulating enough capital to set up in private business, for example as furniture manufacturers or bar owners. But economic realism dictates that this be expected to take twenty years or more. (In most cases, of course, the transition in fact takes even longer, or is never achieved.) Similarly, virtually all railwaymen express the intention of eventually returning to their original, rural or small-town homes. Yet a reasonably deep acquaintance with Sekondi-Takoradi reveals that many retired railwaymen have in fact settled there, either because of their success in developing small local businesses, or simply because they ultimately prove reluctant to leave long-established circles of friends. A fair minority of skilled railway workers – 15 per cent of the sample interviewed, for instance – were born and brought up in Sekondi-Takoradi, and the fathers of most of these themselves once worked in the railways. One suspects that for many of these city-born workers, the reference to a 'real' rural home is little more than a conventional fiction.

The continuing presence of many (even if a minority of) retired railway artisans in such residential areas as Esikado, together with this intergenerational element in recruitment, contributes to the sense of corporate identity so evident amongst the skilled railway workers. Even for the majority whose stay in Sekondi-Takoradi proves more transient, involvement in this community, its shared interests and cultural life, is real and deep so long as it lasts. One major reason for this clearly lies in their geographical concentration. Virtually all of the Sekondi-Takoradi railwaymen work in one of the two large but dense conglomerations at Sekondi Location and Takoradi harbour. The close contact and regular communication experienced there extends, moreover, beyond the bounds of the work-place to their residential situation and leisure pastimes. About a third live in one of the two Administration-owned railway villages situated near the centre of Takoradi and at Ketan, on the outskirts of Sekondi (see Map 2). Another concentration is to be found in private accommodation at Esikado, the home of such famed labour leaders as J. C. Vandyck and Pobee Biney (until his death in 1968). Others live in private accommodation scattered throughout the city, but the relatively small size of Sekondi-Takoradi (population 123,000 by 1960), together with the use of Esikado as a weekend leisure venue, makes for frequent meeting.

No tribal clustering or discrimination is evident within these neighbourhoods. In part, this is because accommodation in the Administration's railway villages has been allocated irrespective of tribal criteria; and because, in areas of private accommodation, the large majority are in any case Fantis (or members of other Akan groups) in accordance with their proportionate representation in the work force. But, in addition, residential areas such as Esikado are characterised by a distinctly supra-tribal, proletarian ethos. Thus, the small numbers of Ewes, Gas and other non-Akan groups are integrated into the community as fully accepted and often popular members. Workers from the same home village or town

17

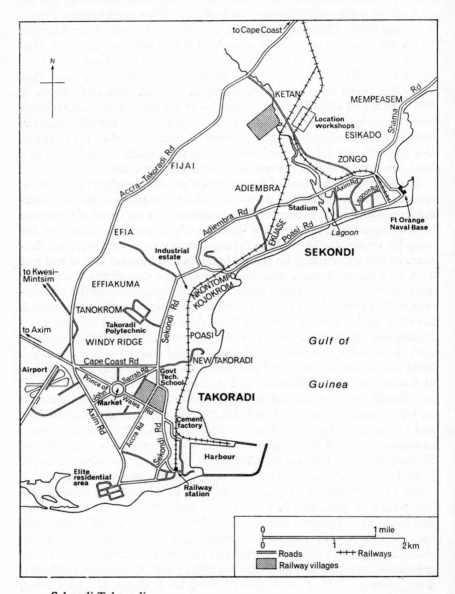

Sekondi-Takoradi

After a map in Margaret Peil's *The Ghanaian Factory Worker* (Cambridge, 1972)

frequently maintain particularly close ties but, in general, tribal differences present no barrier to friendship as such.

The surrounding urban environment

The skilled railway workers of Sekondi-Takoradi therefore constitute a distinct social and cultural community; but, it is important to stress, this is not (and never has been) sharply cut off from the larger surrounding urban community. During the early part of the century, Sekondi, while more than an isolated workers' concentration of the kind one finds in some of the mining townships, was numerically and economically dominated by the growing railway labour force. Similarly, Takoradi was a village of a few hundred persons prior to the construction of the harbour. The 3,500 railway and harbour workers of 1936 clearly constituted the economic and social centre of a twin city whose total population amounted to only just over 22,000 in 1931, though this had almost doubled by 1948.[5] More recently, with the development of several medium-sized manufacturing industries, it would be an exaggeration to describe this group's structural position as one of dominance or centrality. Yet it continues to form a particularly large, cohesive and ideologically influential subsection, closely assimilated to the rest of the city, and sharing many of the concerns of other residents.

Sekondi-Takoradi has always been a predominantly 'working-class' city, populated largely by lower-paid, manual wage-earners and their relatives. Unlike Accra (Ghana's administrative centre) and Kumasi (a trading centre), the city of Sekondi-Takoradi owes its growth almost entirely to industrial development. The 1955 Household Budget Survey estimated that 90 per cent of earnings in Sekondi-Takoradi came from wage employment, compared to 67 per cent in Accra and 22 per cent in Kumasi (see Table 1.6). In 1961 the skilled and unskilled workers employed in the railway and harbour installations constituted approximately one sixth of the city's total male labour force of 43,000. One quarter were employed as skilled or unskilled manual workers by the City Council, the government departments (e.g. Public Works, Posts and Telecommunications), the shipping companies, or in one of the several medium-sized manufacturing industries located there.[6]

Taking into account also the junior clerical workers, this means that approximately one half of the total male labour force was in the lower-paid worker category, earning less than N₵50 per month.[7] Approximately 20 per cent were self-employed, mostly as small-scale traders, craftsmen and providers of 'services'. Another 22 per cent were classified as unemployed, though many of these probably derived some income from

19

casual work or 'informal' activities.[8] The proportion of middle-class or elite elements was very small (see Table 1.5).

This occupational structure, with a much higher preponderance of lower-paid workers than in Accra or Kumasi, was reflected in the difference in average earnings between the three cities. In 1955, average earnings in Sekondi-Takoradi were £11 10s. per month, compared to £16 8s. in Accra and £17 18s. in Kumasi (see Table 1.6).

Sekondi-Takoradi was then a relatively poor urban community, dominated both numerically and in terms of general ethos by lower-paid manual workers. Moreover, this labour force was relatively stable – a high

Table 1.5. *Composition of the 'employed'ᵃ Sekondi-Takoradi adult male labour force, 1960* (percentages; N=42,691)

Professional, technical	4
Managerial, administrative	2
Clerical	14
Sales	6
Farmers, fishermen	7
Transport, communications	12
Craftsmen and production process workers	25
Labourers and longshoremen	21
Service and sport	9
Total	100

Source: Ghana, Census Office, *1960 Population Census of Ghana* (Accra, 1961), Special Report A.

ᵃ Those who did any work for pay or profit during the month preceding the census. Of the adult male labour force 22% were classified as unemployed. Of the 'employed' 20% were classified as self-employed.

Table 1.6. *Average earnings and expenditure in Ghana's three cities*

		Average family size	Average earnings	Wages as % of earnings	Average monthly expenditure
Sekondi-Takoradi	(1955)	3.98	£11 10s.	90	£12 9s.
Accra	(1953)	4.24	£16 8s.	67	£15 14s.
Kumasi	(1955)	4.15	£17 18s.	22	£14 2s.

Source: Gold Coast, Office of the Government Statistician, *Sekondi-Takoradi Survey of Population and Household Budgets, 1955*, Statistical and Economic Papers no. 4 (Accra, 1956).

proportion of workers were committed to urban wage employment as a relatively permanent occupation rather than considering themselves as short-term migrants. According to Margaret Peil's survey, 69 per cent of Sekondi-Takoradi workers planned to stay in their jobs for at least three years, compared to 36 per cent for Accra, or 43 per cent for Kumasi; and almost as many in fact stayed for as long as five years.[9]

The residential pattern is characterised, as in the railway villages, by a remarkable lack of ethnic prejudice or tribal conglomerations. The majority of southern Ghanaians are scattered throughout the city on a socio-economic basis, and, to some degree, by considerations of proximity to the place of work, rather than concentrated in tribal sub-communities. This, again, is partly to be explained by the history of property development in the city and the factors governing accommodation allocation. The National Housing Corporation has generally allocated its houses on a non-tribal basis, and the City Council has similarly distributed land for development. This has been facilitated by the fact that, as the city grew, the local Ahantas were rapidly outnumbered by incoming Fantis, and, since the establishment of the Municipal Council in 1921 (to become the City Council in 1954), the Ahantas have never really succeeded in dominating it or other local institutions.[10] In consequence, the main neighbourhoods rapidly became multi-tribal, and newcomers simply took whatever accommodation they could find and afford rather than heading for particular clusterings of co-ethnics. But, in any case, ever since the early decades of this century Sekondi-Takoradi has been characterised, according to observers, by a distinctly cosmopolitan ethos.[11] As it was the country's major seaport, its inhabitants quickly grew accustomed, and came to look forward (largely no doubt for financial reasons), to the regular visits of foreign seamen. In addition, one might give some credit for the development of this ethos to the attempt of the railway workers and other groups to organise, from the first, on a strictly non-tribal basis (though, obviously, their collective industrial experience and the social pattern of the wider community reinforced each other).

There are two minor exceptions to this pattern. The Ewe people from the Volta Region of Ghana have tended to cluster in a small area along the coast road between Sekondi and Takoradi, and other citizens frequently accuse them of displaying favouritism to co-ethnics in job recruitment and promotion whenever they have the opportunity. But the Ewes comprise only a small proportion of the total city population, no more than 6 per cent (or 7,700 out of 123,000) by 1960 (see Table 1.7). Secondly, the northerners and non-Ghanaians still tend to live together in the zongo areas, one being situated on the northern outskirts of the central residential area of Sekondi, the other out at the suburban village of Kwesi-Mintsim, to the

21

Table 1.7. *Composition of the Sekondi-Takoradi population by tribe* (*1960*)

Main tribe	Sub-group	Numbers	Percentage of total
Akan	Fanti	42,610	34.5
	Ahanta	22,210	18.0
	Nzima	3,340	2.7
	Asante	3,340	2.7
	Other	5,970	4.8
Ewe		7,720	6.3
Mole-Dagbani		6,540	5.3
Ga-Adangbe		5,310	4.3
Various Nigerian		9,480	7.8
All other tribes		16,740	13.6

Source: Ghana, Census Office, *1960 Population Census of Ghana* (Accra, 1961), Special Report E, Appendix D.

north of Takoradi. Here, a modified version of the traditional northern community structure persists, with headmen and, above them, a 'sarkin' (or 'supreme chief') settling disputes and organising communal activities. Although very considerable economic differentiation characterises the northerners, some of them being wealthy butchers and traders, others unskilled labourers, this does not find expression in perceptible differences in style of living. Scarcely any northerners live in other, non-zongo, areas of the city. Even the most eminent northerner in the city, the Regional Government's publicity and liaison officer, a highly educated and sophisticated man, lived in a simple two-roomed house in Sekondi zongo. Elsewhere, he pointed out in explanation, it would prove impossible for him to maintain observance of the Moslem religion and the life style it dictates.[12] Also, he claimed to gain more satisfaction from assisting his (mostly illiterate) fellow Moslems to cope with the problems of city life than he could possibly obtain from setting himself off as a member of the elite. In effect, he and other eminent northerners act as 'brokers' on behalf of the zongo community, intermediaries between its culturally disadvantaged, semi-encapsulated citizenry and the local government bureaucracy.

It would be misleading, however, to overemphasise the degree of northerner encapsulation, or to identify this with social conflict. The zongo areas are geographically integrated with the rest of the city and perfectly open to non-northern visitors. Southerners often attend their cultural festivities, such as wrestling competitions and the visits of prominent Moslem preachers, and the northerners in turn are enthusiastic supporters of the local football teams. There have been many cases of close friendship and even marriage, between young northerners and southerners.[13] Moreover, with the departure of many non-Ghanaians, in consequence or anticipation of the Aliens Compliance Ordinance of June 1970, large numbers of young southerners, mostly unemployed, have moved into the cheap accommodation in Kwesi-Mintsim zongo. Many of these make a living from petty theft or prostitution and pimping, operating in 'rings' frequently composed of southerners and northerners together. In other words, one finds in Kwesi-Mintsim the development of a multi-tribal criminal lumpenproletariat.

At the other end of the socio-economic scale, the small proportion of middle-class and elite elements live mostly in the relatively secluded 'garden city' areas. One is on the escarpment rising above the north-western side of Sekondi; the other flanks the palm-lined beach on the eastern side of Takoradi, set off (somewhat symbolically) from the centre of the city by the hill-topping outlines of the luxurious Atlantic Hotel. While the flamboyant foliage lends particular beauty to these areas, the rest of the city, too, is markedly different in visual features from the standard image of an industrial centre or modern seaport. Takoradi is a spacious, spread-out, slow-moving city. From its main centre, wide tree-lined roads run out to the suburban, semi-rural neighbourhoods where the majority of inhabitants reside. The centre of Sekondi is more cramped but, in some respects, more markedly rural, with goats and fowl roaming the streets leading up to the zongo. Out at the Location workshops, old steam engines lie rusting in the humid heat, half-enshrouded by the encroaching jungle. The single-storey houses of the workers at Esikado open out on to each other's doorway or small backyard but more in the traditional manner of a Ghanaian village than of a working-class street in a Western industrial city, or, for that matter, Ghana's other main industrial centre, Tema.

As Margaret Peil has remarked, this quasi-rural character and atmosphere of Sekondi-Takoradi probably makes for easier adjustment to its life and culture on the part of immigrants from the countryside or small towns than is generally the case in, for example, Accra or Tema.[14] It would nevertheless be wrong to see any incompatibility between this and the development among workers resident there of a strong proletarian identity.

2

The origins and dynamics of Railway Union development

The Sekondi-Takoradi railway and harbour workers were the only group of Ghanaian wage-earners to establish union organisation on a durable footing prior to the commencement of the Second World War. There were several characteristics of this labour force and features of its situation which might be considered especially congenial to spontaneous collective organisation. Yet, in order to gauge their relative historical peculiarity and importance, it is necessary to understand the major obstacles which confronted other groups of workers who attempted to form unions during this period.

That there were numerous attempts, as well as obstacles, is a point deserving emphasis in view of the still current myths as to the process of union formation in Ghana and other ex-British colonies. On first sight, it would appear that the major role in the development of trade unionism in Ghana has been played by government initiative, involving the imitation, whether voluntary or compulsory, of governments' preferred models. It might even be thought that Ghanaian workers have shown little spontaneous inclination to organise in furtherance of their collective interests. For, although there have been instances of strike action and labour organisation dating from the early days of colonial commerce,[1] it was not until the Second World War, and then with the encouragement of the Colonial Labour Department, that any substantial expansion of official union membership occurred – from 500 registered members in 1943 to 6,000 in 1945, and then to 38,000 by 1949 (see Table 2.1). Superficially, at least, the initiating activity of the Nkrumah Government appears to have been even more far-reaching and crucial in character. Under the compulsory structure established by the 1958 Industrial Relations Act, the Ghana TUC introduced union organisation to virtually every group of wage-earners in the industrial and commercial sectors. This created a total union membership of 320,000, or some 17 per cent of the total male labour force, by September 1961.

Table 2.1. *Trade unions and membership in Ghana, 1943–70*

Year ending	Number unions a	Paid-up members (approx.) b	Number African wage-salary employees
3/1944	11	482	
3/1945	14	6,030	
3/1947	24	10,976	
3/1949	41	38,135	
3/1950	56	17,985	
3/1951	61	28,170	
3/1952	65	32,908	
12/1952	73	35,129	
12/1953	69	46,309	
12/1954	66	44,092	240,000
3/1956	91	67,173	261,849
3/1957	95	57,845	271,714
3/1958	95	50,583	286,266
3/1959	85 (24)	116,000	313,566
9/1960	24	201,991	326,664
9/1961	16	320,248	343,752
9/1962	16	320,295	350,111
9/1963	16	324,648	367,832
9/1964	16	351,711	381,326
9/1965	10	n.d.	387,643
9/1966	16	n.d.	357,031
12/1967	16	270,149	357,249
6/1968	16	338,154	387,170
6/1970	17	342,480	402,500

Sources: J. I. Roper, *Labour Problems in West Africa* (Harmondsworth, 1958), p. 107, for early years; Gold Coast (later Ghana) Labour Department, *Annual Reports*, 1951–67, and Ghana TUC, *Report on the Activities of the TUC, 3rd Biennial Congress* (Accra, 1970), p. 1, for 1967–70 figures. The estimates of the number of wage and salary-earners are drawn from Kodwo Ewusi, *The Distribution of Monetary Incomes in Ghana* (Legon, 1971), p. 17.

a Fluctuations in the number of unions reflect not only growth/decrease but amalgamations.

b Labour Department figures include only those members the Department considered paid-up, and are therefore incomplete. TUC estimates were considerably higher, but, for obvious reasons, must be considered unreliable in the CPP period.

Nevertheless, this picture of reliance on government initiative and education in trade union establishment is largely misleading. In the first place, the figure for 1943 substantially understates the number of wage-earners already in effect possessing organisation, since, prior to that year, there was no official provision for trade union registration; and, thereafter, many previously organised groups, displaying understandable caution, were slow to register. In practice, moreover, spontaneous and government-initiated processes overlapped in the growth of unions after 1943. The Colonial Government initiative was a matter not simply of introducing unions where no intrinsic potential was apparent, but rather of responding with the government's preferred alternative to indications of widespread labour unrest and indigenous organising activity. This was specifically designed to counter the threat that union organisation might spread outside government influence, under the leadership of nationalist politicians, or, even worse, the radical leadership of the Sekondi-Takoradi unionists. In any case, even where Colonial Government encouragement was clearly crucial in the original establishment of union organisation – and the same, we shall see, might be said of the Nkrumah Government's initiatives – the rank and file showed themselves quite capable, in many cases, of taking over such tutelary organisation and moulding it to express their own, rather than the government's, conception of union operation and objectives.

Obstacles to unionisation in the pre-Second World War period

If, then, the initiating and educative activity of the government was less crucial and less effective than has sometimes been suggested, why was union development so limited and weak in the pre-war period? A number of factors must be considered here. In the first place, there simply were not many non-agricultural wage-earners prior to the huge expansion of employment opportunities during and after the Second World War.[2] In the second place, those who did work for wages, with the exception of the mineworkers and the railway and harbour workers, were generally employed in very small businesses or highly dispersed amongst the various branches of the civil service and the expatriate firms. Such a situation was not congenial to the development of collective organisation or a sense of labour solidarity. Thirdly, even where large concentrations of workers were to be found, in the mining townships for example, the short-term migrant character of much of the labour force militated against the growth of interest in trade union activity. (This, of course, is the one element of truth in the suggestion that trade unionism did not come naturally to Ghanaian workers.)

As late as 1939, some 54 per cent of the mines' work force continued to come from the Northern Territories, Northern Nigeria or the French colonies.[3] These workers generally aimed merely to save a certain financial 'target', and then to return home. Those who stayed longer in

Southern Ghana tended to change their job frequently, and the mining companies, adapting themselves to this fact, operated a card system by which an employee could have a friend or relative substitute for him. In consequence, the mines' labour force was (until very recently) characterised by an extremely high turnover rate. By 1940, for example, annual turnover in the mines amounted to nearly 80 per cent of the labour force, and about 40 per cent of those leaving the mines had been employed for less than six months.[4] This did not, of course, make either for industrial efficiency or for strong labour institutions. As Richard Wright has remarked, 'The lessons learned last year are washed down the drain of tribal life.'[5]

Additional obstacles faced those who might have wished to organise the mineworkers for united action. The migrant northern workers organised themselves in the mine townships in a modified form of their traditional system, dividing into small groups under a 'headman', who acted as their intermediary with the management.[6] This arrangement had to be radically transformed, if not entirely destroyed, before a more efficient, centralised organisation could be developed.[7] Furthermore, while most of the underground and unskilled labour was supplied by northern Ghanaians or aliens, the majority of skilled workers were from the south. This tendency for ethnic and cultural divisions to coincide with occupational divisions exacerbated sectional jealousies and vitiated labour solidarity. (Such features, as we have seen in the previous chapter, also characterised the railway labour force. A crucial difference, however, lay in the proportion and strategic importance of migrant northerners employed in the main mining centres.)

Finally, the labour surplus conditions which obtained in the Gold Coast after 1925 placed wage-earners in an extremely weak bargaining position. Employers could dismiss agitators, or even whole groups of workers, without fear of being unable to replace them. Isolated strike incidents did occur in the mines, the first recorded being in 1924, and there were several reports of attempts by the skilled workers to organise the labour force in the mid-30s.[8] But, in such cases, the repressive policy of the mining companies, made possible by the labour surplus conditions of the period, provided, as it were, the final straw which broke the back of the miners' organisation. A. B. Holmes has described the mining companies' policy: 'The general reaction of the mines toward strike activity was to dismiss all the leaders as well as any persons who remained adamant after deadlines for returning to work. Political officers were strongly pro-management and backed anti-strike activity with arrests of leaders as rioters or intimidators.'[9] A significant factor in the railway workers' early organisation was thus the reluctance of a paternalistically minded Colonial Government to utilise such methods with respect to its own employees.

It was in this more limited sense, also, that the Colonial Government's introduction of protective legislation for union activity was really crucial to the development of durable trade unions. Without some such compensatory support, labour organisers stood no chance of success in a straight contest of power with management in prevailing market conditions.

Origins of the Railway Union

The first recorded strike by Ghanaian railway workers occurred in June 1918 following the granting of a war bonus to European and 'permanent' African staff in the civil service in belated recognition of the wartime increase in the cost of living. Skilled and unskilled manual workers were not included in this award, it being argued that the greatest increases had occurred in the prices of imported goods which only the 'permanent' staff were expected to consume. Incensed at such discrimination, the artisans and labourers in the Railway Administration downed tools for a week, but with no success save an assurance that wages rates would be reviewed in the near future. By the end of 1921 these manual workers were understandably impatient at the government's inaction, and in December they staged another week-long strike. The management refused to negotiate. But Governor Guggisberg intervened to appoint a committee of enquiry which reported in favour of a wage increase for all lower-paid servants of the government.[10]

Several other groups of wage-earners were stimulated to collective action by the economic conditions of 1918–21. A boom in cocoa production coincided with an extension of public works programmes to precipitate a serious shortage of labour. Urban and industrial employers were most seriously affected as workers rushed back to the cocoa farms. At the same time, wages for urban workers generally failed to keep pace with the rise in prices.[11] Recognising their increased bargaining power, and dissatisfied with the falling value of their wages, the artisans and labourers of Accra founded a union and went on strike when their demand for a wage increase was refused.[12] Numerous other strikes were reported. Yet, with the exception of the railway workers, all such attempts at collective organisation rapidly collapsed. This can only in part be attributed to Governor Guggisberg's skilful handling of the situation and to the growing prosperity which wage-earners experienced in the mid-20s as prices declined from their 1921 peak. Such considerations did not, after all, prevent the railway workers seeking to express their growing sense of common interest and social identity in associational form.

In 1923 a railway official wrote, 'Men are forming into associations in the Railway Workshops, which will probably form the nucleus of the

28

trade union in years to come.' [13] These first attempts at formal organisation were clearly modelled on the guild-type associations of self-employed
craftsmen – gold- and silver-smiths, blacksmiths, carpenters and masons –
which had sprung up in the expanding urban centres of the southern
Gold Coast during the previous decade.[14] The early organiser of the
Workshop Association, Atta Payine, was himself a carpenter, and, as
in the craft associations, members were required to take an elaborate
oath, and various traditional ceremonial trappings were adopted.[15] But,
in spite of the use of these traditional trappings, the main function of the
association was to help workers adjust to unionised life in an industrial
community. Arrangements were made for the provision of funds to members who needed to travel or meet expenses incidental to funeral and wed-
ding ceremonies. The leaders would sometimes help newcomers to find
accommodation. And, in 1926, the association even attempted to bring
cinemas to the Location. This, like many other schemes, failed because of
inefficient management. There was no provision for regular dues collection, and meetings became increasingly irregular. Hence, the Workshop Association seems to have been barely active by 1928 when the
Railway Association was established. This latter organisation was, from
the start, less influenced by traditional cultural forms, and more specifically concerned with industrial grievances. Nevertheless, it made use of
what organisational infrastructure remained from earlier days in the creation of its own structure, and maintained the concern of the Workshop
Association with the general social and cultural welfare of its membership.[16]

The establishment of the Railway Association perhaps owed something
to its organisers' knowledge of the operation of British trade unions. The
Railway Administration's Apprenticeship scheme for artisans entailed
sending some to Britain for experience in the workshops at Crewe. But
it was not simple imitation of British practice which motivated these
trainee artisans to develop a union at Sekondi. Rather they wanted a
vehicle to express their frustration at the Railway Administration's refusal to accord them equal status with clerical staff. As one of the founders
explained:

> I was among the first batch of Africans to be given proper railway
> training. I was even sent overseas. Yet, when we educated people
> became acquainted with technical work, we found ourselves regarded
> as inferior to the clerks, even though we had as much qualifications.
> Those on the clerical side were on monthly salary and enjoyed
> leave, but we were given only a daily rate with no leave. We
> apprentices decided to do something about it.[17]

In November 1928, J. C. Vandyck, H. B. Cofie, W. A. Adottey, H.

Renner, F. H. Wood, S. W. Owiredu and J. Eshun formed a Railway Association Committee, and set out to incorporate all the African artisans and apprentices at Sekondi Location in a single body. Their principal immediate objective was to attain for themselves 'permanent' status, thereby gaining entitlement to monthly pay (a generous conversion from the daily rate being assumed) and annual leave. They soon found themselves on the defensive rather than the aggressive, however, and accordingly sought to extend membership to the unskilled workers, so as to attain greater solidarity in the face of threats of dismissal.

The 1931 and 1939 strikes

In 1928–32 the Gold Coast suffered a severe economic depression related directly to that which hit Europe in the same period. Cocoa prices fell drastically, prices of imported foods rose in spite of a reduction in customs duties, and a severe restriction on the import–export trade culminated in the staging of a remarkably widespread and effective hold-up of cocoa during the 1930–1 season. The Colonial Government was forced to cut back its expenditure, and several hundred government workers were dismissed, including, in May 1930, the whole of the labour force employed on the construction of Takoradi harbour.

The Railway Administration itself suffered a drastic reduction in the volume of its traffic, and a corresponding decline in revenue (see Table 2.2). Alarmed at this growing threat to the job security of its members, the Railway Association demanded improved and more secure conditions of service. The Administration responded with the elimination of some existing benefits and a warning that some dismissals could be expected, while the more fortunate could be employed only four days per week. The association leaders organised a mass meeting of all non-permanent railway workers in Sekondi-Takoradi at which agreement was reached on a proposal to withdraw their labour entirely until they could all be re-employed

Table 2.2. *Gold Coast railway revenue*

Year	Net revenue
1928/9	+£644,566
1929/30	+£539,323
1930/1	−£120,543
1931/2	−£181,930
1932/3	−£204,576

Source: P. R. Gould, *The Development of the Transportation Pattern in Ghana* (Northwestern University Studies in Geography No. 5, 1960), p. 58.

full time. This met with the Administration's consent, on the condition that a small skeleton staff should continue to work. The rest of the men then retired to their home villages and towns for two months. On return, they were all re-employed, though at slightly reduced rates of pay (see Table 2.3).

It hardly requires stating that the sense of strategy, and level of solidarity, displayed by the railway workers in 1931 was extremely impressive. Nevertheless, the whole experience had been a somewhat daunting one, and it was not until toward the end of the decade that the taste or confidence for aggressive assertion of demands was regained. In addition, the economic conditions of the mid-30s, with the world depression only gradually lifting, and labour in abundant supply, were hardly propitious for effective strike action. The Railway Association did petition the management for the restoration of the 1929 rates of pay in April 1934, and again in November 1936. But, when they were requested by the management to be patient, the railway workers apparently felt unable to press their demands more forcefully. During this period the efforts of the association leaders were primarily directed to the gradual improvement and extension of their organisation. Dues payment was introduced and branches were established all along the line from Sekondi to Kumasi. In November 1938 the association was renamed the Gold Coast Railway African Workers Union. According to the general manager of railways at the time, 'it is claimed to be the representative of the whole of the daily-rated staff of the Railway, and has delegates from all Branches on the Committee'.[18] Although the union could not be accorded official recognition (there was no legal provision for union registration at this date), its leaders helped aggrieved groups of employees to draw up petitions to the management, and were sometimes allowed to participate in the settlement of disputes on an informal basis.

Table 2.3. *Railway wages, 1910–39*

Occupation	1910	1921/2	1929/30	1931/2	1939
Labourer	0s. 9d. to 1s. 3d.	2s. 0d.	1s. 6d. to 1s. 9d.	1s. 3d.	2s. 0d.
Artisan	2s. 0d. to 3s. 0d.	3s. 6d. to 5s. 6d.	3s. 0d. to 5s. 0d.	2s. 8d. to 5s. 0d.	3s. 6d. to 5s. 6d.
Engine-driver	n.d.	n.d.	3s. 8d. to 7s. 0d.	2s. 8d. to 7s. 0d.	4s. 0d. to 7s. 0d.

Source: L. A. Lacy, 'A History of Railway Unionism in Ghana' (MA thesis, University of Legon, 1965), p. 48.

In November 1938, with the cost of living rising rapidly, the GCRAWU again petitioned the government, via the general manager of railways, for 'the restoration of the 1929 rates of pay, and an increase in the number of pensionable posts'.[19] There were a number of subsidiary points connected with the age of retirement, annual leave, uniforms and the like. When no reply had been received by the beginning of May 1939, the union threatened strike action. On 9 May 'all classes of workers, from the highly paid engine drivers and artisans to the porters and labourers, with the exception of twenty drivers who were on the pensionable establishment, downed tools'.[20] Two days later, the governor agreed that the 1929 rates of pay should be restored (no increase had been granted since the reductions of 1930–1), and promised to establish a board of enquiry to investigate the remaining grievances. But the men refused to return to work, according to the management 'intimidated by the ringleaders',[21] until the union leadership had had time to consider the proposals. Certainly, these leaders saw the strike as an opportunity to elevate the status of the union and not simply as an economic protest. On 15 May, J. C. Vandyck, the union secretary, informed the general manager that they would return to work on the one further condition that the general manager 'recognise the Gold Coast Railway African Workers Union as the body to which all matters affecting the interest of individual workers in his employment should be referred'.[22] When the general manager replied that existing laws did not provide for the recognition of trade unions, the strike continued. Eventually, a demonstration of workers was routed, with considerable violence, by the police, and eighteen unionists were imprisoned.

The severity of the government's reaction was clearly intended to reduce the likelihood of similar occurrences amongst other government employees. As an official report stated,

> There were naturally repercussions in other government department[S] and there were one or two cases where anxiety was caused. Steps were taken immediately to put into effect the decisions of the Wages Board and, so far as possible, to place other departments on the same footing as the Railway. Any danger of a general upheaval died away though it has taken time to settle down, and even yet petitions are being received from Government employees, the principal demand usually being to be made pensionable.[23]

Against the background of the beginning of the Second World War, with instructions arriving from London 'to take every possible step to guard against the contingency of the possibility of friction between employers and workers in Colonial Dependencies',[24] it was essential to control this unrest and channel the development of union organisation by Ghanaian workers. For this had received considerable impetus from the large measure of success of the 1939 strike.[25] It is in this context that the establishment of a Labour Department by the Colonial Government to assist the formation of unions must be seen.

Dynamics and divisions in early Railway Union development

At this point, it is worth considering some of the salient features of early Railway Union development. Of particular interest from the general perspective of this study are the differences in union orientation and degree of participation displayed by the various categories of railway employee. Attention should also be paid to the most serious sources of divisions which manifested themselves during this early period. For, generally speaking, these differences and divisions have continued to characterise Railway Union politics down to the present day.

The Railway Union was essentially the creation of a dynamic, elementary school educated, labour elite of artisans. Unlike many of the so-called skilled workers in the mines and other industries, these artisans were genuinely highly skilled, many having been sent abroad for training. It was perhaps in part out of concern for the considerable capital investment they represented that the Railway Administration adopted a far more progressive policy towards its skilled workers than did the mining companies. Aiming to achieve a high degree of labour stabilisation, the Railway Administration proved relatively responsive to demands for improved conditions of service, and disinclined to resort to mass dismissals when the artisans sought to organise themselves. In turn, the latter, who were mostly literate Fantis from the nearby coastal towns of Cape Coast and Elmina, looked to skilled technical work to provide a relatively permanent and prestigious form of employment, a suitable alternative to clerical work.[26] Indeed, the skilled African railway worker, and especially the engine-driver, was a figure of very considerable status, certainly of great popular admiration, in the Gold Coast society of the inter-war years. He was the pioneer of technological progress, familiar with the white man's magic, opening up the country to a new pace of social and economic life. It was natural that he should expect official recognition of his high social status in terms of an appropriate financial reward.

The railway artisans were concentrated in large numbers in the Sekondi Location workshops. This situation made for the rapid development of a sense of solidarity, and of the power they possessed as a corporate group. It also facilitated communication and organisation. It was fairly easy, moreover, to communicate quickly and secretly with fellow workers

33

stationed at the up-country branches through the agency of the itinerant engine-drivers.

One further factor which encouraged the spontaneous development of trade unionism amongst the railway workers, and lent the union such significance for its members, deserves brief mention here. As we have seen, Sekondi was a new town, or, as the railway general manager described it in 1912, 'an upstart town, practically the creation of the railway'.[27] As young workers floated in, beyond the control of the local chiefs, and without the close supervision which the mining companies provided in the mine townships, new forms of social organisation, or mutations of traditional organisation, were required. For the Fanti and other southern Ghanaians who predominated in the skilled and semi-skilled railway labour force, traditional associational forms were of distinctly ambiguous relevance. The Fanti 'young men' (i.e. 'commoners' as distinct from elders and chiefs) were heirs to a tradition of popular political participation through membership of 'asafo' companies, semi-military organisations which also had recognised political functions. During the first half of the twentieth century the asafos were frequently and centrally involved in political disputes over the legitimacy of particular chiefs and their policies, and sometimes, implicit in this, over the institutional reforms the Colonial Government sought to introduce.[28] While the rules governing asafo politics were vague and highly changeable – as one historian has observed, 'they were little more than a reflection of the existing balance of power in the state'[29] – there can be no doubt that they were, in an important sense, democratic institutions, both in internal structure and as regards their function in the wider political system.

There are clear indications, however, that the operation of the asafos in Cape Coast, Elmina and other Fanti chieftaincies was characterised by intense and increasing inter-company rivalry, often over issues only marginally related to twentieth century economic and political realities.[30] The overriding need in the Sekondi situation was for an organisation promoting co-operation and solidarity amongst the mass of skilled railway workers. On the one hand, therefore, no simple adaptation of traditional organisation appeared practicable or adequate to the new circumstances. This need was rather met through the creation of the Workshop Associations and subsequently the Railway Union, with officials acting as organisers, arbitrators and spokesmen for the railway workers in many areas of social life other than the narrowly occupational. On the other hand, certain stylistic characteristics of the asafo companies were to find expression in the developing cultural idiom of the railway workers' union. The union's borrowing of asafo cultural elements can be seen in the use, from early days, of an asafo 'gong-gong' (literally, a gong), an asafo battle-cry ('Kyor-be' – 'Prepare yourselves for the coming struggle'), and, more generally, in the quasi-military atmosphere of mass meetings, with speakers trying to outdo each other in bravado. The asafo tradition may well have influenced the railway workers' understanding of union organisation and operations, and certainly provided a cultural referent for the concept and practice of solidarity.

However, these same factors making for solidarity among the skilled workers set them off the more sharply from the unskilled workers, mainly illiterate Nigerians and northerners speaking little or no Fante, and firmly attached to their own cultural traditions. As we have seen, the artisans extended their union organisation to the unskilled workers in a particular situation of common grievances and insecurity, and essentially for the opportunistic reason of enhancing their own bargaining position. But it was perhaps to be anticipated that, once granted the permanent status and conditions of service they desired – monthly salary, two weeks annual leave etc. – they would then be inclined to practise a more particularist ('elitist') form of unionism.

Certainly, cultural differences and social distance between unskilled and skilled worker strata were such as to make any deeper and more lasting solidarity seem unlikely. As a senior colonial official remarked in 1936:

> The manual labourer has no standing in the social scheme. He is regarded by the educated classes as an inferior – also the term 'labourer' is closely associated with the word 'strangers' which defines the status of the natives of neighbouring countries and the Northern Territories. Under the present order of things it would not be possible for the son of an educated man to become a labourer.
>
> The artisan class is on a different footing, for this worker has his niche in the social life of the colony, and there is a tendency for sons to follow the vocation of their fathers.
>
> It is obvious that it will be some time before any labour movement is created. The probability of any co-operation between the artisan and the labourer is remote.[31]

Surprisingly, this coincidence of ethnic, cultural and economic lines of division was not to be a source of serious political disunity within the Railway Union. Labour unity, however, has implied the condition that the unskilled workers and their representatives (generally speaking their gang headmen) should accept second-class status, and a subordinate role in the union's power and policy-formulating structure. This they have generally been prepared to do out of recognition of their dependence on the powerful bargaining position and collective strength of the artisan class. In turn, the artisans have been concerned, in nearly all their strike actions, to fight general battles for an improvement in the wage-levels of all 'lower-paid workers' (i.e. skilled and unskilled manual workers). This might be explained in part by the artisans' continuing failure to attain that distinct economic and occupational status which they have long felt themselves to deserve, and which, once attained, might have served to differentiate their interests more clearly from those of the unskilled labourer. But their relationship to the unskilled workers has certainly also come to involve a genuinely protective, paternalistic attitude.

The most serious lines of division within the Railway Union (or the Railway Union's potential membership) have been, firstly, between the skilled workers and the clerical workers and, secondly, between the workshop artisans and the engine-drivers. Both were clearly presaged in the early period of the union's history. Firstly, the establishment of the union owed nothing to the activity of clerical workers, nor did members of this occupational category seek to participate in union affairs prior to the protective trade union legislation of the early 1940s. In part, no doubt, this was because unionisation was of particularly dubious legality, and most clearly guaranteed to meet with official disapproval, in the case of white-collar members of the civil service. These people were certainly not without their grievances but felt it advisable to articulate them by petitioning the government in an informal, ad hoc and expressly respectful fashion. This did not, however, reflect merely a difference of official attitude toward unionisation for manual and clerical employees. When union membership was declared legitimate for African clerical staff in the civil service (as it was in the early 1940s legislation), clerical unionists continued to display a marked moderation, even humility, in their approach to grievance representation. Indeed, many clerical workers chose not to join the union, while those who did rarely attended mass meetings. In explanation of this attitude, it should be observed that the career structure for clerical workers was not (and has not been) such as to encourage a high level of trade union activism. They enjoyed greater mobility opportunities – both in number and degree – than the skilled workers, and recognised that the path to promotion lay in examination-passing and the good opinion of supervisors. They focused their efforts accordingly, showing little inclination to collective action, and avoiding involvement in disruptive trade union activity. Hence they followed the management's instructions to refrain from participation in the 1939 strike. In addition, they were, of course, highly conscious of their superior status to the artisans, and therefore inclined to regard the 'rowdy', militant style of unionism of the latter as very much beneath them. In their own view, no doubt, they were also sufficiently well versed in the bureaucratic processes and

36

financial problems of government to understand the reasons for delay in settling grievances. Manual workers' militancy might be seen as resulting from pure ignorance, and consequent impatience at what they (incorrectly) saw as deliberate delaying tactics on the part of the government or management.

The artisan–enginemen division derived not so much from attitudinal or cultural differences as from the almost inevitable sectionalist tendencies of militant craft unionism. The enginemen, being the most highly skilled of the railway manual workers, were at an early date accorded special privileges which they guarded jealously. In 1939 they were initially amongst the most militant advocates of strike action. Yet they later opposed prolongation on the grounds that it might cause the loss of pensions and other privileges (which very few artisans enjoyed). In the event, the strike was maintained, but shortly afterwards the formation of a separate Railway Enginemen's Union was announced. With the exception of two brief periods (1943–9 and 1962–6), the enginemen have continued to maintain a separate union, evidently believing that their own grievances over increment rates for example, or promotion opportunities and job classification, are sufficiently particular to require specialised handling.

Nevertheless, the enginemen have generally been in accord with the artisans on major, general issues, and have acted solidly with them at times of political crisis – the 1950, 1961 and 1971 strikes, for example. At such times it has been the practice to establish a Joint Council of Railwaymen to co-ordinate activity between the two unions. The maintenance of this artisan–engineman cohesion, as of that between artisans and unskilled workers, owes a great deal to the ideological influence of Pobee Biney's leadership in the nationalist era.

3

The railway workers in the nationalist movement – the meaning of political commitment

Most of the literature on African trade unionism emphasises the influence of the nationalist experience on the subsequent development of relations between post-Independence governments and labour movements.[1] The close affiliation of the labour movement to the ruling party after Independence, as in Ghana, is held by some writers to have resulted from the close ties forged between such parties and the unions in the period of nationalist agitation. Other writers, notably Berg and Butler, have argued that, in Ghana as in most other African countries, the unions displayed a marked lack of political commitment in the nationalist period.[2] This is said to explain their reluctance to accept party control in the period immediately after Independence, a control successfully asserted only because of the unions' inability to resist.

Both positions, it should be noted, tend to assume that political involvement in the nationalist movement, where it existed, implied commitment to a particular political party. Such an assumption should perhaps not be so glibly made. Both also posit a simple continuity in relations, or preferred relations, between unions and parties in the two eras. Yet it should be fairly obvious that such ties as predated Independence (or the period of 'diarchy') changed radically when the party became the state, and the superficial unity of the nationalist period gave way to an increasingly manifest differentiation of interests.

The case of the railway workers of Sekondi-Takoradi brings home in vivid manner the false simplicity of both of these arguments. The foremost proponents of political unionism in the nationalist era (when they staged a two-week strike in support of Nkrumah's 'Postive Action' campaign), the railway workers were subsequently to lead union resistance to control of the labour movement by the Convention People's Party. Why did they become the leading opponents of party affiliation, and how did this relate to their conception of nationalist aims? In short, what was the meaning of political commitment for the railway workers?

38

This question assumes importance not only from the perspective of general arguments as to the nature of union politics in Africa, but also within the particular context of Ghanaian politics. In 1949–50, it is apparent that, in as far as Nkrumah possessed a radical, organised mass basis of support, this consisted above all in the railway and harbour workers of Sekondi-Takoradi. One looks in vain, as did Nkrumah himself during these years, for any alternative, organised section of the masses, able or willing to back up his demands with direct physical threats to the continued stability of the colonial regime. This is not to cast doubts on the extent or enthusiasm of popular support for Nkrumah's programme; but only the railway workers were able to make this support conspicuous and politically telling. It is important, then, to understand just what this politically most crucial of groups conceived to be the aims of their nationalist activity.

The impact of the Labour Department's model of trade unionism

In 1938, against the background of serious labour disturbances in the Caribbean colonies, the Gold Coast Government established a Labour Department. As the Colonial Secretary had noted in October 1937, 'The recent spread of labour unrest throughout the British Colonial Empire points to the necessity of an organisation with accurate knowledge of labour conditions should the day come when we have to face serious labour disputes in the Gold Coast'.[3] Within eighteen months, the government had to deal with a major strike action by the railway workers, and there were clear indications of mounting unrest among other workers. In November 1941 the railway artisans and labourers again came out on strike in support of a demand for more speedy implementation of the 1939 agreement. The governor, shocked at the railway workers' failure to give advance warning of their intention, and, even more, at the lack of consideration for the war effort their action implied, instructed the police and management to deal severely with the strikers.[4] Many were imprisoned, and temporary labourers were taken on by the Railway Department, thereby inducing some of the unskilled workers to return to work.[5] The workshop artisans remained solid, however, and retaliated against the government by persuading workers in the Public Works and Posts and Telecommunications Departments in Sekondi to join them. There were even reports that the strikers were intending to storm Sekondi prison 'to release the prisoners and so obtain their help'.[6] After twelve days they were forced to capitulate and report back to work in return for the release of most of their imprisoned fellow strikers. J. C. Vandyck and John Ashun, president and secretary of the union, were detained until May 1942, and then, predictably, the Railway Department refused to reinstate them. The union approached Nana Kobina Nketsia, chief of British Sekondi, and later Dr J. B. Danquah, to lobby for their reinstatement, and they did so, but to no avail.[7]

In the aftermath of the December 1941 strike, government representatives visited Sekondi Location and gained an assurance that the railway workers would refrain from further strike activity until the conclusion of the war.[8] Then, the railwaymen were promised, the government would give speedy and sympathetic consideration to their claim for a compensatory wage increase. Nevertheless, the Colonial Government was understandably anxious to take additional measures to prevent similar disturbances. Accordingly, in February 1942, the Labour Department recruited I. G. Jones, a former official of the British Union of Mineworkers, to man the trade union section. It was his responsibility to organise, or reorganise, Ghanaian unions along the most suitable lines (from the government's point of view), and to instruct local unionists in the proper procedures to be followed.

These procedures had already been laid down in outline. In February 1941 the Colonial Government had issued a Trade Unions Ordinance authorising the combination of five or more persons, and subsequently it issued a series of legislative orders, modelled largely on equivalent wartime measures in the United Kingdom, defining a 'trade dispute', the proper settlement procedures, and the circumstances in which strike action was illegal.[9] Initially, the Labour Department stipulated that industrial disputes be settled through the local chiefs and elders in the Native Councils, in the hope that these councils would moderate the demands of workers and keep them from approaching the government directly. The railway workers immediately protested at this idea, however, and in compromise the Labour Department suggested that the more exalted Provincial Council of Chiefs should act as a mediating body.[10]

The Colonial Government's conception of legitimate trade unionism was aptly summarised in a pamphlet written by the special adviser to the Kenyan Labour Department which was widely circulated to union organisers throughout the British Colonies: 'A trade union is not an organisation with political aims. It is an association which has as its main objective the regulation of relations between workers and their employers.'[11] Such regulation, it was stressed, was better achieved through peaceful negotiation than through strike action. This was the lesson which I. G. Jones set out to teach, though with considerable sympathy for the predicament of Ghanaian unionists and employing a rather more flexible approach than the preceding quotation suggests.

40

The Labour Department's report for 1942 noted that

> Early in this year, this officer toured the country holding informal meetings with groups of people in order to explain the principles of Trade Unionism and the Provision of the Trade Unions Ordinance. In the early stages this officer met with considerable suspicion as to Government intentions and with a great deal of ignorance as to the aims and objects of trade unionism. He has been successful in obtaining the confidence of all those with whom he has come into contact and his advice on procedure has been willingly accepted by the Railwaymen whose Union – the Gold Coast Railway African Employees' Union – shows the most promise of those so far registered.[12]

The Railway unionists were indeed highly suspicious of government intentions at first, and informed I. G. Jones that they would co-operate with him only if he helped them to secure the reinstatement of J. C. Vandyck and John Ashun as railway employees. This he was able to achieve towards the end of the year, and the railway unionists kept their promise to follow his advice on reorganisation.

The remarks of H. B. Cofie, assistant secretary of the union at this time, testify to the confidence which I. G. Jones managed to establish in his intentions: 'It was a surprise to us that he really fought for us, showed us the proper channel to pass, and was most energetic on our behalf in many ways.'[13] Jones' plans for reorganisation involved incorporating the African clerical staff in the renamed Gold Coast Railway African Technical and Clerical Employees' Union (1943). Clerical staff representatives (or 'clerical unionists' as I shall henceforth refer to them) soon came to dominate the union executive, partly through the numerical predominance which ex officio representation gave them, and partly through their possession of the literary and administrative skills required by more sophisticated procedures.[14]

This development was largely responsible for giving considerable currency in Railway Union deliberations to the peaceful, apolitical model of unionism propounded by the Labour Department. Most of the skilled worker, or 'technical', unionists, while appreciating the usefulness of the advice I. G. Jones had to offer, listened to this apolitical line with increasing cynicism as the decade progressed. The clerical unionists, on the other hand, took the reasoning behind it more seriously. There were a number of possible reasons for this. The skilled workers were later to argue that the clerical staff were relatively contented with their situation under the colonial regime, and more particularly with the pay increase awarded them in 1946 by the Harragin Commission. But this was no adequate explanation, since the clerical workers, too, suffered a severe subsequent decline in living standards from the inflation of 1947–50, and the slow rate of Africanisation of senior posts in the civil service provided a source of real resentment. More important were the general situational considerations and cultural characteristics, outlined in the previous chapter, which made for moderation among clerical workers and a marked concern to do things 'the correct way' – i.e. by emulation of British ways and institutions, as communicated to them by the British in the Gold Coast. Viewed from their own perspective, they were sufficiently well educated to understand the reasoning behind the model of strict separation of trade unionism from politics. In particular, they adopted the argument that, since not all Railway Union members were supporters of the Convention People's Party, it would be undemocratic to stage strike actions in support of Nkrumah's nationalist campaign.[15]

Most of the leaders of the new unions established in 1943–50 might also be classified as clerical unionists and, since they owed their institution largely to the education and assistance of the Labour Department, they were similarly inclined to uphold the apolitical model. The most important, though only partial, exception was the Mines Employees' Union. The story of the founding of the MEU illustrates the continuing obstacles to effective organisation presented by the character of the mines' labour force, as well as the rather ambiguous role played by the Colonial Labour Department. According to J. B. Blay, the official historian of the Union, the initiative came from skilled workers at the Abosso mine, where a strike in the electric shop against a white supervisor in June 1944 proved successful and encouraged the creation of a general union.[16] The Abosso mineworkers summoned a delegates' meeting at which J. H. Sam was elected president. In December, Sam toured the rest of the mines stressing labour's unity of interest and the benefits of organisation. An attempt was made to register the embryonic union, but I. G. Jones, as labour inspector for the Western Province, expressed his opposition to an amalgamated union and urged a separate union for each mine. At a second delegates' meeting in January 1945 it was nevertheless decided to insist on a single miners' union, and in September the Gold Coast Mines Employees' Union was officially registered with 1,780 paid-up members. Six months later, however, the union could claim to represent no more than 5,000 of the 40,000 workers then employed in the mines. It was not until the first successful strike was staged in October 1947 that the paid-up membership grew to a more impressive figure. Even then, the control of the union leadership over its northerner members was extremely fragile, being dependent on the intermediary role of the tribal headmen. The accountability of these headmen to the chiefs of their home areas provided an indirect but effective channel of influence for colonial district officers stationed in the north. Accordingly, the southerner leaders of the union, though often themselves sympathetic to the militant style of nationalism represented by Nkrumah, were deterred from seeking to mobilise their membership in overtly political action by the risks of internal and possibly long-lasting division which such a policy would inevitably incur.[17]

By 1945, unions with a total paid-up membership of 6,030 were registered, and in that year the Railway Union took the initiative in establishing the first Gold Coast Trades Union Congress to co-ordinate their activities. The TUC central office was at Sekondi, and this fact, together with the greater experience and dynamism of the railway unionists, assured them a large measure of influence over the growing trade union movement as a whole. In spite of the militancy and radical nationalism of the skilled worker rank and file, however, Railway Union leadership of the TUC did not make for direct involvement of the whole trade union movement in the nationalist struggle. Delegates from most other unions on the TUC Executive Board, including C. W. Techie-Menson, the first president (1945–8), opposed such a policy, and the Railway Union Executive was itself far from characterised by singularity of purpose.[18]

The Colonial Labour Department succeeded, then, in raising considerable obstacles to trade union involvement in the nationalist movement. And, although the militant nationalism of the skilled railway workers eventually gained expression in the 'Positive Action' strike of January 1950, this requires explanation in terms of leadership politics as well as the strength of rank-and-file feeling.

Railway worker nationalism: economics and ideology

The factors making for an upsurge of popular unrest and nationalist consciousness in the immediate post-war period in Ghana have been admirably discussed elsewhere.[19] Here it is necessary merely to point out certain salient features of the railway workers' conception of nationalist aims and the most important influences on their thinking.

In the first place, nationalism, for the railway workers as for most Ghanaian nationalists, was in large part an expression of acute economic discontent, a response to post-war conditions of rapid price inflation and falling real incomes. The Colonial Government signally failed to produce the increased prosperity or financial opportunities for Africans that had been expected. In 1941, we have seen, the railway workers had been assured that their refraining from strike action during the war would be rewarded with improved conditions at its conclusion. But these did not materialise without the pressure of a major strike action (in 1947), and

43

even the wage increase of that year proved to be only a temporary hiatus in the general pattern of declining real wage-levels. This may be seen from the evidence presented by W. B. Birmingham on fluctuations in the real value of the government minimum wage.[20]

In such conditions of rapid inflation, as David Apter has cautiously put it, rightly avoiding any simple equation, 'the urban population suffered the most. It is in the urban areas as well that the most aggressive feeling for independence resides'.[21] More specifically a number of groups were especially severely frustrated. Ghanaian businessmen, or would-be businessmen, chafing at the virtual monopoly of trade enjoyed by European firms, were inclined to lay the blame directly on oppressive discrimination by the Colonial Government. The rapidly expanding class of elementary school leavers, finding themselves with little hope of employment in government clerical service, were anxious for increased mobility opportunities, and therefore more rapid economic and political development. The skilled railway workers, while better off than many of their fellow elementary school leavers, were still without the improved conditions of service and life style, equivalent to those of the clerical workers, to which they had long aspired. Such frustration could be greater for those to whom the goal seemed nearer, and greater still when, as their situation deteriorated, that goal became increasingly remote. Living in the city of Sekondi-Takoradi, moreover, the railway workers were very aware of the worsening situation and mounting discontent of other groups. Most

Table 3.1. *Fluctuations in the real value of the minimum wage, 1939–50*

Date	Daily wage	Money wage index	Cost of living index	Real wage index	Food price index
May 1939	1s. 6d.	100	100	100	100
Nov. 1945	1s. 10d.	122	186	66	202
Nov. 1947	2s. 9d.	183	212	86	250
Dec. 1948	2s. 9d.	183	227	81	264
Dec. 1950	3s. 3d.	217	285	76	391

Source: W. B. Birmingham, 'An Index of Real Wages of the Unskilled Labourer in Accra,' *Economic Bulletin of Ghana*, 4, 3 (1960), p. 6.

disturbing was the growing number of 'pilot boys', a semi-criminal group of unemployed young school leavers.[22]

Indeed, several of the phenomena which Meyer Fortes identified in 1945 as making for mounting unrest in the colonies after the war, were to be found in particularly acute form in Sekondi-Takoradi.[23] The influence of foreign soldiers and sailors, calling in at the colonies, for example, was clearly most strongly felt in the harbour towns. The British and American soldiers who drunkenly toured the brothels of Takoradi hardly conformed to the colonial stereotype of the dignified, self-disciplined white man, and might have done much to undermine respect for whites in general (though it is unclear to what degree such a stereotype had ever been widely prevalent). More important perhaps, the radical discontent of the American negro troops seems to have had a considerable impact on many of the young people and workers of Sekondi-Takoradi, offering them a new social and ideological dimension in which to conceive of their own situation and sense of grievance. Many of the older railway workers interviewed in 1971 spoke of exciting and influential meetings with some of these American blacks during the war years.

The nationalist activism displayed by Ghanaian ex-servicemen has often been remarked upon.[24] Recently, it has been questioned whether they were, proportionately, much better represented in the ranks of CPP activists than any other section of the population.[25] But the important point, for our purposes, lies in the influence which some of them, at least, had on the thinking of the railway workers. A number of ex-railway workers and other inhabitants of Sekondi, after serving in the Allied Forces in 1943–5, were prominent in the organisation of the Gold Coast Ex-Servicemen's Union. Many returned to Sekondi to communicate something of their sense of power and their scorn for the fragility of British Colonial Government to friends still working in the railway:

> I can remember when my friend Francis came to see us on Christmastime, just after the war. We were expecting just to celebrate, but after much akpeteshie [local gin] he wanted to talk about how we were going to throw out the government. I can honestly say it astonished me, because I had started thinking politically but he had not been serious at all when he left us but just a cheerful sort of fellow. And when I asked him, 'How can we possibly throw out the British Government which has shown it can beat the Germans?,' he just said, 'There is an army of us here who helped defeat the Germans, and we show the British our strength on our own land, with all the people behind us'.[26]

It might appear, therefore, that railway worker nationalism was simply an extension of economic grievance, lent what ideological dimension it possessed by a growing sense of confidence and of solidarity with other blacks against the white man. It is significant in this context that the personal qualities which, in the railway workers' view, distinguished both Nkrumah and their own great nationalist leader, Pobee Biney, were simply 'courage' – the courage to act out boldly their sense of grievance, challenging the colonial authorities directly – and 'understanding' – 'it was as though he could tell us our thoughts before we ourselves knew them'.[27] At the same time, however, this identification with the courageous 'strong man' leader entailed defining the struggle as being against the 'effete' detached African educated elite, as well as against the British. Progressively, it also involved a vision of a new, more brotherly and egalitarian order, 'self-government' meaning government by and for the 'common man' rather than a mere taking over of colonial structures.

Some of the radical railway unionists conceived of the struggle in overtly Marxist terms. J. S. Annan, for example, a member of both Railway Union and TUC Executive Councils, attended the 1945 World Federation of Trades Unions Conference in Paris, and returned to report:

> I believe that the time is now ripe when organised labour in the Gold Coast should commence to struggle against economic and socially militating forces: there should be no room for fear: we know these reactionary forces – the might of Imperialist Capitalism that has exploited the working-classes for years must be stayed. Let me say, however, that our struggle is not only against foreign capitalism and merciless exploitation – it is also against unbridled Capitalism of our own people, the Africans: we do not intend to remove foreign Capitalism that exists to make excessive profits at the expense of African cheap labour and put similar Capitalism in black skin: our fight is directed against Capitalism of any description that refuses to give fair and adequate remuneration to labour. Our slogan must be, 'Workers of the Gold Coast unite: You have nothing to lose but your Chains'.[28]

The influence of Marxist ideas with some of the railway unionists can be traced back to the activity of Wallace-Johnson's West African Youth League in the mid-1930s. Born in Sierra Leone, and trained for a time in the Soviet Union, Isaac Wallace-Johnson attempted between 1933 and 1937 to introduce a socialist, anti-colonialist mass movement to the Gold Coast.[29] To this end, he combined the articulation of radical anti-imperialist ideology with the representation of local grievances (for example, miners' grievances over the lack of compensation for industrial injuries), making use of his contacts in the British parliamentary left. By

December 1936, the Youth League claimed a total membership of 7,000. This was probably an exaggerated figure, and the movement largely collapsed when Wallace-Johnson himself was forced out of the country in 1937. But there can be no doubting the continuing influence of his ideas and strategy on many members of the Gold Coast sub-elite of skilled workers and their leaders. In particular, Pobee Biney, the railway workers' great nationalist leader, was a local organiser of the Youth League, and the branch at Sekondi-Takoradi is reported to have been one of the largest and most active.[30]

Nevertheless, the most striking aspect of the history of the Youth League in the Gold Coast is its failure to attract a larger or more militant following. Admittedly, economic and political conditions in the mid-30s were, as we have seen, hardly propitious for self-confident political assertion. But one might also hazard the suggestion that, for many of the railway artisans, with their love of plain speaking, Wallace-Johnson's Marxist rhetoric was more a handicap than an attraction. Certainly, Pobee Biney, though himself apparently influenced by a vulgar form of Marxism, found it necessary, when mobilising the railway workers in support of political action in the late 40s, to speak in common words which the ordinary artisan could readily understand. This involved articulating the class element in the nationalist revolution only in somewhat vague terms, and playing down the differences between Biney himself and the right wing of Nkrumah's followers. Only after 1950 did the full extent of these differences clearly emerge.

Biney's ideology will receive more detailed treatment later in this chapter. Here, the important point is that in the immediate post-war period, the class element in railway worker nationalism, though real enough, was generally speaking more implicit than explicit, and somewhat narrowly defined. Hostility to elitism was directed specifically against the existing educated elite and was primarily expressed in terms of non-attendance at meetings of the United Gold Coast Convention.[31] The two leading representatives of the UGCC in Sekondi were especially unappealing political figures from the railway workers' point of view. The lawyer R. S. Blay had on more than one occasion attempted to intervene with the railway unionists to persuade them of the advantage of official arbitration procedures, and was therefore cast (by the militants) as a government sympathiser.[32] And the lawyer F. Awonowoor Williams was well known locally for extreme and somewhat eccentric elitist views which, to his credit, he made no attempt to conceal from the masses.[33]

Kwame Nkrumah was a startling contrast with this kind of politician. Nevertheless, he appears to have remained suspect with the railway workers so long as he remained within the fold of the UGCC. It was not until 1949, when he broke with the elite, and came to speak to the railway workers in the streets of Sekondi (rather than the chambers of the UGCC) that he made any great impact.[34] Only then did he come to express radical nationalist ideas, already current among the 'common men', in a sufficiently extreme form to give the impression of courageous and genuine leadership. Interviews held with the older railway workers in 1971 left little doubt that Nkrumah's rhetorical ability endowed him, for a time at least, with truly charismatic status. Even some of the leaders of the 1961 strike against the Nkrumah Government described his impact in terms as rapturous, if not quite so poetic, as those of Ayi Armah's hero in *The Beautyful Ones Are Not Yet Born*:

> I stood there staring like a believer at the man and when he stopped I was ashamed and looked around to see if anybody had been watching me. They were all listening. The one up there was rather helpless-looking, with a slight, famished body. So from where had he got this strength that enabled him to speak with such confidence to us, and we waiting patiently for more to come? Here was something more potent than mere words. These dipped inside the listener, making him go with the one who spoke.[35]

Yet it would be wrong to overemphasise Nkrumah's personal hold over the railway workers. The militant artisans, unlike most other Ghanaian social groups, already possessed in Pobee Biney a leader of similar rhetorical power and equal charismatic stature in their own eyes to that of Nkrumah himself. Indeed, many of them came to hold the view that he was greater than Nkrumah, more courageous and more consistent in his principles. Certainly, his influence was more continuous and direct, and his leadership as crucial to the success of the 1950 'Positive Action' strike (from which, the railway workers claim, Nkrumah would have backed down had not Biney forced his hand). Since his role in Railway Union politics in 1945–50 was so central and illustrates so vividly many of the continuing characteristics of rank-and-file attitudes, it is worth focusing on his part in these events. The following account presents the way in which Biney's character, role and ideology were perceived (or, more accurately, subsequently perceived) by the skilled railway workers themselves. Although this runs the risk of overemphasising his personal importance, and over-glamorising his real character and personality, such an account is the more informative about subsequent attitudes and behaviour. For the legend of Pobee Biney still provides an ideal model of railway unionism for many members.

Pobee Biney and the politics of the 1950 'Positive Action' strike

Alfred Pobee Biney was born at Cape Coast on 13 January 1914.[36] Educated at the Government Boys' School there, he left in 1932 and took a series of jobs with the mining companies before entering the training scheme for engine-drivers in the railways in 1935. He soon took an active interest in trade union affairs, becoming a member of the Enginemen's Union Executive in 1941. Two years later, he appears to have been influential in persuading the enginemen to reamalgamate with the main Railway Union. His militant style of unionism was to earn him the nickname 'Let Go the Anchor' – a reference to the phrase he himself coined for declaring strike action, and intended to express the idea of downing tools (or 'dropping anchor'), thus bringing the railways to a grinding halt.

His initial participation in trade union officialdom was no doubt inspired by the ideological stimulus he received from membership of Wallace-Johnson's West African Youth League, and can be seen as clearly directed to building up a powerful radical political following. But, even more clearly than Wallace-Johnson, he was no mere ideologist but was sincerely concerned to right particular grievances. From the point of view of the skilled railway workers, his career is seen as having developed from that of mere branch unionist to that of major nationalist leader, and emphasis is placed on the fact that he was not a politician in the conventional derogatory sense, but a real workers' leader. To this is often added the significant qualification, 'He was a real workers' leader, but not just the railway workers' leader, rather a community leader. I should say he was a fighter for the suffering masses, a real humanitarian'.[37]

Biney initially developed this reputation as a 'fighter for the suffering masses' on the basis of his bold and successful, if constitutionally improper, spokesmanship for the railway workers' grievances. As we have seen, the Railway Union emerged from the Second World War period as the Gold Coast Railway African Clerical and Technical Employees' Union, its executive dominated by clerical unionists who mostly accepted the British model of apolitical unionism and favoured a policy of peaceful negotiation rather than direct action in the settlement of grievances. This policy proved markedly ineffective and, to many of the rank-and-file skilled workers, their officials seemed insufficiently concerned, urgent or courageous in their handling of grievances.

It was in this situation that Pobee Biney began to lead groups of aggrieved employees, skilled and unskilled, irrespective of their job category and proper channel of representation, to impromptu interviews with foremen and other supervisors to press for redress. He held no official executive rank in the union at this time: in 1945–9 he was merely Takoradi

49

branch representative for the enginemen on the Working Committee (with the exception of a brief period in 1946 when he stood in as interim president on the retirement of S. Wood). But he is remembered as having been almost invariably successful in gaining some redressive action. His main resource for this role seems to have consisted simply in his personal qualities of persistence and courage. He scorned red tape and other (as he saw them) delaying tactics of the management, and was able to overawe even senior executives with 'his huge magical frame' (Biney stood 6 ft 3 in tall and was extremely muscular). He was in a sense a bully, but a highly idealistic one.

> Soon his fame spread far and near and aggrieved railway employees would mob him during the brief spell his shunting engine stood in steam. They would state their grievances to him in great detail and retire, highly optimistic that their petition was in capable hands. Or they would travel to his residence from the farthest railway station to present their case and seek advice.[38]

On the basis of this approachability and success, and his 'stirring speeches at mass meetings, in which he advocated the correction of injustices merely from an impelling desire to see such injustices righted',[39] Biney's stature was such as to enable him to intervene decisively in the strike of 1947. The skilled and unskilled workers had still not received the benefits promised them in 1941 and were feeling the sharp pinch of inflation. Nevertheless, the executive proved slow and shy to press its case. By February 1947 'a rift is developing between the labouring and clerical classes, the former accusing the latter of resting content because of the awards which they have gained under the recommendation of the Harragin Commission'.[40] In October, the executive was pressurised into threatening strike action, and, on the 22nd, 5,900 workers – the total skilled and unskilled labour force – went on strike.

After two days, the Provincial Council of Chiefs sent a delegation to Sekondi to request that the strikers return to work while their leaders conducted negotiations. At a mass meeting, the union president, A. K. de Veer, declared himself in favour of the chiefs' suggestion. Biney stood up and expressed his contempt for such a back-down, attacking the chiefs ('our little gods of times past, now become messenger-boys of the Colonial Government')[41] for attempting to interfere. On a virtually unanimous vote, the strike continued for thirteen days more. The official executive was further embarrassed when, again largely at Biney's instigation, the rank- and file rejected the first communiqué produced after negotiations with a government-appointed commission, and it was compelled to return and fight for certain amendments.[42]

50

In spite of this demonstration of his substantive leadership of the rank and file, Biney was not elected to the union executive, until in 1949 the enginemen seceded yet again, and Biney became president of the Railway Enginemen's Union. (In the same year, he was also elected vice-president of the Gold Coast TUC.) There were two main reasons for his failure to achieve executive status. The executive was selected by delegates from the various branches at the annual conference, and few of the disproportionately high number of clerical delegates admired Biney's personality or ideological tendencies. Some of the skilled worker representatives, too, secretly disapproved of Biney's demagogic behaviour, involving frequent improper excursions into their official territory of jurisdiction. Secondly, rank-and-file pressure for Biney's election as president was tempered by general recognition of his possession of qualities more suitable to the role of leader in times of crisis than to the performance of continuous administrative functions.

Nevertheless, his reputation continued to grow with his leadership of demonstrations of discontent over issues extending from management–worker relations into the wider field of community politics. An interesting example of this occurred in early 1949 during the funeral of an ex-railway worker, a Mr Banka. Several hundred workers were participating in the customary procession from Location to Sekondi city centre. In the words o one of them,

> A white man came speeding along in his car with no intention of slowing down for the procession. Pobee jumped in front and stopped the car and beat on it, telling him to show due respect. Some of us joined in. Unknown to us he was a chief of police. He instructed his force to come and arrest the leaders in the procession. When we were brought to court, we were fined £15 by the magistrate, but Pobee Biney told us not to pay. We were not to pay the government anything because we were in the right and we had the solidarity of the workers behind us. Realising this, the government first reduced the fine, and later dropped it altogether. This was a great victory for Pobee.[43]

During 1948–9 Biney organised several rallies in Sekondi to communicate his radical nationalism to a wider audience. Hundreds of railway workers would ride into Sekondi on a hijacked train and disperse throughout the city urging people to come and attend the rally, thereby expressing in practical form Biney's belief in the political vanguard role of the organised, enlightened workers. Biney's rhetorical skill is frequently described in terms similar to those used of Nkrumah: 'We always felt he was simply revealing our own thoughts and needs to us. It was as though he was

51

able to penetrate our consciousness and extract out of it the feeling of solidarity.' [44]

The ideology he communicated might best be termed 'African populism'. He attacked the evils of colonialism on the grounds not only of economic exploitation but also of its destructive effect on the traditional culture and social relations, the sense of brotherhood of the Ghanaian people. The true 'people' he defined as 'the common people', as distinct from the elite of lawyers, civil servants, and other collaborators with the colonial regime. He derided the latter's cultural separatism, their 'White African' dress and manners. He was therefore strongly opposed to the United Gold Coast Convention and its leadership of 'lawyers who would not risk their wigs for the sake of the common man'.[45] Accordingly, he was totally unsympathetic to the view, prevalent among many Railway Union and TUC officials in 1949–50, that to stage a strike in support of 'Positive Action' [46] would be to confuse trade unionism with party politics and to misrepresent those workers, mainly clerical staff, who favoured the UGCC rather than the Convention People's Party.

This did not mean that Biney wished to tie the Ghanaian labour movement to unconditional support of Nkrumah's Convention People's Party. He emphasised in his speeches the idea that the railway workers were fighting for a new, independent and more just society, not for the CPP as such. It is likely that he was already aware of the divergence between the skilled railway workers' aims (as he conceived them), and those of many leading members of the CPP. Accordingly, his notion of the vanguard role of the organised, enlightened workers in leading the Ghanaian people to independence involved the corollary that they should continue to act thereafter as defenders of the nationalist movement's aims, checking degenerative tendencies in the party-become-government. Admittedly, this implication became far clearer to the rank and file from Biney's speeches and behaviour after the 'Positive Action' strike and the CPP's accession to a share of government power. In 1949–50, the issue of party commitment was not squarely faced. Nevertheless, the highly conditional nature of railway worker support for the CPP deserves emphasis even during this early period.

In retrospect, it might seem strange that Biney was at all prepared to back the CPP and the melange of social forces it represented. There was talk in 1949 amongst the radical railway unionists of forming a separate Labour Party, but this was rejected as being unrealistic.[47] Of course, the full extent of Nkrumah's willingness to compromise with the colonial authorities and the right wing of his own party could not have been apparent at this time. Nor could the weakness of the UGCC's challenge have been fully anticipated. A further consideration might have inclined

Biney to throw his weight behind Nkrumah. It is possible that Sacki Scheck, personal secretary to Nkrumah at this time and a close acquaintance of Biney, was influential in persuading the latter of Nkrumah's sincere intention to back the radicals in the trade union movement.

In any case, the immediate problem for Biney and the radicals in 1948–9 was to secure control of the Railway Union and the TUC. Of crucial importance here was Biney's success in developing a close friendship and ideological accord with Frank Woode, himself a clerical unionist, and general secretary of both organisations in 1947–9. The ascendancy which Biney's political line had achieved on the Railway Union Executive by April 1949 (illustrated in the following communiqué) was due in considerable measure to Woode's support and his influence with the clerical unionists:

> This Union wants it to be resolved at the Conference that the Trade Union Congress must force Government to reduce inflation. If the Government fails, the working class will back any Government who accepts this on principle. If the government-to-be (self-government) indicates better living for the working classes, there should be no alternative but to back it.
>
> A responsible Government officer recently said that Trade Unions must not go into politics. This in our opinion is a deliberate attempt to make Trade Unions in West Africa impotent. Instances can be quoted from the West Indies where labour and politics have shown a better way to the world.
>
> We cannot stand out of politics. Our demand can serve as an avenue to lay pressure on the Government in our legitimate demand for self-rule.
>
> Your faithful Brother Secretary,
>
> F. Woode.[48]

By 1949, the position of the political unionists had also been strengthened on the TUC Executive Board in consequence of the 'Big Six' episode. In response to the Accra riots of 28–29 February 1948, the Colonial Government arrested six leaders of the UGCC. Frank Woode, as general secretary, convened an emergency session of the TUC Executive which resolved to call a general strike unless the detainees were released within three days. In subsequent discussions with the government, C. W. Techie-Menson, president of the TUC and leader of the non-political unionists, accepted the government's explanation for the arrests, and its assurances that the six would be released on the arrival of a commission of enquiry from Britain. He agreed to call off the strike, and Woode and the other

53

militants, though unconvinced, felt bound to demonstrate solidarity. Shortly afterwards, however, they made such an issue of Techie-Menson's unrepresentative leadership that he was forced to resign from the presidency.[49] This facilitated the election of Pobee Biney as vice-president and Anthony Woode as general secretary of the TUC in August of the same year.

Anthony Woode (no relation to Frank Woode) was just twenty-three years old at this time. He had risen to sudden prominence in the trade union movement through his highly successful leadership of the oil storage workers of Takoradi, gaining important benefits for his membership through aggressive bargaining. He held radical nationalist views of similar complexion to Biney's, and the two became close friends. Anthony Woode was by far the more sophisticated thinker of the two, and increasingly assumed the role of political strategist to Biney's 'man of action'. Woode was also the good friend and political mentor of E. C. Turkson-Ocran, a young clerk in the Railway Union office. These three met regularly in Sekondi during 1949 to discuss and co-ordinate plans for a general strike, with Ocran acting as intermediary between Nkrumah on the one hand and Biney and Woode on the other.

In spite of the predominance of radical nationalist views in both Railway Union and TUC Executives in 1949–50, anti-political attitudes had not been totally overcome, and united support for an overtly political general strike could not be anticipated from either executive. At the TUC level, the Mineworkers' Union, most importantly, refused to be won over. Within the Railway Union, the president himself, J. C. Vandyck (who was also president of the TUC but delegated most of his duties to Biney), was unprepared for such dangerous action as Biney was proposing (perhaps recalling his incarceration in 1941–2), and resigned rather than involve himself in it.[50] When the time came, therefore, Biney and Woode concentrated their efforts on the railway workers and other workers in Sekondi-Takoradi, and called the strike without even consulting the other members of the executive or gaining formal approval at a mass meeting.

The excuse (and it was really little more than that) came with the government's dismissal of some sixty Meteorological Department workers for staging an illegal strike in October 1949. Anthony Woode forwarded a telegram to the government on 13 November, protesting about the dismissals, and threatening a general strike. It seems probable that this threat was regarded by most members of the TUC Executive as an indication of concern rather than a serious expression of intent. Biney and Woode had no intention of backing down, however, and at a meeting with the Joint Provincial Council of Chiefs on 6 January 1950 raised their demands instead to include '(a) the withdrawal of the government circular concerning the political activities of civil servants', and '(b) the immediate granting of Dominion status'.[51] On 6 January Pobee Biney announced a general strike to start at midnight and called out the railway workers. On 8 January Nkrumah announced the commencement of his 'Positive Action' campaign.

There is evidence to support the railway workers' contention that Nkrumah was reluctant to go ahead with 'Positive Action' but found his hand forced by Biney and Woode. Sir Charles Arden-Clarke, governor of the Gold Coast at the time, has written:

> The party leaders had been officially informed and were well aware that they had a perfectly constitutional way of achieving power and gaining their objective, if their candidates at the forthcoming election were returned. I have good reason to believe that some at least of the party leaders would have preferred not to resort to 'positive action' but to await the results of the general election, of the outcome of which they were fairly confident. But they found themselves enmeshed in the coils of their own propaganda. The tail wagged the dog . . .[52]

Reginald Saloway, the Colonial Secretary, has been even more explicit:

> Nkrumah publicly called off 'Positive Action' [. . .and] tried hard to get the Trades Union Congress to call off the general strike, but the TUC no longer had any control over the wild men. [Moreover] Dr Danquah taunted Nkrumah with having sold himself to the Colonial Secretary and thus infuriated the rank and file of the CPP who forced Nkrumah to retract.[53]

Railway worker participation in the strike was virtually one hundred per cent solid and lasted until 20 January. Some intimidation was certainly used – Biney had groups of his most enthusiastic supporters stationed along all routes to the railway work centres in Sekondi-Takoradi to dissuade would be strike-breakers, mostly clerical staff, from going to work. But the extent of spontaneous support for the strike was impressive. Workers in most parts of the country, on the other hand, participated for only a few days, and the mineworkers did not come out at all.

Ideology and significance of the 'Positive Action' strike

The reasons for this difference have already been outlined. It is important, however, to emphasise the distinctive idealistic dimension to railway worker militancy. This dimension is perhaps most accurately characterised

55

as 'populist' in the sense in which Peter Worsley uses the term.[54] That is to say, ' "Populism" is best conceived as a style of popular participation rather than a systematic ideology', but one involving 'a high valuation of the virtues and culture of the uncorrupted, simple, common folk, and a converse distrust of the wealthy, over-educated . . . and fundamentally corrupt urban elite'.[55] The social structure is conceived of dualistically in terms of an elite–mass division and opposition. Often, populism is a form or style of nationalism, in which the native elite are seen as the stooges of an external imperialist power.

Worsley's description of the typical structure of leader–follower relations in a populist movement is clearly applicable to the case of the railway workers and Nkrumah. The populist leader is generally a 'charismatic' figure, and often characterised by a 'strong man' image and by acceptance of violence as a legitimate means of effecting political change. On assumption of power, however, the leader is likely to be faced with the familiar problem, but in especially acute form, of 'institutionalising' a new and in some ways inevitably disappointing order. Increasing separation of leadership from rank and file and attempts to defuse the movement and substitute control for orderly development are likely to be seen as a 'revisionist' betrayal. This is particularly the case because of the vagueness and/or diversity of the movement's positive policy aims.

This provides important insights into the subsequent process of railway worker disillusionment with the Nkrumah regime. After the 1950 'Positive Action' strike, the railway workers naturally felt they had a right to expect much of the Nkrumah regime. This had, after all, cost them dearly. The Colonial Government declared a state of emergency and arrested a number of trade union leaders, including Biney and Woode, as well as Nkrumah and several other CPP leaders. These were brought before the courts, convicted and sentenced, Biney to six months' imprisonment, Nkrumah to one year on each of three separate counts. All government employees participating in the strike were dismissed and later re-employed only on conditions which entailed their losing long-service increment and other benefits. Understandably, many workers lost interest in trade union participation for several years to come, the TUC collapsed, and most of its constituent unions became moribund.

On the other hand, the general strike was successful in intensifying determination for political emancipation in the country as a whole, in stirring the Colonial Government to more progressive policies, and so in hastening the CPP's accession to power. During 1950 the Coussey Constitution was formulated, giving Ghanaians a measure of self-government, and arrangements were made for a general election to be held in February 1951. At this election the CPP was successful in winning thirty-four out of thirty-eight seats in the Legislative Assembly, and Nkrumah was released from detention to become leader of government business.

The beginnings of a new social order were therefore in sight, and the leaders and participants in the 'Positive Action' strike had high expectations of it. They expected, firstly, some recognition of their own contribution to the nationalist cause, some reward for services rendered. Apart from individual rewards, this meant aiding the revival of the trade union movement and according it an important role in the political life of the country. The railway workers expected a strong trade union movement to bring them benefits, and anticipated that their representatives would play a leading role in it, but did not desire this out of purely selfish motives. The aim of their nationalist participation had not been simply their own economic advancement, certainly not if this meant maintaining the existing socio-economic and political structure and simply stepping into the white man's shoes. The new order should be more egalitarian, more brotherly than that of the past: it should be government in the interests of the common man. The political role of the trade union movement should be directed to ensuring that such a new order was in fact instituted.

4

The politics of TUC reorganisation under the CPP regime

The repercussions of the 'Positive Action' strike of January 1950 virtually destroyed the Gold Coast TUC and many of its constituent unions. Particularly affected were those unions which had participated in the strike under the radical leadership of Pobee Biney and Anthony Woode. The Mineworkers' Union and the United Africa Company Employees' Union, having remained aloof, were less seriously disturbed and the Colonial Labour Department decided to encourage the resuscitation of the TUC around these moderate, apolitical unions, with affiliation to the International Confederation of Free Trade Unions (the Western liberal trade union centre). The new headquarters were to be based in Accra rather than in troublesome Sekondi. A new constitution prohibited Congress from initiating general strike actions, and allowed the Labour Department supervisory powers over the use of Congress funds. In July 1950, J. H. Sam, the Mineworkers' Union president, became president of the resuscitated Gold Coast TUC, and Charles Techie-Menson, former president and leader of the moderates in 1945–8, now stood in as general secretary.

At the same time, the Convention People's Party, under the direction of Komla Gbedemah during Kwame Nkrumah's detention, turned its attention to the Mineworkers' Union for the purpose of 'capturing' it and ensuring its participation in 'Positive Action no. 2'. For, in 1950–1, Gbedemah and Nkrumah had little reason to think that the apparent failure of the 'Positive Action' strike would soon become a glorious victory for them. They blamed what they saw as the dismal failure of that strike on Biney's and Woode's failure to bring out the mineworkers, and, judging that a further, more solid bout of 'Positive Action' was required, Gbedemah instigated a drive to capture the Gold Coast Mines' Employees Union.[1] In a series of elections, the old officers were driven out, and staunch CPP men such as D. K. Foevie and J. K. Arthur took over control. These men lacked sufficient prestige with the rank and file, however, to contemplate staging a strike immediately. Moreover, the shrewd generosity

58

of the Chamber of Mines in its negotiations with these new leaders hindered their attempts to whip up militant feeling. In the event this proved unnecessary since, by September 1951, 'Positive Action no. 2' was cancelled. Nkrumah was out of prison and leader of government business, having decided to co-operate with the Colonial Government and its schedule for self-government.

This co-operation came to extend to the Labour Department's reorganisation of the TUC into a more moderate, manipulable, Accra-based labour movement. The CPP leaders were now more interested in consolidating their newly acquired political power than in continuing to develop a movement of opposition. It was obvious to them that they could not immediately fulfil all their campaign promises, and during this tricky period of transition from nationalist agitation to executive responsibility, Nkrumah had no more desire than Governor Sir Charles Arden-Clarke to have to deal with serious industrial disturbances. Party loyalists should now direct their efforts to cooling down the unions. CPP men were already in control of the Mineworkers' Union, and in 1952, A. Allotey Moffatt, a Kumasi railway unionist who was 'closely linked to the Hon. Dr Kwame Nkrumah',[2] was elected general secretary of both the Railway Union and the Gold Coast TUC. It was to this Gold Coast TUC also that such able and ambitious CPP organisers as John K. Tettegah (subsequently TUC general secretary, 1954–9 and 1960–2) and Joe-fio N. Meyer (TUC president, 1956–8, chairman of the executive board, 1958–9, and secretary general, 1959–60) directed their efforts – men with little initial supporting base in the rank and file of the labour movement, but close to Nkrumah, and possessed of very considerable political and organisational abilities.[3]

This sudden switch in official CPP policy alienated the radical unionists and their followers, who had been pursuing a course of escalating opposition to the Colonial Government and now found themselves required to cool down and take a back seat. Anthony Woode, for instance, had been continuing his efforts to stir up the mineworkers, touring the mines townships in the summer of 1951 making inflammatory speeches. He attacked the leadership of the Gold Coast TUC and the Gold Coast Mines Employees' Union, in spite of the fact that CPP men were already in control in the latter organisation. Woode still believed that, ultimately, it would be necessary to drive the British out and was therefore angered by Nkrumah's decision to co-operate. Pobee Biney, meanwhile, on his release from gaol in August 1950, similarly felt that further 'Positive Action' was required to force the government's hand, and organised the Ghana Calling Association, a group of ex-servicemen, unemployed and other militants in Sekondi who apparently aimed to obtain explosives and initiate a terrorist campaign of property destruction.[4] By October, the Sekondi police had succeeded in gaoling several of its members and disbanding the associa-tion. Very few railway workers, it would appear, however radical in their aims, were prepared for such guerrilla-type revolutionary activity. Here, as on several subsequent occasions, the mass of railway workers perhaps proved more realistic in their political thinking, as well as more peaceable, than Biney himself.

During 1951 Biney assumed the seat in the Legislative Assembly with which the CPP rewarded his nationalist contribution, and attempted to lobby his way back into the Gold Coast TUC. The reconstituted Congress rejected his approaches on the grounds that he was no longer employed in the railways or a member of any constituent union. Nevertheless, he and Anthony Woode insisted on standing as candidates for president and gen-eral secretary in the 1952 Congress elections, but were defeated by Larbi Odam and A. A. Moffatt, the former a moderate apolitical unionist and the latter a reliable CPP loyalist.

It is difficult to judge whether Biney's and Woode's candidature in this election was serious, or simply intended to impress on the rank and file of the Railway Union and other workers in the Western Region that the resuscitated Gold Coast TUC was the work of imperialist intrigue. Cer-tainly, this was the interpretation placed on the elections, with Biney's and Woode's encouragement, by many of the Sekondi-Takoradi workers, who continued to stand aloof from their official unions and to adhere instead to the leadership of the Gold Coast Unemployment Association, some-times also known as the Dismissed Workers' Assembly.[5] This Association had originally been formed to campaign for the re-engagement of those workers dismissed after the 'Positive Action' strike. Having achieved this objective, its leaders, E. C. Turkson-Ocran and I. K. Kumah (a former harbour worker and later chairman of the Sekondi-Takoradi City Coun-cil), decided to expand the aims of the organisation to opposing the resuscitated 'collaborationist' TUC and developing an alternative radical trade union centre. In July 1951 its title was changed to the Ghana Fed-eration Trade Union Congress, with Kumah as president and Ocran as general secretary. Anthony Woode and Pobee Biney, too, though not officials, were known to be closely linked with it. The GFTUC policy programme consisted primarily of pressing for radical redistribution in the existing wage structure, and switching the international and ideologi-cal affiliation of the Ghana trade union movement from the ICFTU (the Western liberal centre) to the World Federation of Trade Unions (the Communist centre).

Contrary to some accounts, the CPP loyalists had nothing to do with the establishment of this radically anti-imperialist centre (even though some later sought to infiltrate it), nor did Nkrumah lend it his support. At a meeting in Sekondi in October 1951, Nkrumah accused the GFTUC of 'dividing the workers' and apparently gained the agreement of the executive to its dissolution.[6] At a mass meeting two days later, however, 'Hundreds of workers decided to oppose the dissolution of the Ghana TUC – "We do not want any imperialist tactics. Nkrumah should come and tell us what good thing he wants to do for the workers" – The members decided to maintain the Congress and to await what would come out of the proposed conference of all trade unions'.[7]

Encouraged by this demonstration of rank-and-file support, the GFTUC leaders decided to stand their ground and fight the party bureaucrats for control of the labour movement. On October 27 they announced, 'The Ghana TUC has asked the Government to review all laws inimical to the interests of the workers in the country. The Congress would not be affiliated to any political party. This new Congress considers the existing Gold Coast TUC as lifeless because its officers are always under the influence of employers'.[8] Turkson-Ocran was able to use his personal influence with Nkrumah – he acted as Nkrumah's personal secretary for a brief spell in 1951–2 – to impress upon him the need to accommodate the left-wing unionists if large numbers of the Western Region rank and file were not to be alienated from the official labour movement. In mid-November Nkrumah publicly agreed with the Ghana TUC that the Gold Coast TUC was inefficient and suggested they form 'one strong TUC which will be independent of Government interference'.[9]

Nevertheless, the rivalry between the two TUCs continued throughout 1952. This was against the wishes, it must be said, of Nkrumah, who was probably thinking in terms of CPP influence rather than formal control over the unions at this stage. He was accordingly prepared to accommodate the energies of the left-wingers if only they would be more realistic about immediate requirements and possibilities. Biney and Woode, however, were determined to force the issue of CPP (or non-CPP) left-wing versus centre at both TUC and parliamentary levels, and in this they showed marked political ineptitude.

After the rejection of his candidature as general secretary of the Gold Coast TUC in August 1952, Anthony Woode accepted the presidency of the Ghana Federation TUC in direct defiance of Nkrumah's expressed wish that he should work informally for a merger of the two bodies. And both he and Biney, having failed to secure such far-reaching socio-economic reforms as they had hoped for through the Gbedemah Commission, mounted increasingly extreme and personal criticism of the party's loss of idealism and momentum from their seats in the Legislative Assembly. As Biney himself put it, he became 'rapidly unamenable to the strange discipline and policies of this party'.[10] While there was no doubt considerable justification for this view of the party's rapid degeneration, it was in the interests of neither Woode nor Biney, given the continuing adherence to the CPP of most of the Sekondi-Takoradi workers (on whose support their prominence depended), to force an open split. Yet their criticisms became so extreme that they were not renominated by the party in 1953 for seats in the subsequent Legislative Assembly. Partly in consequence, neither retained sufficient respectability to gain any position of influence in the new Gold Coast TUC which, under government pressure, was eventually forged out of an amalgamation of the old Gold Coast and Ghana TUCs in July 1953. The composition of the new executive, reflecting an agreement to share out senior positions between the previously competing TUCs, was as follows: president, F. E. Techie-Menson; vice-president, I. K. Kumah; general secretary, E. C. Turkson-Ocran; assistant general secretary, John K. Tettegah; and treasurer, J. C. Rudolph.

At the first conference, a resolution disaffiliating the Gold Coast TUC from the ICFTU was moved by John Tettegah and carried by the majority. The new TUC was to be neutral between the ICFTU and WFTU. It was also to remain strictly independent of the government:

> The Trade Union Movement of this country shall always be free to formulate and advocate its own policies. In the future, as in the past, we shall continue to urge on the Government those policies which from our experience we believe to be in the interests of the country and we shall retain our right to disagree and publicly to oppose the Government where we think it necessary to do so.[11]

This statement of intent was hardly borne out by the TUC president's announcement in October 1953 that the popular Turkson-Ocran, ideological protégé of Biney and Woode, had been relieved of his duties as general secretary. Allegedly, this was for being a communist and a channel of WFTU funds into the Ghanaian labour movement. This accusation may possibly have had some basis; the WFTU has at times been generous in its aid to Ghana, not least to the Nkrumah–Tettegah inspiration, the All-African Trade Union Federation.[12] But the main reason for Ocran's downfall (and that of several other alleged communists) appears to have been Nkrumah's desire to stage a left-wing purge so as to increase his respectability and reliability in the eyes of the British. The British Government had recently suspended the constitution of British Guiana on the grounds that its nationalist leader, Cheddi Jagan, was following a communist line. Nkrumah wished to insure himself against the possibility of similar charges. This was, of course, a strategy commonly adopted by nationalist leaders in the 'collaborationist' phase of the movement. For example, Houphouet-Boigny broke with the communists in the Ivory Coast, and Azikiwe with the Zikists in Nigeria, in similar circumstances and for essentially the same reasons.

Turkson-Ocran was also in Nkrumah's disfavour at this time for his over-sympathetic attitude towards strikers, and, more particularly, his handling of the September 1953 strike at the African Manganese Company in Awaso. On visiting the mine, Ocran did little to restrain the workers or their more militant speakers and, as a result of the continuation of the strike, several hundred workers were dismissed. Such incidents were extremely embarrassing to Nkrumah, who was thereby placed in a difficult position between the Colonial Government on the one hand and Ghanaian working opinion on the other. There was a danger that further incidents of this kind would play into the hands of the left-wing critics of the regime. Hence his readiness to clamp down on Ocran and the extremists.

In February 1954 the Gold Coast TUC reaffiliated to the ICFTU with John Tettegah as its representative on the Executive Board, and soon afterwards Tettegah was appointed full-time general secretary to the Congress, the headquarters of which were accordingly transferred from troublesome Sekondi to Tettegah's town of residence, Accra.[13] It was at the 1954 conference of the Congress also that Tettegah first canvassed the idea of a highly centralised trade union movement with increased finances and authority at the top of the structure. His reasoning had in principle much to recommend it: 'The fault of the incapacity of the TUC is due to its weak structure and the unfortunate registration of a multiplicity of Unions numbering over 80, some with membership of just over 50, and cannot therefore have any hope of providing any service to the membership except protecting them from dismissals and victimisations.'[14]

Many of the more experienced unionists, however, in addition to reacting against the threat to their autonomy which a more centralised structure would entail, suspected a CPP manoeuvre to assert party control over the trade union movement. While it may be doubted whether either Nkrumah or Tettegah envisaged a formal alliance at this stage, the political background of Tettegah and his leading followers – decidedly 'party' rather than 'unionist' – encouraged such notions, and enabled opponents to draw on widespread feelings of resentment at the dominance of officials with little or no rank-and-file supporting base. In turn, Tettegah was impelled, in order to counter such opposition, to call on the services of reliable CPP 'apparatchiks'. These were largely responsible for the creation of numerous small (and mostly Accra-based) unions, many of them little more than paper organisations, others 'splinters' from established unions, which emerged in 1954–7 without any corresponding increase in the proportion of workers unionised.[15] In reality, Tettegah's professed aim of union amalgamation was far from consistently pursued during this period. The later administrative secretary of the TUC was quite frank about the nature and purpose of the loyalists' intermediate strategy: 'Up to 1957 we encouraged the mushrooming of splinter unions to undermine the power-base of reactionary elements such as the UAC [Employees' Union] leadership. Each new union also increased our voting strength in the Congress.'[16]

Tettegah, it is clear, was dependent on Nkrumah's personal support and a good deal of dirty work to defeat several attempts to undermine his leadership during these years. Early in 1955 he was voted out of the secretary-generalship by a meeting of the executive board, but he simply refused to vacate his office physically, and later secured his re-election by a quite unconstitutional version of the board packed with CPP loyalists.[17] Shortly afterwards, at the April 1955 delegates' conference, the Railway Workers', Mines Employees', Dockworkers' and UAC Employees' Unions joined in an attempt to overthrow the incumbent TUC leadership. Although these unions still represented a large proportion, possibly a majority, of 'active' unionised workers, this strength was not reflected in voting terms in the TUC Council of Delegates.[18] Having got wind of their intentions, Tettegah was easily able to thwart their plans by 'whipping' the votes of delegates from the newly established unions who were in effect his political clients.

The CPP loyalists attempted to brand these dissidents as 'reactionaries' in contrast with their own proclaimed 'socialist' ideals. In reality, the alliance they confronted was ideologically highly disparate. The UAC Employees' Union might fairly be described as 'conservative' and 'economist' in orientation in the sense that its members, predominantly clerical, appear to have been strongly influenced by the Colonial Labour Department's model of apolitical unionism. In addition, they wished to preserve the autonomy of their relatively wealthy 'house' union, an aim in which they received strong support from the paternalistic United Africa Company itself. Several other unions – the Hospital Workers' Union, for example – supported the dissidents out of a similarly rigid adherence to the separation of politics from trade union affairs. The railway workers and various other Sekondi-Takoradi unionists, alienated from the CPP by the downfall of Biney, Woode and Turkson-Ocran, represented by contrast a highly political and industrially militant left-wing challenge, the particular nature of which will later be analysed more extensively.

The mineworkers' orientation poses far more difficult problems of classification. The participation of their leadership in the reorganisation of the Gold Coast TUC in 1951 should be seen less as an indication of conservative leanings than as a strategy to gain Colonial Labour Department assistance in building up the union's membership under extremely inimical conditions. This entailed persuading the mining companies to adopt measures for stabilisation of the underground labour force. Labour Department support was also sought to strengthen the union's legitimacy vis-à-vis the Chamber of Mines. It must be admitted that the relative isolation of the mineworkers from the main urban centres continued to make for a certain parochialism of concerns and an extremely guarded attitude toward external (i.e. party political) interference in their affairs. It would nevertheless be misleading to describe them as politically right-wing, and even more so – witness the three months' strike of October 1955 to January 1956 – as 'moderate' in their conduct of industrial relations. Finally, any interpretation of mineworkers' politics during this period must accord a central, even dominant, role to the manoeuvres and motivations of their general secretary, D. K. Foevie. Possessed in the eyes of the mineworkers of a 'strong man' image similar to that which Biney enjoyed with the railway workers, Foevie was nevertheless fired by intense personal ambition. Initially presenting himself as a staunch CPP loyalist, subsequently appearing to oppose Tettegah's plans for TUC centralisation until offered the chairmanship of the executive board, Foevie's manoeuvres are ultimately comprehensible only in the card-playing terms of seeking to reap the maximum personal benefit from his control of a particularly strong political hand; a hand which, as the progress of his career eminently testifies, he was to play with very considerable finesse.

The 'socialist' pretensions of the CPP loyalists have generally been granted a surprisingly uncritical degree of acceptance by left-wing commentators. This has been due in large part, no doubt, to the ideological appeal of the Nkrumah regime's foreign policies. As far as domestic policy is concerned, it is important to note certain distinctions if the use of this term is not to be seriously misleading. In Western parlance, 'socialist' generally denotes a primary identification with the economic interests of labour, normally involving advocacy of government ownership or control of industry in order to serve those interests. Modernisers in underdeveloped countries sometimes advocate nationalisation and a major role for government in the economy for quite different reasons: namely, to develop industry where there is as yet little or none, rather than to secure economic benefits for the already existing (and proportionately minute) wage labour force.[19] Although its advocates might term themselves socialists, such a strategy is perhaps more appropriately described as one of state capitalism where, as under the CPP in Ghana, it involves less in the way of economic egalitarianism than deliberate restraint of lower-paid workers'

65

wages. Many CPP–TUC officials were undoubtedly sympathetic to the situation of lower-paid workers and, even more clearly, committed to the development of an industrialised national economy. Yet, judging from numerous personal interviews, the dominant motivation in nearly all cases consisted of a combination of intense personal loyalty to Nkrumah together with the advancement of their own financial and political status. This latter aim in particular was to be achieved through the construction of a well-financed (and excessively well-staffed) TUC trading its own supposed control of the workers for government subsidies and increased representation on various governmental bodies. Herein lay the essential rationale for Tettegah's 'new structure'.

The 'new structure'

In October 1957, Tettegah returned from Israel effusively espousing the centralised model of the Israeli Histadrut:

> Despite all our efforts there are [sic] still too great multiplicity of Trade Unions in a small country like Ghana with a population of only 5 million. We must now positively consider the feasibility of merging the various registered Trade Unions with the Trade Union Congress so that Congress could become a negotiating body. Departments can be created and a centralised Executive to direct our affairs throughout Ghana . . . We must turn to something like the General Federation of Jewish Labour in Israel [Histadrut].[20]

This diverged in several respects from Nkrumah's preferred policy of encouraging strong individual unions and a consultative TUC, and, although Tettegah's projected changes were not actually opposed, the government informed Congress that they were expected to be voluntary and not to require legislation.[21] By 1958, for reasons already elaborated, Tettegah could rely on a majority vote in favour of his 'new structure', but the resulting body would be pretty meaningless if the Railway Workers', Mines Employees', and UAC Employees' Unions opted out of it as they threatened to do. The exact form of the constitution was supposed to be worked out after a special committee had listened to objections from these and other unions. These objections centred on the degree of centralisation envisaged for the TUC, which would effectively deprive them of many of their powers and of negotiating functions which they had already shown themselves able to perform efficiently. Behind such objections also lay a deep distrust of the sincerity (as workers' representatives) and financial probity of the TUC elite whose position would be the more firmly entrenched by such measures. None of these objections was met in the new

66

constitution: indeed, they were not deemed significant enough to merit a formal reply. There seems little empirical justification for Ioan Davies' assertion that the 'new structure' 'was the result of four years of hard negotiation with the Ghana unions'.[22]

The opposition of the mineworkers was nevertheless overcome by coming to terms with the personal ambitions of their general secretary, D. K. Foevie. (He was made chairman of the executive board in 1960 and was later to become managing director of the State Mining Corporation.) Foevie was able to contain the discontent of his members at this policy volte-face, in part through the hero's status he had attained after the successful conclusion of the 1955–6 strike, but increasingly through the use of a wide range of quasi-fascist techniques, including the use of spy networks and physical intimidation.[23] The railway workers were not to be so easily controlled, however, even if some of their leaders might be won over. The UAC Employees' Union was also determined to retain its independence. Hence the need to enforce the 'new structure' proposals by legislation, first by the 1958 Industrial Relations Act and later, in the fact of continuing railway recalcitrance, by the 1959 and 1960 amendments.

Under the Act, a Trades Union Congress was established with twenty-four constituent national unions (reduced in 1961 to sixteen, and in 1965 to ten). All negotiations – for registration, failure of collective bargaining procedures, and introduction of the 'union shop' and the 'check-off' – were to be conducted through the Ghana TUC, which was thereby responsible for the direct conduct of all major trade union affairs. To carry out these duties, a large permanent secretariat was to be established at the headquarters in Accra, from which nine executive secretaries, appointed by the executive board, were to sit, together with representatives from each union, on the Supreme Congress, thus greatly strengthening the hand of the TUC bureaucrats. While officials were in theory to be elected, a Cabinet Minister made it quite clear that all senior posts were to be occupied by CPP loyalists – 'It is an ideological heresy for Party members to elect a non-Party worker as a leader of their organisation – the CPP and the TUC are one'.[24] In practice, the railway workers soon discovered, the freedom of election was further restricted by the presence of senior TUC and CPP officials at the delegates' conference (where executive members were elected by 'open' voting) in order to ensure the appointment of a particular official candidate as general secretary. Later (in 1961) union membership cards were replaced by party cards.

This extensive central organisation, including special education and publicity departments, was to be financed by the establishment of union shops and a check-off system according to which virtually all wage-earners in Ghana were compelled to become dues-paying members of the TUC (giving a total official membership of some 500,000 in 1962). Of these membership dues (2*s.* per month) 45 per cent were to go directly to the Ghana TUC, with 40 per cent going to the national union, and 15 per cent to the local branch.[25] The railway unionists pointed out that the requirement that they should pay 5 per cent of their dues to a central TUC strike solidarity fund seemed a little unnecessary in view of the fact that they, together with other public-sector employees, were prohibited from going on strike.[26] But again their objections were ignored. Strikes in the private sector were to be legal only after the exhaustion of an elaborate (and practically inexhaustible) negotiating machinery.

For workers in private industries, and especially those formerly ineffectively organised, this 'new structure' had something to recommend it. Prior to the 1958 Act, many private employers had refused to recognise workers' representatives or meet them for negotiation. They were now compelled to recognise unions and negotiate industrial agreements with professional TUC officials. The practical benefits of these new arrangements were considerable. A legal minimum wage was introduced in 1959, and its enforcement in the private sector, though far from universal, was doubtless more extensive than would otherwise have been the case. In the period 1960–6, moreover, TUC officials succeeded in negotiating substantial wage increases for many private-sector employees which at least mollified the effects of rapid inflation on real living standards.[27]

For previously organised government employees such as the railway workers, however, the advantages of the 'new structure' were far less clear.[28] They lost the right to strike absolutely, and, with this, a great deal of their bargaining strength. They enjoyed no arrangement for regular negotiation with their employer – the government – and therefore depended on TUC initiative for bringing attention to their grievances. The TUC leadership argued that through its participation in the top government and party decision-making bodies – Tettegah was to have a seat in the Cabinet as ambassador plenipotentiary – it could safeguard the workers' real interests, bound up as these were with the interests of the nation as a whole. The various questions of housing, education, inflation and unemployment could be tackled far more effectively through TUC influence on government policy-making than by strike actions for higher wages. Anyway, the workers should be less concerned with immediate standard-of-living increases than with working 'consciously for the development and strengthening of the new socialist sector of the national economy', and acting as an ideologically conscious vanguard 'to create a state based upon the socialist pattern of society adapted to suit Ghanaian conditions'.[29]

In abstract, the railway workers' rejection of this 'progressive' argument

68

might well appear reactionary; but such an interpretation would assume the existence of a credible national leadership. The railway workers viewed the TUC's 'socialist' argument as little more than a confidence trick, and, in retrospect, it appears that they were not entirely mistaken. Their distrust derived in part from their past experience that government generally, including the Nkrumah regime, had to be forced into considering its employees' demands for improved conditions of service. TUC officials, who were also CPP 'apparatchiks', would, it was thought, be less than enthusiastic to jeopardise their positions by pressing the government too strongly. Recent experience provided confirmation for the view that the maintenance of the strike weapon (at least as a threat) was essential to the protection of workers' interests. During the summer of 1955 there had been mounting pressure from lower-paid workers for the government to increase its minimum wage.[30] The Lidbury–Gbedemah award of 1952–3 had already been eroded by inflation. Several powerful groups of workers, including the railway workers, threatened strike action, but the TUC leadership refused to voice support for their demands. Eventually, Nkrumah announced the appointment of the Waugh Commission on the day immediately following the mineworkers' commencement of strike action. Neither they nor the railway workers were likely to be convinced by TUC President Techie-Menson's defensive assertion that 'the Prime Minister's statement is the outcome of the efforts of the Gold Coast Trades Union Congress as a whole, and not of a single or individual union'.[31]

The introduction of so great a degree of centralisation and party control as the 'new structure' proposed could only, it was felt, result in an even more pronounced subservience of the leadership to the party and its detachment from the rank and file. A more detailed assessment of the performance of the TUC in 1961–6 will be made in a subsequent chapter: hindsight should not be unduly allowed to colour consideration of the railway workers' conflict with the CPP loyalists in the earlier period. It might fairly be pointed out, however, that already by 1961, with hundreds of officials seated in the N₡250,000 Hall of Labour donated to the TUC by President Nkrumah, and little achieved (by the TUC leaders themselves at least) in the way of rank and file benefits, it was understandable that the elements of self-enrichment and empire-building in the loyalists' motivations should be widely perceived to outweigh any other concerns. One might also observe that, since the TUC lacked the sympathy of the most dynamic and class-conscious group of workers in Ghana (i.e. the Sekondi-Takoradi workers), all talk of socialist mobilisation was fairly empty rhetoric.

This is not to deny that, at least as late as 1962, the TUC leaders enjoyed considerable rank-and-file support, especially in Accra, the home base of the majority. (It is of significance here that most of the Accra rank and file were clerical or commercial workers, and that Accra had seen a great deal more of CPP 'development' than any other part of the country.) This support, together with the expanding size and increased visibility (e.g. the numerous TUC cars touring the city) of TUC organisation, helps to account for the fear of CPP right-wingers that the TUC was becoming too strong, threatening to turn the CPP into a workers' party.[32] The most powerful explanation of this fear, however, lies in the fact that the majority of MPs were even more detached from social realities, that the factional conflicts of the CPP and its various wings were conducted in a kind of political ivory tower. The prevalence of such anxiety on the part of CPP right-wingers was perfectly compatible with a growing sense of class-antagonism to the TUC elite on the part of workers in the Western Region. For them, as we shall see, the Borgward cars were less a sign of the TUC's growing 'socialist' influence and power than of their supposed representatives' happy participation in the corrupt politics and ostentatious living of government leaders.

5

The railway workers' response to CPP socialism: the strike of 1961

In the 'Positive Action' strike of January 1950 the Sekondi-Takoradi railway and harbour workers had demonstrated their enthusiastic support for Nkrumah's nationalist campaign. In September 1961 they staged a seventeen-day strike against the Nkrumah Government's July budget, a strike in which, according to St Clair Drake (who was present at the time), 'the Government saw its very existence implicitly challenged', and which 'drastically altered the entire character of political activity in Ghana'.[1] This latter strike action, while certainly motivated in part by economic grievances – most obviously, opposition to the budget proposals for a property tax and a compulsory savings scheme – was also undoubtedly informed by wider political motivations. The staging of an illegal strike in so determined a manner, in opposition moreover to measures which the government had made clear it considered essential to the achievement of its major objectives, and in what was politically an extremely sensitive moment – with Nkrumah out of the country visiting the Eastern Communist bloc, and widespread popular unrest in Ghana at the budget's austerity measures – suggests that, at the very least, the 1961 strike expressed a far-reaching disillusionment with the Nkrumah regime.

This opposition, it should be remembered, came from the former vanguard supporters of Nkrumah. If political allegiance in the Ghanaian nationalist movement entailed more than a purely immediate economic alliance, then the reasons for the railway workers' disillusionment merit extensive consideration. What, then, were the sources and nature of this disillusionment, and, in more positive terms, the aims, explicit or implicit, of the strikers?

The preceding two chapters have described, firstly, the leading role played by the Sekondi-Takoradi railway and harbour workers in the pre-1950 development of a Ghanaian trade union movement; and, secondly, how between 1950 and 1961 the leaders of the railway workers and other older-established unions were displaced by the dominance of CPP acolytes in a 'new structure' modelled on a very different conception of the proper role of labour. This chapter traces the development of an increasingly bitter political and ideological conflict between the local leadership of the Sekondi-Takoradi rank and file and the CPP loyalists (the national officials of the union sometimes being seen as allied with the latter), and shows that the 1961 strike was essentially a further episode – the decisive encounter in fact – in this struggle.

As Ioan Davies has suggested, the 1961 strike was in part the reaction of an old-established union – the Railway Union – against the takeover of the labour movement by CPP bureaucrats with little or no supporting base in the working rank and file.[2] In certain important respects, however, Davies' formulation is inadequate. A warning has already been voiced against identifying the railway workers' opposition to the 'new structure' too closely with that of other old-established unions such as the Mines Employees' Union or the UAC Employees' Union. Members of these unions played no part in a strike which was almost entirely a Sekondi-Takoradi affair. Workers in other parts of the country, including the railway workers of Accra and the up-country branches, participated, if at all, for only a day or two. On the other hand, the Sekondi-Takoradi strikers received the active or moral support of virtually all the inhabitants of the twin city – unskilled workers who would not be directly affected by the budget measures, the market-women and even many of the unemployed. These considerations suggest inadequacies also in St Clair Drake's and Lacy's account of the strike as the reaction of a 'labour aristocracy', operating with an 'economist' ideology, to the austerity measures demanded by Nkrumah's newly radicalised regime.[3] It certainly does not seem to have been seen this way by other, decidedly non-aristocratic groups within the community.

The beginning of an explanation of the Sekondi-Takoradi workers' quite singular militancy is to be found (superficially somewhat paradoxically perhaps) in the nature of their nationalist experience. In so far as this section of the proletariat was simply in advance of working opinion in other parts of the country – and sympathy for the aims of the 1961 strikers certainly did spread widely in the later years of the CPP regime – it is readily understandable that disillusionment should have first set in amongst precisely those who, in the early days, had been the most militant and radical supporters of the nationalist movement. Additional factors were nevertheless clearly involved.

Among the most important of these was the ideological influence of Pobee Biney and his followers. It was their view, we have seen, that the trade union movement should be especially concerned to check degenerative tendencies in the political system as a whole. With the erosion of the democratic principle in so many institutional areas in 1957–61, the trade union movement represented, as it were, the last line of defence. From this perspective, the growth of elitism and authoritarianism within the TUC itself was especially staunchly opposed, but only as part of the matter. Obviously, this was the politico-economic institution which most directly affected and involved the railway workers. But the range of abuses they were concerned to protest against was indicated by the fact that some strike leaders went so far as to threaten to disband parliament forcibly. If this general notion of asserting the popular accountability of the government indeed constituted the subjective significance of the 1961 strike action, then it is far easier to understand why the skilled railway and harbour workers, although formally protesting against measures which would directly affect only themselves and higher-paid workers, conceived of themselves as acting on behalf of all the 'common people'. In turn, the urban poor of Sekondi-Takoradi looked to the more highly articulate and organised workers to lead expression of a generalised sense of social injustice and exploitation.

The prevalence of such a conception of common interest cannot, of course, be understood in a social vacuum. It is necessary, therefore, to consider those specific situational factors which lent it such powerful tenability, before proceeding to an analysis of the struggle waged by the railway workers for control of the trade union movement in 1950–61.

Sekondi-Takoradi: a working-class community

Sekondi-Takoradi, we have seen, was (and remains) a relatively poor urban community, dominated both numerically and in terms of general ethos by lower-paid manual workers. This labour force was already by 1961 comparatively stable by African standards – a high proportion of workers were committed to urban wage employment for at least a decade or more, rather than being short-term migrants. These factors made for the development of a strong sense of working-class identity and solidarity, stronger most probably than could be found in any other West African city. Even the casual workers, who in most countries and strike situations tend to be cast as blacklegs, have in Sekondi rather been concerned to display solidarity with their 'brothers' in direct actions. Maxwell was a casual labourer in the docks in 1961: 'Oh, yes, I joined in the strike and demonstrations. I even carried a placard and led my fellow workers. After all, the railway workers are my brothers, and we are all here for the same reason, to earn a living wage, and we have to unite to tell the government what it should be doing to help us.'[4]

More generally, the predominantly working-class composition and

73

ethos of Sekondi-Takoradi tended to foster the strong development of 'proletarian' attitudes – anti-elitist, anti-corruption and anti-authoritarian – which were likely to become prevalent among lower-paid workers generally as correlates of their situation in the national politico-economy, but whose growth and articulation might be inhibited in less congenial environments.

Yet this 'working-class' identity was often formulated, especially by the skilled railway workers, not in terms of 'the working class versus employers', but rather of 'the common people versus the big men in government'. As one railway artisan described the background to the 1961 strike, 'us poor common people, we were being cheated by those big men in Accra, and anyone who tried to speak up for us was detained or hounded out of the party'.[5] The notion of acting as 'the spokesmen of the common people' was in part no doubt conceived by the railway workers to strengthen their claim to represent a large body of opinion. It reflected, in other words, their awareness of the minority and relatively privileged position of urban wage-earners in the larger national society. But, judging from the support they received from other occupational groups in the 1961 strike, this was not mere rhetoric. In so predominantly working-class a community, the unemployed looked largely to their worker fathers and brothers for assistance, and were therefore directly dependent on the workers' financial capacity.[6] Similarly, the market-women and the small businessmen relied very largely on the custom of the workers, and therefore had an indirect, but clearly perceived interest in the lower-paid workers' financial prosperity and the politics of the TUC.

This sense of common interest was not, however, simply a matter of other local groups recognising their dependence on the railway workers. The railway artisans were also socially and culturally very much a part of the 'masses', and their growing hostility to the CPP elite was fuelled by resentment at abuses of power which hurt other sections as much as themselves. Since they identified with Sekondi-Takoradi as a relatively permanent 'second home', they shared the general sense of disillusionment of the 'common people' of that city with the conduct of CPP officials and the lack of benefits accruing to the city (and the Central and Western Regions more generally) from the attainment of independence.

It would be somewhat misleading, therefore, to portray the 1961 strike as simply a manifestation of relatively highly developed class-consciousness. Implicit in the strike and the 'populist' consciousness of its participants was a fairly strong communalistic element. The despised elite were, in the main, the 'big men' in, or from, Accra. The corruption of official institutions emanated, and was directed, from there, to the exploitation of the people of Sekondi-Takoradi. Accra alone, it appeared, had benefited from elite wealth and patronage, with its fine roadsteads and plush hotels. Sekondi-Takoradi had been consistently refused development grants (with the sole exception of that for a new market-centre), and seemed to lack any representatives sufficiently influential with the Nkrumah Government to secure fair treatment for the city. Resentment at such relative deprivation sometimes found expression in openly regionalistic sentiments: 'We westerners especially, the government doesn't mind us, yet we have all these industries, bauxite and gold and things, and we work much harder than all those office workers in Accra, drawing their fat salaries. If they don't look out, it will be another Biafra.'[7] The open expression of such sentiments is atypical, and even frowned upon in Railway Union culture, which is itself markedly free from tribalism, and generally disapproving of communalistic movements in national politics. Nevertheless, the Accra/Sekondi-Takoradi dimension certainly served to intensify the railway workers' sense of social distance between the 'big men' and the 'common people', as well as to create widespread local support for the 1961 strike. Minister Tawia Adamafio's denunciation of the strikers as 'western rats' was indicative of some well-grounded government feeling in this regard. As has generally been the case in the post-Independence politics of African states, an explosive situation resulted from the coincidence of class-type and communal lines of conflict.

Communal grievances and the elite–mass gap

In the relatively small and poor urban community of Sekondi-Takoradi, the corruption and high living of CPP officials was both highly visible and particularly provocative to the ordinary resident. A. Y. Ankomah, a leading organiser of the 1961 strike, though earlier an enthusiastic admirer of Nkrumah and 'his sugar-coated words', described the process of his own disillusionment in terms similar to those used by nearly all railway worker interviewees:

> We had union leaders imposed on us, men like H. W. Mensah [regional TUC general secretary] with no trade union background. We heard they were buying Borgward cars with our money. They tried to persuade us the TUC was doing a good thing by establishing these shops for the workers, but the leaders took things on credit and never paid, so the shops had to close down. And they went with other people's wives. Really, there was so much corruption and wife-stealing.
>
> Then there were the brigade officers coming home with cars loaded with foodstuffs, the Ghana women held big, big parties every Saturday, and Young Pioneers were being flown to Russia for courses and indoctrination. Then rumours about corruption in the City Council

started coming out through some of the junior officers. But the worst people were the Farmers' Council leaders. They would come into Takoradi and throw their money around in the bars, boasting about how they had cheated our brothers and sisters in the rural areas. This was too much.[8]

One of the areas in which CPP corruption most directly hurt the interests of the railway workers was housing. Between 1950 and 1960 the population of Sekondi-Takoradi almost doubled (rising from 44,000 to over 75,000), thereby exacerbating a serious housing shortage which dated back to the early part of the century. In 1912 the then railway general manager wrote that 'Seccondee is an upstart town, practically the creation of the railway, and an ever-expanding institution requires constant additions to the staff. Houses are now almost impossible for new men to find, rents are exorbitant, and incidentally the cost of living is very high . . . The men live all over the place in wretched conditions.'[9] Later, two railway villages were built, one at Ketan (on the outskirts of Sekondi) and the other near the centre of Takoradi, but these at no time provided accommodation for more than one third of the railway employees. Busia's Social Survey of 1950 gave a vivid picture of the overcrowding which still persisted there,[10] and the 1955 survey revealed little improvement, with an average of 3.3 families and 11.8 persons occupying each house.[11] In 1952, Takoradi landlords and tenants were complaining that a law forbidding tenants to live in kitchens would result in thousands of people being homeless.[12] Two years later, the Town Council, under the chairmanship of the popular I. K. Kumah (a former harbour worker and president of the Ghana Federation of Trade Unions), announced plans to build two housing estates, consisting of some 800 houses in all ('in the bourjois style' – i.e. two rooms and a hall), 'to provide fitting accommodation for our workers and their families'.[13] Soon after completion, however, these houses were taken over for allocation and administration by the National Housing Corporation which, as the 1966 commission of enquiry into its affairs clearly showed, proceeded to allocate them to local officials of the various CPP wings and organisations, or those who could afford the bribes demanded by corporation officials (which certainly did not include the lower-paid workers), or even in some cases to Accra-based MPs and their girlfriends.[14] In consequence the lower-paid workers of Sekondi-Takoradi found the housing situation deteriorating rather than improved, and were forced either to pay exorbitant rates for small rooms, or else to band together with relatives or friends to build or rent a house to accommodate several families.

Closely related to such abuse of power was a steady diminution in the channels of mass communication with the government, both central and local. Indeed, it was this factor, the people of Sekondi-Takoradi's lack of access to government patronage or to channels for making their sense of deprivation known, rather than the extensiveness of bureaucratic irregularity itself, which might be held to account for their especial sensitivity to the evils of corruption. The most important issue for the railway workers in this respect was the connection perceived between the corruption of top officials and the growing disregard for democratic processes within the TUC. But the significance of this phenomenon was lent greater urgency and wider relevance by the operation of similar tendencies in other institutional areas.

The city councillors, originally local people pushed forward as local representatives, became increasingly unapproachable and unresponsive to local needs. There was no change in the composition of the City Council between 1954 and 1960 with the exception of four new members out of a total of twenty-one in the 1959 elections. This certainly did not reflect satisfaction with the representation the electorate were receiving. There were several instances of councillors being dragged out of their houses at night by the local 'young men' to 'explain' what had happened to the money for facilities the ward had promised. In fairness, the council was not receiving the money it required for constructing much-needed roads and schools because of mutual distrust between it and the Ministry of Local Government.[15] This fact, together with the council's loss of much of its authority and financial resources to the district and regional commissioners, meant that there was no longer much point to the CPP ward meetings. Whereas in the first half of the 50s the fortnightly ward meetings had been genuine mass forums, held out of doors, with opportunity for the articulation of local needs and grievances in some hope of remedial action, by the late 50s they had come to consist of irregular, small, indoor meetings, largely conspiratorial in nature.[16]

Very few of the new industries established under CPP rule were located in Sekondi-Takoradi. Now (i.e. in 1961) the government was building a new harbour at Tema – fifteen miles from Accra – to the inevitable disadvantage of Sekondi-Takoradi. The people of that city felt, with some justification, that the Accra area benefited disproportionately from government-induced development, while the Central and Western Regions were neglected. The available statistics suggest that employment opportunities in the Eastern Region (including Accra) rose by some 56 per cent between 1956 and 1963, compared to a mere 16 per cent in the Western and Central Regions combined (see Table 5.1). Naturally, this lack of significant economic development in Sekondi-Takoradi was blamed on the ineffectiveness, or unconcern, of the MPs and commissioners for the area.

77

Table 5.1. *Changes in Ghanaian employment by region, 1956–63*

	1956 (thousands)	1963	Index of change (1956=100)
All regions	267.4	374.1	140
Ashanti/Brong-Ahafo	53.6	75.1	140
Eastern (inc. Accra)	105.7	164.6	156
Northern/Upper	13.4	21.4	160
Volta	10.3	15.5	141
Western/Central	84.3	97.5	116

Source: Norman Uphoff, 'The Expansion of Employment Associated with Growth of GNP: A Projective Model and Its Implications for Ghana', *Economic Bulletin of Ghana*, 2, 4 (1972), p. 9.

The regional and district commissioners generally proved unapproachable and extremely unpopular:[17] 'Go to see them? They would not even speak to you unless you were a big man in the party. And anyhow, how could you approach them as they flashed past in their big cars? They did not have time to throw a pesewa to a beggar.'[18] On the parliamentary level faith in the representative character of the assembly was not strengthened by the expulsion of the Sekondi-Takoradi workers' outspoken heroes, Anthony Woode and Pobee Biney, nor by the subsequent appointment of two women with little local standing, support or contact, as representatives for the Western Region.[19] These were not the kind of people to voice popular discontent with the government at any risk to their own positions. Dissatisfaction with the style and structure of parliamentary politics was clearly expressed in the strike leaders' threat that, if parliament did not give way to the demands of the people, they would disband that body by force.

This general issue of popular resentment at the widening socio-economic and communications gap between the CPP elite and the 'common people' who had brought them to power was not, of course, articulated as a formal issue in union politics. But it was much discussed in the bars of Sekondi-Takoradi in the months leading up to the 1961 strike, especially by Pobee Biney, whose political demise after 1956 came to symbolise the failings of the regime for many of the railway and harbour workers.

The railway workers versus Tettegah

In consequence of the 'Positive Action' strike of January 1950 and the government's subsequent reprisals, the majority of skilled railway workers either were temporarily unable or else refused to rejoin their own official union. Many of the strikers were suspended from their jobs in the Railway Administration, leaving clerical staff in electoral control of what remained of the former organisation. Accordingly, in August 1950, A. T. Foley and F. K. Balfour were elected as president and general secretary respectively. Foley and Balfour were both moderate clerical unionists who denied personal involvement in 'Positive Action' and were concerned to 'send an assurance of co-operation and loyalty to the Colonial Secretary, Accra'.[20] They further proposed to affiliate the union to the resuscitated Gold Coast TUC. At a mass meeting on 15 August 1950 the 'Technical Men, Takoradi branch' resolved 'that we are unanimously not in favour of the new officers. The old officers should function.' [21] Two weeks later, the Takoradi branch secretary informed the general secretary that 'The situation appears to confirm the desire expressed at certain quarters to split the union into two sections: Technical and Clerical'.[22] In the event, no formal division occurred, but the majority of 'technical men' – the skilled and unskilled manual workers – took membership of the Ghana Federation Trades Union Congress on an individual basis or lent it their moral support.

The continuing rivalry between the GFTUC and the Gold Coast TUC in 1950–3 gave rise to some bewilderment, however, amongst growing numbers of the Railway Union rank and file, whose confidence in Nkrumah and his political strategy was revived somewhat by the publication in April 1952 of the Lidbury–Gbedemah Commission Report recommending a large wage increase for the lower-paid.[23] Many were also concerned to concentrate for the moment on union reunification and reorganisation. In short, there appears to have been considerable confusion amongst the skilled worker rank and file at this stage over whether to remain outside the official Railway Union and adhere to the old left-wing leaders or rejoin the union and at least displace the existent inefficient clerical leadership:

> I would say most of the men in my shop [one of the Location work-shops] were refusing to pay union dues though we attended the meetings sometimes to see what they were proposing to do for us. The way we saw it, Pobee Biney had brought us a lot of progress, and the Unemployed Association people had tried to make sure we would not . . . suffer for our part in it, so they were the people to be our union leaders just as Nkrumah was now the Prime Minister. And anyway they did not know anything about our problems or how to tell the management what should be done.[24]

The feeling that someone who 'knew about our problems' should be elected to run the Railway Union, even if this were not Pobee Biney or one of the GFTUC leaders, was sufficiently strong to induce many of the manual workers to rejoin the union and participate in the 1952 elections. John Eshun, an artisan and an early organiser of the union, was elected president on the platform of 'centralising all efforts on the betterment of the manual staff which forms the greater bulk of the Union.'[25] One of the resolutions passed at the delegates' conference was to the effect that there should be an increase in the representation of the associations (as distinct from the branches), and thereby in the number of 'technical' (as distinct from 'clerical') unionists, on the Working Committee.[26] The new general secretary, A. A. Moffatt, was an experienced branch and regional trades council organiser from Kumasi, who had been imprisoned for his part in the 'Big Six' protest of 1948, and was expected to be a 'forceful' leader. The primary issue in this election, therefore, was seen at the rank-and-file level as that of technical versus clerical unionists, and of the lack of dynamism of the outgoing clerical leadership.

There was considerable dismay later in the year, however, at A. A. Moffatt's acceptance of the secretary-generalship of the Gold Coast TUC, especially since this involved his standing against the candidature of Pobee Biney and Anthony Woode. Biney and Woode attempted to interpret their defeat to the Railway Union rank and file as the work of 'imperialist intrigue' on the part of Nkrumah in collaboration with the Colonial Government, and thereby to force the issue of radicals versus CPP moderates back into the forefront of Railway Union politics. This strategy met with only limited success, since at this stage, it would seem, Biney and Woode were outpacing majority rank and file opinion. Many of the railway workers were inclined to place more faith than they in the sincerity and good intentions of men such as Moffatt and Tettegah, and in Nkrumah's assurance of government non-interference in trade union affairs. This division of opinion together with considerable confusion as to the real motivations and intentions of the leading actors was, we shall see, to persist at the rank-and-file level of the Railway Union between 1952 and 1958, with first one view – confidence in the CPP and its favoured union leaders – and then the other – identification with Biney's criticisms of the subservience of the CPP unionists – gaining the ascendence. Ultimately, Biney's view was to win out, but in 1952 the issue was not so clear, and tended to cross-cut that of Railway Union and labour movement reunification.

There can be no doubt that the majority of railway workers welcomed the merger of the two TUCs into a single body in 1953. They were equally antagonised, however, by Turkson-Ocran's dismissal from the secretary-generalship soon after its formation. In spite of Tettegah's growing prominence and popularity as an apparently radical spokesman for labour's interests, his part in engineering the former's downfall was obvious to all but the most credulous, and inevitably lent itself to cynical interpretations of his own (and Nkrumah's) motivations: 'He spoke what the workers were feeling in those early days, how the workers were being cheated by the colonialists and that they should enjoy the fruits of their labour. At that time we thought the TUC was going to be independent. But we began to have our suspicions over the Ocran business. Tettegah was getting too ambitious.'[27] An additional source of confusion (or complexity) arose from the railway workers' desire to distinguish, as far as possible, between 'party' and 'union' affairs. On the parliamentary front, for example, their clear preference for the CPP over any alternative political leadership disinclined them to support Pobee Biney's candidature as an independent for the Sekondi constituency in the 1954 general elections. Here, as in 1952, Biney miscalculated the strength of their personal allegiance to him, or, more accurately perhaps, the sophistication and realism of their political thinking. As one railway worker recalled, 'All the workers here at Location knew that the election was very important for CPP self-government, and as we were still strong for CPP, we couldn't vote for him. We could see his reasons, and appreciated the truth in them, but it was the wrong time to contest the issue.' [28] Their concern at Turkson-Ocran's dismissal, and what they suspected of being a manoeuvre to eliminate the left wing of the labour movement preparatory to asserting party control, nevertheless induced them to press for Biney's reinstatement as union president. At the 1954 conference of the union, Moffatt and Eshun were successfully pressurised to resign, and Biney was elected in the latter's place.

From his base in the Railway Union Biney then set about forming an alliance with those various and varied elements in the labour movement which were opposed to the leadership of the CPP loyalists. When the attempt to displace the incumbent TUC leadership at the 1955 delegates' conference failed in the face of Tettegah's powerful clientele network,[29] Biney and Victor Narh (general secretary of the Hospital Workers' Union) led six unions in breaking away to form a rival Congress of Free Trade Unions based at Sekondi. These were the Public Works Department, Hospital Workers', Maritime and Dockworkers', UAC Employees', Sekondi-Takoradi Municipal Council, and Railway Employees' Unions.[30] Contrary to some accounts, the CFTU did not align itself with the major opposition party during 1954–6, the Ashanti-based National Liberation Movement.[31] From one point of view, this antipathy might be explained in terms of the very different communal interests which the NLM and the CFTU represented. But there was also perhaps some truth to the railway workers' own explanation that they were sufficiently clear as to their reformist aims to avoid involvement in oppositional party politics, particularly when this opposition party consisted of the elitist and tribalistic

NLM.[32] They were concerned at this stage to press for reform of the CPP and the TUC (and of the relations between the two organisations) along the lines of a loose informal alliance providing for free expression of rank-and-file opinion and greater accountability of the leadership. Recognising the need to work within the TUC to this end, one year after their protest disaffiliation the railway workers reaffiliated 'in order to consolidate the forces of Trade Unionism in the emerging independent Gold Coast'.[33]

The CPP–TUC leadership was nevertheless not prepared to leave so stubbornly incorruptible an opponent as Biney at the head of the country's most powerful union.[34] As the Railway Union's chief clerk at the time (1956) recalled,

> After his attempt to form a rival TUC, the CPP became very annoyed with Pobee and some of the union leaders started attacking him, charging him with being a drunkard and not attending to his duties. Most of us did not believe this [that he was not attending to his duties], but some did, and Pobee felt betrayed by us. He insisted on resigning. It was a very sad day for us.[35]

Biney's resignation from the Railway Union presidency marked the end of his formal political career. Yet his ideological and stylistic stance of persistent (if drunken) opposition to autocratic and elitist tendencies in the CPP regime continued to exert a powerful influence on Railway Union politics. Biney epitomised that process of disillusionment which was to culminate in the 1961 strike. This influence operated on several levels and through various channels. He continued to meet many of the railway workers in the houses and bars of Sekondi, leading the criticism of CPP policies and elite behaviour in these informal (and often inebriated) political discussion groups. Moreover, his influence naturally increased as his interpretation of the direction of development of the CPP proved ever more accurate. If in 1952 and 1956 his own views on CPP degeneracy had outpaced those of the majority of railway workers, by 1958–61 Biney's rejection by the party seemed to symbolise the failings of the regime: on the one hand, Pobee Biney, still outspoken, still in touch with the 'common people', still dressed in a simple traditional cloth and pair of sandals; on the other, the wealthy, party-subservient, incommunicative TUC bureaucrats. Biney, everyone knew, was a drunkard; but he was a popular drunk, a frequenter of the low bars of Esikado and Ketan, unlike the elite souses in their plush hotels. And, though it might appear to a more cynical outsider that Biney's political and financial demise was decreed rather than chosen, he nevertheless appeared to many of the railway workers as 'a consistent spokesman for the suffering masses, for the aims of our independence revolution – he was the only Ghanaian who had the courage to stand up to Nkrumah, who could not be won over with bribes'.[36]

A third, less direct, channel of Biney's influence was through the continuing prominence of his followers and apprentices in Railway Union politics in 1956–61. For this was, relatively speaking, a highly stable labour force in which there was no great expansion in size over the period 1950–61. The annual labour turnover rate among the skilled workers was less than 10 per cent. Even by 1970, 17 per cent of the Location skilled workers could claim to have participated in the 1950 'Positive Action' strike.[37] Equally important, a high degree of stability characterised the union middle-level leadership between 1955–6 and 1961. These branch and association officials who sat on the Working Committee exerted a powerful influence on rank-and-file interpretation of events, and, as the 1961 strike was to illustrate, possessed a far greater degree of control over rank-and-file behaviour than did the top-level leadership. They were likely to be forceful, opinionated personalities in the Biney mould; that was why they had been elected. Moreover, Biney had directly influenced the thinking of many of them during his own Railway Union career. Almost all of the middle-level leaders who staged the 1961 strike – V. K. Quist, W. N. Grant, A. Y. Ankomah, J. K. Baaku, K. G. Quartey, S. Winful, T. Hagan, K. Imbeah and T. Bentil – had become union officials during his presidency and through his encouragement. Many still speak of the heroic status he possessed in their eyes, and of the dominant influence he exerted on their understanding of trade union principles and methods:

> Biney taught me all I know about trade unionism. I lived only a few doors from him in Esikado, and we would often sit talking. He told me I had the right qualities for a union leader – boldness and being straightforward – and he persuaded me to stand for election in my association. To my astonishment I was elected and he instructed me how to go about my duties, how I should always speak truthfully and stand up for what I believe in. I can truly say, he was a great humanitarian. Trade unionism and humanitarianism, they are the same thing.[38]

This is not to say that all Biney's 'apprentices' followed his example strictly, or maintained his distinction between left-wing reformism and party politics under the pressure of increasing CPP autocracy – though most were concerned to do so. But it is hardly to overestimate his personal influence to suggest that, in 1956–61, Biney's movement of reformist opposition to the CPP–TUC was carried on by others in his absence.

Immediately after Biney's resignation J. K. Bohann, vice president under Biney and a staunch CPP loyalist, took over as president, but at the May 1957 delegates' conference I. E. Inkumsah was elected in his place. Inkumsah was a long-time friend and supporter of Biney, apparently possessed of a similarly forceful character, and it was expected that he would maintain the union's stance of opposition to the CPP–TUC leaders and their plans for greater centralisation and party control of the labour movement.

By 1957–8, it should be observed, the railway workers' chances of successful resistance by constitutional means had significantly diminished, and their policy alternatives were correspondingly restricted. The officers of the vast majority of Ghana's ninety-five registered unions of 1957 were, as we have seen, political clients of Tettegah and thereby committed in advance to support any programme presented by the TUC leadership. Confronted with this situation, the railway workers had three possible alternatives. They could abandon their stance of overt opposition to the TUC leadership and attempt to work within the proposed 'new structure' to make, as it were, the best of a bad job; they could retreat to an isolationist stance of non-affiliation to the TUC, thereby evading the controls and demands of the 'new structure', but giving up their struggle to reform the national labour movement; or they could turn to mobilising the activist rank and file of the movement in direct and open opposition to the 'new structure'. Collectively, the workers of Sekondi-Takoradi could bring the country's transport and communication system to a halt. For less narrowly practical reasons, also, the notion of a communal Sekondi-Takoradi protest-action possessed great relevance and appeal. However, the successful staging of such a protest would require the occurrence of a general and deeply felt issue.

The railway workers' response – the Joint Council of Railway Unions and the 1961 strike

As we have seen, I. E. Inkumsah became president of the Railway Union in May 1957 on the platform of his determination to oppose the TUC leadership's plans for extreme centralisation and party affiliation. At the TUC Conference in Cape Coast on 25–26 January 1958, Inkumsah led the criticism of the proposed 'new structure', supported most prominently by representatives of the Mineworkers' and Public Works Department Unions. Afterwards, he reiterated to the Working Committee his view that there were 'too many flaws in it to be acceptable'.[39] At the end of February, he gave his full support to the staging of a demonstration against the 'new structure'. But on 15 June he attended an informal TUC meeting in Accra and on his return commenced to argue the case for a greater degree of co-operation with the TUC leadership and its plans. At a Location mass meeting he declared

> that since it was to be a Government Bill, it will come whether you like it or not. He said the opportunity was there for discussing the clauses and make representation to Government before the matter reached Parliament, and he really felt that if they could not make good use of the chance, then whether or not they like it, its tentacles would embrace the workers.[40]

This met with hooting and catcalls from the Location workers: 'We thought those TUC boys must have bribed him. Or else his cousin [A. E. Inkumsah, the Minister of the Interior] had persuaded him to betray us.'[41]

This judgment may have been unfair. Certainly the 'new structure' offered an indirect bribe to the presidents and general secretaries of national unions in the form of vastly increased salaries of £840 and £750 per annum respectively. But it is arguable that Inkumsah also had a firmer grasp than the rank and file of political realities. His reconsideration of the position did not, he stressed, lead him to support the new structure unconditionally but merely to hold the opinion 'that it was better to be in there and have our views expressed, and by the strength of our arguments to win them over to our viewpoint'.[42] His fellow executive officers, with the important exception of V. K. Quist, agreed with him. That Inkumsah was not 'selling out' to the TUC was suggested by the attitude taken towards him by the TUC leadership which, as he pointed out, 'was at the same time branding him as being reactionary and working against them in the interest of a political clique'. This distrust persisted right through to September when Inkumsah was detained in spite of his official stance of opposition to the strike; and on his release from detention, the TUC leadership prohibited his reinstatement as president of the union.

Still, the majority of the Sekondi-Takoradi rank and file and their branch and association leaders would not agree to any compromise, and at the July Working Committee meeting, the Location Branch submitted a resolution 'disavowing the leadership of Comrade Inkumsah'.[43] They listed five charges, of which the last and most important was that 'he has committed this union to accept the Histadrut structure prepared by Mr John Tettegah'[44] (the use of 'Mr' rather than 'Comrade' here was clearly pointed). The executive officers and up-country (i.e. non-Sekondi-Takoradi) delegates sided with Inkumsah in conformity with an oft-recurring pattern in Railway Union politics, and carried the resolution that 'there was no substance in the charges preferred against the President – and that the President should remain in office'.[45] But the Location representatives insisted that their stand was irrevocable and that 'although

85

Comrade Inkumsah has the personality for leadership and is bold, yet since the Location masses do not appreciate his services they wish that he should resign or they secede'.[46] At the end of September, having once more failed to win over a majority of Working Committee members, the Location Branch of the union did in fact secede, and, together with the Electrical and Traffic Associations (based at Takoradi), the Marine Association (which had broken away earlier in the year) and the Enginemen's Union (which was maintaining its opposition to incorporation in the central Railway Union), formed a Joint Council of Railway Unions.

From the perspective of the structure of power and communications in the Railway Union, it is significant that the secession was limited to these groups. It did not include any of the up-country workers, with the exception of those in the Traffic Association, nor all even of the Takoradi workers. The up-country workers and their representatives were (and indeed remain) relatively insulated from many of the influences which engender militancy among the Sekondi-Takoradi workers. More particularly, the ease with which they have been controlled by the official union leadership derives from their isolation from the centre of union activity (all negotiations being carried on between association leaders and departmental heads based in Sekondi-Takoradi). Lacking close familiarity with union affairs, they generally follow the official line as communicated to them by branch representatives. These are in turn easily cultivated by the executive officers on their tours of the line.[47] A different and more complex explanation is required in the case of the decision of many of the Takoradi workers not to join the secession. Highly active, well informed, and independently minded in their trade union participation, they could not so readily be controlled by union officials, whether local or national. But in confused situations, where a difficult decision between conflicting aims and principles had to be made, long-serving or particularly esteemed local leaders were often able to exert a subtle but decisive influence over rank-and-file behaviour through the respect accorded their opinions.

So, in 1958, although the Sekondi-Takoradi workers had been united in their opposition to the 'new structure', many were confused, when it came to the difficult question of secession, as to whether such a transgression of the basic principle and motto of the union ('United we stand, divided we fall') could be justified. In this situation, the rank and file tended to follow the line of their association leaders, partly on account of patronage ties in the sense of gratitude for past services rendered, but primarily because the opinions and sincerity of their local leaders could, it was felt, be most trusted. As one former association leader put it, 'The thing about the railway workers, especially here in Sekondi-Takoradi, is that you really have to persuade them with good arguments. You must never take their support for granted. But of course it helps a great deal to persuade them if they know you personally and have reason to respect you.'[48] Whereas the association and branch leaders at Sekondi Location were united in their determination to secede, and A. Y. Ankomah (Electrical Association secretary), W. N. Grant and A. K. A. Bello (chairman and secretary of the Traffic Association) persuaded their members to follow, no significant inroads were made among those Takoradi workers whose association leaders refused to support the secession. This refusal appears to have derived very largely from their long-standing friendship with Union President Inkumsah, who had been the Takoradi branch secretary for several years; though, as the secessionists claimed, lack of courage may also have had something to do with it.

The subsequent history of the Joint Council of Railway Unions was lucidly summarised in a bulletin issued to the rank-and-file membership in July 1959:

At the 3rd Annual Conference of the Federation of Government Industrial Trade Unions held in Kumasi, we were invited to attend and discuss the new TUC structure. After a very lengthy and thorough research on the constitution of the structure we were able to extract 13 articles from it to which we objected and forwarded to the Secretary of the TUC for amendments – but he did nothing about it.

Some time later, we received copies of the Industrial Relations Bill from the Minister of Labour, requesting us to study and submit our objections. We all welcomed this idea but the . . . time given us was so limited . . . we were forced to sit one whole day to construe the whole Bill: this done, we further submitted 11 articles in the Bill which we found was straining the Freedom of Trade Unionism, to the Minister of Labour and Co-operatives for necessary amendments to be made in the Bill. He did not even reply to our letter sent to him, but all that we would hear was that the Bill had been passed into law by the Parliament.

Later, the Prime Minister met us again to discuss some naughty points in the structure and the Bill. We did not however reach any vital conclusions – the next thing we heard was the inauguration of the new TUC.

The four Unions in the Railway decided to stay out and operate as it was and in accordance with a section in the same Industrial Relations Act which states: 'Unions not affiliated to the TUC can meet their employers, provided the latter has no objection, but will have no legal bargaining.'

. . . But according to the General Manager, he has received a letter from the Government stating that it is now the Government policy to stop meeting all unions that are not affiliated to the TUC.

We have sent a letter to the Minister of Labour to confirm whether this policy is correct. We are patiently waiting for a reply.

I am asked by your leaders to thank you for your unflinching support you have given our march towards freedom of Trade Unionism.[49]

The following month the secessionists received a reply from Nkrumah in person. After expressing his continuing concern for the interests of those who 'played so large a part in the struggle for Independence', and giving an assurance that he would oversee the TUC's use of its funds, the Prime Minister reasserted his belief in the advantages of the 'new structure'. He concluded, 'From now on I and my Government recognise only two national unions in the Railway establishment – the Railway and Harbour Workers' Union and the Railway Enginemen's Union.'[50] Shortly afterwards, the government passed an amendment to the Industrial Relations Act decreeing that no unions were permitted to exist outside twenty-four constituent unions of the TUC.

Between then and the end of the year, the splinter groups formally reamalgamated with the official union, but the seriousness and bitterness of the 1958–9 division had been such as to prevent any real, lasting reunion, and the conflict between national and local (Sekondi-Takoradi) leadership continued with hardly a respite. In October 1959 the national executive officers were re-elected without change, having refused to allow the splinter unions' members to vote. And in January 1960 the leaders of the former splinter unions were re-elected to their positions in the branches and associations. They resumed their attack on the top-level leadership by proposing a resolution that only the associations, and not the branches, should be represented on the National Executive Council (which would have assured them of majority control there), and that national officers should forfeit the right to vote on major issues since they were 'officially classified as Government back-benchers'.[51] This was, not surprisingly, overruled. The national officers countered by tabling an amendment to the union constitution, recommended by the TUC leadership, according to which, 'Any member who endeavours to create dissension among the members shall upon conviction thereof be punished by expulsion from the Union.'[52] This too failed to gain majority support (it was considered not to be conducive to the proper and peaceful working of the union), though the president's disciplinary and executive powers were vastly increased in the new 'model' constitution adopted in February 1960, and the malcontents had to tread more cautiously for a while.[53]

88

Below the surface of relative quiescence in the Railway Union in 1960–1, however, opposition to the TUC and the regime it served was growing amongst the rank and file, fuelled by further examples of the detachment and insensitivity of top-level officials. President Nkrumah's presentation of the N₵250,000 Hall of Labour to the TUC was regarded as a bribe to oblige TUC officials to restrain workers' wage demands, and as a symbol of their social distance from the working masses. The pseudo-Marxist ideology propounded by TUC officials, and by visiting speakers at TUC seminars, was not simply ineffectively communicated to the rank and file and their middle-level representatives. Rather, this 'Soviet-ism nonsense', as Pobee Biney termed it, was itself a positive irritant to unionists who valued, above all, the qualities of 'straightforwardness' and 'plain talking'.[54] As one branch official recalled,

I must be frank, we never understood what they were telling us, we were just following them blindly. The ideas seemed foreign to us, and although the speakers were obviously very brilliant, a lot did not know the workers' real situation. They would tell us, 'The workers of Ghana will never have any difficulty getting milk and margarine', when there was a shortage in the market at the same time. If we had tried to talk that way to the masses – well, a few did and the workers just hooted with laughter over it. Especially the 'isms'. Everything was with ' isms'.[55]

In so far as the TUC ideologists' attacks on 'bourgeois opportunists and self-seekers' were understood, they could only serve to highlight the hypocrisy of those making them. A student of the ideology of the Nkrumah regime concluded from his interview with CPP–TUC leaders: 'For many, socialism was not even a perspective within which to bring about modernisation, it was merely a means to rationalise the acquisition of power. Most tended to see socialism in a favourable light in terms of the expansion of their own departments.'[56] The Sekondi-Takoradi railway workers were not slow to perceive this reality and to contrast the socialism of Tettegah and Meyer with that of Pobee Biney.

The 1961 budget

For the Nkrumah Government, an austerity budget was imperative in 1961 if it was not to abandon its development objectives.[57] The Second Development Plan (1959–64) aimed at an ambitious programme of industrialisation, farm mechanisation and agricultural diversification designed to break the nation's excessive economic dependence upon cocoa, which it was estimated would require a total expenditure of N₵980 million over a five-year period. Almost half of the required revenue was expected to come from the export tax on cocoa (about 40 per cent of the government's annual revenue was secured from this tax up to 1959) and from loans from the Cocoa Marketing Board – a public corporation which had its own invested reserves built up by the monopoly it held on buying the entire cocoa crop each year at a fixed price and selling it on the world market at a highly variable price.

In 1960 a sudden and drastic fall in the price of cocoa on the world market threatened to wreck these development plans. The government's loan from the Cocoa Marketing Board was N₵9 million less than had been anticipated because the board had to pay out this sum to farmers who had been guaranteed a fixed price, while the world price had tumbled below that figure. Ghana's bumper crop of 1961, it became clear, would yield several million less than had a smaller crop the previous year – world production was at an all-time high and, in 1961, the world market price reached its lowest point in thirteen years. If a serious slowing down in the pace of development was to be prevented without resort to dependence on foreign loans and the further exhaustion of national reserves (which had already fallen from N₵235 million in 1955 to about N₵120 million in 1961), then it was clearly necessary to increase the proportion of revenue from other sources.

With the agreement of the Ghana Farmers' Council, cocoa farmers were required to contribute 16 per cent of the price owed them by the Cocoa Marketing Board to the national coffers and also to accept a government bond, maturing in ten years, to cover 10 per cent of the total sum owed them for their crop. The urban populace were to contribute their share to the development effort through various measures introduced in the July budget: a property tax on houses larger than the average size (two rooms and a hall); a new purchase tax on durable consumer goods, such as cars and refrigerators; increased import duties on a wide range of commodities; and a compulsory savings scheme suggested by the Cambridge economist Nicholas Kaldor. Under this scheme, all persons earning over N₵336 a year would have to accept 5 per cent of their wages or salaries in national investment bonds drawing 4 per cent interest and redeemable after ten years. This figure was set so as to exempt the lower-paid category of unskilled workers. Hardest hit would be the skilled workers, economically situated just above the exemption ceiling of N₵336 per annum, and therefore least able to afford the compulsory savings exactions. However, as Kaldor saw it, 'the advantage of the scheme as against straightforward taxation is that people are merely asked to postpone their consumption and not to forego it altogether'.[58] This overlooked the fact that the increasingly unaccountable character of the CPP regime, together with the highly undiplomatic suggestion made by some CPP leaders that patriots should be prepared to make their contribution without expectation of repayment, completely undermined confidence in the scheme's working according to plan. It was certainly generally regarded not as an investment but a form (devious, perhaps, rather than 'straightforward') of direct taxation.

Nevertheless, relative to the sacrifices being demanded of the cocoa farmers, and to the skilled workers' own rise in prosperity in 1957–61, the level of exaction imposed was not so high as inevitably, or by itself, to provoke such stern resistance as was in fact encountered. The government had some reason to anticipate its being accepted as reasonable. The Minister of Finance, presenting the budget to parliament on 7 July, declared that

> Any increase in burdens imposed by this budget will be small in comparison with the increase in incomes and living standards which the people of this country have enjoyed since Independence – as Osagyefo [Nkrumah] said in his speech, the increase in the total wage and salary payments since 1957 has been 49 per cent. Last year we granted a general wage increase of approximately 22 per cent.[59]

Such figures say little, of course, about real wage-levels, which, for the skilled and unskilled workers, appear to have risen by approximately 14 per cent in 1957–61. Over the whole period of the 1950s these workers had enjoyed a rise of some 45 per cent in real incomes (see Table 5.2).

Table 5.2. *Fluctuations in the real wage-level of unskilled workers, 1950-61*

Date	Daily wage rate	Money wage index	Cost of living index	Real wage index
Dec. 1950	3/3	217	285	76
Dec. 1951	3/3	217	333	65
Apr. 1952	4/6	300	326	92
Dec. 1952	4/6	300	324	93
Dec. 1953	4/6	300	324	93
Dec. 1954	4/6	300	324	93
Dec. 1955	4/6	300	344	87
Apr. 1956	5/2	344	351	98
Dec. 1957	5/2	344	351	98
Dec. 1958	5/6	367	354	104
Oct. 1959	5/6	367	364	101
Dec. 1960	6/6	433	367	118
Dec. 1961	6/6	433	390	111

Source: Kodwo Ewusi, *The Distribution of Monetary Incomes in Ghana* (Legon, 1971), p. 43.

This at least enabled skilled workers to meet the cost of basic necessities, but hardly provided a life of even relative luxury. The Sekondi-Takoradi Household Budget Survey of 1955 suggested that skilled workers and others, earning around £11 per month, often experienced difficulty in living within their incomes, even though the average expenditure pattern included little in the way of luxury items.[60] If this was the picture in 1955, then by 1961 the skilled workers should have been able to exist fairly comfortably though with little to spare or save. They were, of course, bound to be unenthusiastic about giving up most of what little economic progress they had achieved since Independence. And, with food prices rising by over 40 per cent in the summer months, it is perhaps understandable that they should have been complaining of 'an already precarious financial situation: it is hard to make ends meet'.[61] They were, however, accustomed to this regular seasonal rise in food prices which therefore presented little cause for disquiet in itself (though the rise in 1961 was rather greater than in earlier years). It would seem reasonable to conclude that, while the compulsory savings scheme was likely to impose some financial strain on skilled workers, this was hardly so great as to be unacceptable if the government and its development plans retained any degree of popular confidence or enthusiasm. The commencement of the 1961 strike, though rationalised by its leaders in terms of opposition to the budget measures, in fact signified a far deeper disillusionment with the CPP regime. W. N. Grant, a leading organiser of the 1961 strike, was quite clear about this:

> Tettegah tried persuading us about the advantages of his consolidation, and we had to agree with this, but we disagreed about party control. The thing was we realised Nkrumah was becoming a dictator. He was already trying to bribe workers' leaders to co-operate in muzzling the workers. Everybody had been put into a frenzy of fear. You couldn't speak your mind. So it was all political really. But we had to be careful not to be too obviously political.[62]

Herein lay an acute dilemma for the railway workers' leaders. It was obvious to Grant and some of his fellow unionists that their objections to the CPP–TUC were so fundamental, and the logic of autocratic politics so inexorable, as to necessitate challenging the very existence of the Nkrumah regime if it was to be resisted at all. Yet an alliance to this purpose with the opposition United Party – a party whose leadership included precisely those elite elements of the old United Gold Coast Convention they had so vigorously opposed in 1948–50 – would be not only distasteful and highly dangerous, but ruinously divisive of railway worker unity.

The commencement of the strike

The budget measures were announced on 15 July. On 20 July the railway workers' middle-level leaders manoeuvred the national executive into supporting a resolution that

> As that aspect of the Budget proposals dwelling on the National Development Bonds strikes at the very root of the income of the workers, we the members of the Working Committee acting on behalf of the National Executive of Railway and Harbour Workers hereby resolve that in view of the extreme hardship that the deductions are likely to throw on the workers at the end of this month and thereafter, the Government, through the TUC of Ghana, be approached to call for suspension of these deductions until such time that the workers' viewpoint of the whole Budget proposals has been heard.[63]

It was most unlikely, the opposition leaders realised, that the TUC would support, or even reply to this demand, but it at least maintained the appearance of following official procedures, and gave the TUC leadership an opportunity to redeem (or finally damn) itself. When the TUC failed to reply by the end of August the middle-level leaders had made their point and resolutions were adopted by the Sekondi, Takoradi and Kumasi Branches calling for secession since 'the TUC has definitely failed to express the true feelings of the working class'.[64] Inkumsah and the other top-level leaders now stood revealed as 'ghost' leaders, having lost all control over the Sekondi-Takoradi rank and file. They could only go along with the forthcoming strike action, or else retire from the scene and make disapproving sounds from afar in order to avoid being held accountable. The opposition leaders 'pointed out that the absence of the National Officers at the Rally of 29th August was conspicuous and urged them to be present at the next one'.[65] None were, and the union chairman, J. Appiah, capitulated entirely by handing in his resignation. On 3 September, the strike leaders took over the union offices – now deserted by the national officers – and sent out messages to the branches to 'let go the anchor' (Pobee Biney's code-phrase for strike action). During the following seventeen days of strike activity, the national officers made it clear to the press that 'the Railway Union as such has not officially declared a strike' and 'did strongly appeal to the workers to work to enable immediate negotiations to be carried out' [66] – but to no effect.

John Tettegah recognised that the strike was centrally concerned with the 'new structure' and its leadership, and not simply compulsory savings. In the second week of the strike he attempted to restore some measure of confidence in the TUC by appealing that 'all outstanding grievances be forwarded to TUC headquarters without delay in order to seek avenues of redress and prompt actions'.[67] The railway workers certainly had a plethora of job-related grievances going back many years – their conditions of service had been brought up to date, and the Africanisation programme implemented, but in a piecemeal fashion which gave rise to scores of inconsistencies and injustices and left them disadvantaged relative to workers in the new corporations. Such grievances were an important factor in generating allegiance to forceful local leadership which 'really understood their situation and problems', and conversely in generating alienation from the Accra-based TUC officials. But Tettegah underestimated the depth of this alienation if he seriously thought that such a gesture could restore the railway workers' confidence in the TUC. In any case, the railway workers' open opposition to the TUC elite had become part of a wider political struggle, attracting the involvement of other social groups: 'The support received from all the people here [i.e. in Sekondi-Takoradi] was so tremendous, we realised we could not back down even if we had wanted to. People felt it was a burning issue to the community.' [68]

Subjective significance of the strike: class-consciousness and communalism

Preceding sections of this chapter have delineated the sources of conflict between the railway workers and the CPP–TUC elite, and have indicated the way in which the economic welfare of other sections of the populace – the unskilled workers, the unemployed and the market-women – depended directly or indirectly upon that of the skilled workers. The unskilled workers were, of course, most directly involved in the railway artisans' conflict with the TUC elite. One of the central issues in this struggle was reform of the wage and salary structure inherited from the colonial period. The CPP, though apparently committed to such reform in 1949–51, had failed to carry it through. The Lidbury–Gbedemah Report of 1951–2 had made only half-hearted reforms in this direction, and it was on this issue primarily that Pobee Biney and Anthony Woode had criticised the party and its leadership. Many of the unskilled railway workers also felt (and still do feel) very strongly about this: 'It all depends on cheating. There are so many people being paid fat salaries without working. I didn't go to school but I know my work. If an educated man comes along to sit in an office and he's given so much more pay than myself, I have to challenge the government and find out what is happening'.[69] The skilled railway workers' association with a militant reformist stance helps to account for the fact that, in 1961, they received the solid support of the unskilled workers, even though these would not be directly affected by the compulsory savings exactions.

Many of the unemployed of Sekondi-Takoradi also joined in the strikers' demonstrations. Some of these were, of course, sons or other relatives of the skilled workers on whom they depended for food and accommodation. They were therefore particularly concerned to unite with the strikers in attacking the proposed property tax. We have already seen how a serious shortage of housing for the lower-paid in Sekondi-Takoradi had been exacerbated by corruption and party favouritism in the National Housing Corporation. In consequence, most workers had either to pay exorbitant rates for privately rented accommodation, or else to band together and struggle to save enough to build a house for several families. It was small wonder, then, that the 1961 strikers demanded that the property tax 'be amended to suit the ordinary worker',[70] since they feared that it would be passed on to those renting accommodation and would inhibit private building where more was needed. It also seemed grossly unfair to impose a tax on 'family houses' in which workers provided free accommodation for the unemployed. As one railway worker put it, 'The government had done nothing to solve our housing problems at all, rather they had cheated us to please their girlfriends. And then, when we struggled to build our own houses, they tried to tax us again, forgetting we were already overburdened with relatives who could not find work'.[71] The property tax issue illustrates how, in Sekondi-Takoradi in 1961, grievances which might superficially appear to have been particular to the so-called 'labour aristocracy' of skilled workers, together with the higher-paid wage-earners, took on the character and significance of a 'mass' communal protest against the CPP elite.

The reasons for the development of a sense of communal deprivation amongst the people of Sekondi-Takoradi have already been treated in some detail. It is worth drawing attention here, however, to the particular grievances of the Sekondi-Takoradi market-women, since they were amongst the most ardent, and certainly the most valuable, supporters of the railway workers during the course of the strike, encouraging them to hold out and raising morale by supplying them with free food. Victims of CPP oligopoly in the market-trade, they identified closely with the railway workers' struggle against similar centralising tendencies in the TUC. Alice Koomson, the leading organiser of the market-women, explained why they had become so disillusioned with CPP rule:

> In the early days, all the market-women were crazy for CPP and joined the Women's Organisation, but once the women's officials had gained control of the distribution of foodstuffs in the market, they

95

used this monopoly to make them a packet. Essie Eluah, the leader of the market-women here [she was actually Vice-President of the Sekondi-Takoradi Ghana Women], she organised it. She gradually moved from selling foodstuffs to cloth and other things. Then she got a pass-book for GNTC [the Ghana National Trading Corporation], the largest wholesalers here in Ghana, so that she could obtain goods on credit, and later recommended her closest friends for pass-books. We found that some of our sisters were moving to bigger things while the rest of us were crippled.

So during the summer of 1961 I travelled round even to Kojo-krom [a village some five miles out of Sekondi] to tell the other market-women I was prepared to stand and fight against this. I told them, 'I have only two children and nothing to lose so I will organise it.' When the strike came, they were all ready to help the railway workers. We spent all the money we had saved on giving them free cassava, and then, as we were running out, Kwesi-Lamptey brought us some more from Danquah and those people [the leaders of the opposition United Party].[72]

It is clear, then, that the motivation of those involved in the 1961 strike went far deeper than that of opposition to the budget measures. Even the compulsory savings scheme issue was as much symbolic as material in significance: 'We knew they were trying to fool us, they would not pay us back, and we didn't trust them to spend it properly. You couldn't believe what they said any more'.[73] The central issue was initially seen by the railway workers as a struggle between the working masses and the TUC elite. But the subjective significance of the strike rapidly widened to take in, implicitly at least, the structure and performance not merely of the TUC, but of the government as a whole. This issue united virtually the whole Sekondi-Takoradi community in support of the strike.

By midweek practically every activity in the port was closed down. Municipal bus drivers had joined the strike, as had the city employees who collected the sewage daily. Market-women dispensed free food to the strikers at municipal bus garages and other strategic points. Red head-bands and arm-bands were in evidence everywhere; they were symbols worn in former days by Fanti tribal fighting men to mean, 'We are ready for War'. Ships were pulled away from the docks and anchored in the roadstead for fear of sabotage. There was an air of excitement and pride throughout the city over the fact that they, the people of Sekondi-Takoradi, had brought business to a standstill, had stopped train service to all of Ghana, and were displaying solidarity in the fight against the budget. Morale was high. The railway

96

workers were heroes . . . W. N. Grant, a prominent strike leader, told the crowd that if parliament did not give way to the demands of the people, they would disband that body by force.[74]

The United Party involvement

The government took an extremely serious view of the strike and, two days after its commencement, declared a state of emergency in the city. This was partly because such strike actions were now illegal under the 1958 Industrial Relations Act, and also because the measures against which the railway workers were (formally) protesting were considered essential to the achievement of the government's major objectives. In an *Evening News* editorial earlier in the year, for example, the government had warned that

> Those who have not the heart for the sacrifices which the Party and Nation will call forth will be swept by the wayside by the wind of change . . . Ghana's economic independence can be achieved only if the party is able to mobilise the masses in town and countryside to tighten their belts, so that a greater proportion of our national income is diverted to financing the construction of the means of production – machines for making machines.[75]

But the government's disquiet also derived from suspicions that the sinister hand of the United Party opposition was at work behind the strike.

The United Party had been inaugurated on 3 November 1957 at a rally in Accra presided over by Dr Kofi Busia.[76] Its executive was drawn from its component groups – the National Liberation Movement, the Northern People's Party, the Moslem Association Party, the Togoland Congress, the Anlo Youth Organisation and the Ga Shifimo Kpee. Executive members included Dr J. B. Danquah, Obetsebi Lamptey, Ashie Nikoe, J. Kwesi-Lamptey, Joe Appiah, M. K. Apaloo, Attoh Okine, R. R. Amponsah and K. Y. Attoh, in addition to Dr Busia. In short, the United Party consisted of an alliance of the major communalistic movements in Ghanaian society under the leadership of intellectuals who had consistently opposed the CPP since UGCC days, or, as in the case of Kwesi-Lamptey and Ashie Nikoe, had broken with the CPP in 1951–3. At its inauguration in 1957 it could claim the support of thirty-two MPs. However, after a series of election defeats, the defection of a number of northern MPs and the 'preventive detention' of some thirty-eight party members, including the executive members Attoh Okine and K. Y. Attoh, the United Party was, by 1960, a much-weakened parliamentary and electoral force.[77] Its only hope of displacing the CPP regime, or even preserving its own existence (and keeping its leaders out of prison), appeared to lie in the use of violent measures. This might, of course, take the form of a coup d'etat, or an assassination attempt such as Apaloo and Amponsah were alleged to have planned in December 1958. It seems probable, however, that there was little basis to this latter charge and that, in general, the UP leaders were less prepared to resort to direct or open violence than the CPP liked to suggest. A more appealing strategy lay in the incitement of civil disturbances by fuelling, or playing on, the intense and growing popular hostility to the CPP regime which existed in many parts of the country. In any case, the leaders of any movement of opposition to the CPP were likely to be drawn into flirtation with the UP, at least in the sense of seeking its financial support.

This undoubtedly occurred in the case of the Sekondi-Takoradi strike. Danquah and other UP leaders met a group of railway unionists in August and sought to convince them that the budget measures were not only harsh and unfair but signalled an impending economic crisis.[78] It is also clear from the testimony of Alice Koomson that she and her husband, A. Y Ankomah, the railway unionist, had developed close links with Kwesi-Lamptey, the UP's leading representative in Sekondi-Takoradi, and arranged for him to channel money to the market-women to aid the workers' strike effort. Ankomah and his wife were, on their own admission, firmly committed by 1961 'to spoil the government'.[79] Yet it is far from clear that the mass of strikers knew anything of this UP involvement, and quite manifestly untrue that the UP actually incited the strike (as a subsequent government white paper claimed), or was capable of doing so. On the contrary, it is clear from a consideration of the background to the strike that the UP's role was marginal, much as its leaders may have attempted to capitalise on an existing conflict between the railway workers and the CPP. Indeed, the most notable characteristic of the railway workers' hostility to the CPP was their consistent refusal to translate this hostility into support for the UP. As late as the plebiscite of 1960, when Danquah and the UP succeeded in winning 35 per cent of the vote in Accra, their electoral support was virtually non-existent in Sekondi-Takoradi. This antipathy to the UP cannot be adequately explained in terms of identification with different, opposing communal interests since, by 1960–1, the UP was far more than an Ashanti-based movement (though also less than representative of Ashanti as a whole). The reason was rather that, although the railway workers' conflict with the CPP was fuelled by a certain communalistic sentiment, this was, for the most part, consciously conceived of in class, or mass versus elite, terms. Railway worker ideology was even nationalistic in the sense that overtly tribal or regional movements were regarded as regressive. The UP still tended to be seen as an opportunistic extension of the old UGCC. In addition, since the

98

central issue in the railway workers' campaign against the TUC elite had been that of party control, many were genuinely concerned for the sake of consistency to resist too close an alliance with, or manipulation by, the opposition party.

Consequently, those railway unionists who had been led by their disillusionment with the CPP regime to develop ties with the UP – A. Y. Ankomah, V. K. Quist, W. N. Grant and K. G. Quartey – were extremely concerned to keep this association secret. The majority of railway workers and their middle-level leaders regarded the strike as a non-partisan reformist protest, and appear to have been either unaware of the UP involvement or, when they learned of it, highly disapproving. At the beginning of the third week of the strike, when President Nkrumah gave assurances of future reforms and ordered the release of all persons arrested in connection with the strike, a split developed between the intransigents – Ankomah, Quist, Grant and Quartey – who wanted to hold out in the hope of precipitating an army coup, and the reformists who felt that, with the president's conciliatory response, the main objectives of the strike had been attained as successfully as could be expected.[80] The reformists were in a majority amongst the middle-level leaders – A. K. A. Bello, K. Imbeah, J. K. Baaku, T. B. Ward, T. C. Bentil, T. Hagan, S. Onyina, G. Essiel and J. Ashielfie were all reformists rather than UP supporters – but had difficulty in convincing the rank and file that their proposal for a return to work did not amount to a back-down. Lacking clear majority support, they were unwilling to undermine the solidarity which had been maintained so impressively until then. By the middle of the week, however, virtually all the rank and file had come round to supporting a return to work for two main reasons. Firstly, the president's warning, on Wednesday of that week, that the strike had taken on an insurrectionary character and that maximum force would be used if necessary to restore the railway and the harbour to normal operation on Friday, intimidated the railway workers into returning on that day. But, in addition, the spread of rumours that some of the strike leaders had indeed accepted money from the United Party undermined the intransigents' support amongst the rank and file, who felt they were now being used against their will by the UP. Hence the aims of the strike became more clearly defined – to awaken the CPP to popular discontent at its increasingly corrupt, autocratic and elitist character, but without dabbling in subversive party politics.

Reprisals and achievements

Soon after the men had returned to work, their leaders and a number of market-women were arrested. On 3 October Danquah, Joe Appiah and

Victor Owusu were detained, together with some fifty members of the UP opposition. The government's white paper on the strike insisted that it was planned from the start as a UP plot to topple the regime, and paid little attention to the genuine grievances of the strikers.[81]

Yet Nkrumah's actions in the month following the return to work clearly indicated that he at least recognised the central importance of anti-elite feeling in the strike's causation. In consequence, it was not only the strike leaders and the UP opposition but many members of the CPP 'old guard' who were to suffer from its occurrence. Admittedly, the president's awareness that all was not well with the CPP's image predated the strike. In April 1961, when preparing for an austerity budget and considering the probable obstacles to its popular acceptability, Nkrumah decided to deliver a 'dawn broadcast to the nation'. In this, he criticised the self-interestedness of some members of the party 'who by virtue of their functions and positions are tending to form a separate new ruling class of self-seekers and careerists'. This was 'working to alienate the support of the masses and to bring the National Assembly into isolation'.[82] He went on to announce measures to curtail the allowances and perquisites of government officials and to compel them to declare their assets and sever their ties with private business.[83] Such a 'clean-up', he insisted, was being demanded by those who were being asked to make sacrifices for development goals.

The Sekondi-Takoradi workers were generally unimpressed with the effectiveness of these measures, however, and the September strike brought home to the president the persisting loss of popular confidence in the sincerity of the regime. In an attempt to remedy this, he purged the party of a number of its leading figures on the grounds that they had abused their position by amassing excessive private fortunes. On 29 September, one week after the strikers had returned to work, the *Evening News* announced that six Ministers had been asked to resign. These included such prominent and long-time party leaders as Komla Gbedemah, Kojo Botsio, and Krobo Edusei, popularly renowned for the episode of his wife's purchase of a gold bed. A number of other leading officials, including A. E. Inkumsah (Minister of the Interior), E. K. Bensah (Minister of Works) and J. E. Hagan (commissioner for the Central Region), were asked to surrender property in excess of the limits laid down earlier in the year. To this degree at least, the 1961 strike was successful, and its significance appreciated in governing circles.

The intransigents among the railway unionists were nevertheless to be proved correct in their belief that such reforms as materialised would be short-lived, and that the major result of any protest which stopped short of 'spoiling the government' would be an intensification of repressive measures. The new men who rose to replace the 'old guard' of the CPP, if marginally less corrupt than their predecessors, possessed an even more regimented conception of 'popular mobilisation'. The main modification in the structure and operation of the TUC after 1961 lay in the introduction of additional measures to deter rank-and-file rebellions. Essentially, the conclusion of the 1961 strike signified the final defeat of the railway workers' attempt to reform the TUC, at least for as long as the CPP regime remained in power.

6

The development of an independent and democratic trade union movement

The Sekondi-Takoradi workers' hostility to the TUC, as expressed in the 1961 strike, derived in part, it has been argued, from particular historical and structural factors. Several other groups of workers expressed their support by striking for a day or two, and tacit sympathy for the protesters was possibly quite widespread, but, generally speaking, the TUC was firmly in control in the rest of the country. The final attempt of the Sekondi-Takoradi workers to reform the structure and orientation of the trade union movement appeared to have failed.

Yet in 1966–71, the Ghana TUC was remodelled along very much the lines advocated by the railway unionists. There were important similarities between Pobee Biney's conception of the ideal role and structure of the labour movement and that of Benjamin Bentum, secretary-general of the TUC during the whole of this latter period. To be sure, Bentum was a more moderate and cautious leader than Biney, and his policy was more closely geared to the practical requisites of both economic development and institutional survival. But, for Bentum as for Biney, the labour movement should be an independent political force, in the vanguard of the struggle for social justice and the defence of democracy. For Bentum too, if rather less clearly than for Biney, the unions should perform the role of populist spokesmen, looking to, and responsible for, a larger constituency than the unionised workers alone.

Certainly, the majority of the railway and harbour workers perceived such a similarity and regarded Bentum's TUC as an approximation to the ideal for which they had consistently fought. This was especially the case in 1970–1, as Bentum became ever more radical in his criticisms of the government and the socio-economic status quo. A substantial minority splinter-group in the ranks of the railway workers clearly took a different view, since it seceded from the TUC and established a separate union and a rival trade union centre. An analysis of the sources and significance of this division will be presented in a subsequent chapter. For the moment,

102

however, the important point to recognise is that the lack of consensus amongst the railway workers in 1970–1 did not imply any lack of enthusiasm for Bentum's TUC on the part of the majority who were members of the 'official' or 'mother' union. With the relatively minor exception of this splinter railway union, moreover, the labour movement was solid in its support for the 'new model' of trade unionism developed under Bentum's leadership. One of the most significant developments in Ghanaian politics during this period was the attainment of a high degree of working-class unity in support of that independent, reformist model of trade unionism which the railway workers had consistently advocated.

There is, at present, an almost total lack of published accounts of this development, and it is therefore necessary to provide a fairly detailed account here. Consequently, the focus of attention in this chapter shifts away temporarily from the railway workers themselves toward the TUC and the Ghanaian unions in general. In chapter 7 the focus returns to internal Railway Union politics, and the role played therein by divergent rank-and-file attitudes to the TUC leadership of Benjamin Bentum.

The CPP regime and the unions: 1961–6

Between September 1961 and the coup d'etat of February 1966 disillusionment with the CPP regime spread to virtually all groups of workers throughout Ghana. This was indicated by the large demonstrations of labour support for the soldiers' intervention in Accra, Kumasi and Sekondi-Takoradi during the week following the coup.[1] It is possible, but unlikely, that these were stage-managed or unrepresentative of the feelings of other workers. In any case, there were more reliable indicators: the fact that the new regime felt it necessary to remove from office only certain TUC officials and the general secretaries of the national unions, it being confidently assumed that support for the displaced regime extended no further; and the intensity and uniformity of pressure from both union rank and file and their leaders for a 'democratic and independent' trade union movement, and their determined unity thereafter in defence of this independent structure against any attempt to force or forge a party political alliance. The experience of 1961–6 had instilled in Ghanaian workers a profound and lasting revulsion against any suggestion of governmental or party political interference in trade union affairs.

Two main factors accounted for the spread of anti-CPP feeling even to those workers who owed their union organisation to the initiative of CPP unionists, and who, in September 1961, had generally sided with the CPP–TUC leadership. Firstly, the rapid price inflation of 1962–6, combined with the government's refusal to raise the minimum wage, had a severe effect

103

on the real wage-levels of lower-paid workers. The TUC did not appear especially concerned to protest at this deterioration in its members' living standards. The real minimum wage index for these years shows a decline of some 42 per cent between 1961 and 1966, from 111 to 64 (see Table 6.1). It is reasonable to assume an equal decline in the average real incomes of skilled workers in the public services. The fall in real incomes of most private-sector employees was considerably less severe, owing to incremental benefits they gained through the negotiation of collective agreements with their employers. According to the calculations in the Mills–Odoi Report, average real wage-levels in the private sector declined by some 20 per cent between 1960 and 1965, compared to 40 per cent in the case of the public sector.[2] It is only fair to recognise here the contribution of TUC officials who, within the limits imposed on their freedom of action by acceptance of the government's development strategy, worked hard to achieve what they could on behalf of Ghana's lower-paid workers, utilising the compulsory collective bargaining machinery established by the 1958 Industrial Relations Act.

To be fully objective, one should also take into account the implicit wage benefits conferred on lower-paid workers by such policies as the abolition of school and hospital fees, and by the CPP regime's continuing commitment to expansion of the level of employment even in the face of the crippling budgetary situation of 1962–6. The TUC leaders were among the foremost advocates of these measures. (Succeeding regimes withdrew some of these concessions to the idea of a welfare state society. Ghana's workers could hardly be expected to appreciate this at the time,

Table 6.1. *Fluctuations in the real value of the minimum wage, 1960–8*

Year	Minimum wage (pesewas)	Index of minimum wage	Accra retail price index	Index of real minimum wage
1960	65 (6s. 6d.)	433	367	118
1961	65	433	390	111
1962	65	433	426	102
1963	65	433	446	97
1964	65	433	502	86
1965	65	433	643	67
1966	65	433	672	64
1967	70	467	623	75
1968	75	500	685	73

Source: Ewusi, *Distribution of Monetary Incomes*, p. 43.

however.) Nevertheless, both public- and private-sector employees suffered a serious decline in living standards during these years, and resentment at this impoverishment clearly informed their growing hostility to the TUC leadership. This was exacerbated by the high living of TUC leaders and by suspicion that TUC dues were being misappropriated – suspicions which post-coup relevations abundantly confirmed.[3] It does not seem necessary to elaborate this point further.

What does require emphasis is rank-and-file antipathy to the growing authoritarianism of the TUC leadership and its increasing resort to police-state techniques of control. This extended to the use of party spies and the deliberate inculcation of an atmosphere of fear at the local level so as to inhibit any open expression of criticism of the TUC or the government. This strategy was resented partly because of the obstacles it raised to pressure for wage improvement. But it produced a sense of humiliation which went far deeper than this, and an attachment to liberal values relatively independent of considerations of economic interest.

An important factor in the adoption of such authoritarian techniques of control was the removal of Tettegah in 1962 from the TUC to the All-African Trade Union Federation. This meant that the TUC lost its one prominent leader who combined organisational expertise and rhetorical ability with a substantial rank-and-file political following (especially in Accra). Magnus-George (TUC secretary-general, 1962–4) and Kwaw Ampah (TUC secretary-general, 1964–6) attempted to compensate for their own lack of any such following with a form of ideological emanation which, as Tettegah himself realised, was wholly inappropriate for Ghana's workers, being far too academic and Soviet-based, and incorporating a 'regimentation' strategy.[4] Kwaw Ampah (a member of Nkrumah's tribe, the Nzima, and a former district commissioner) was perhaps less 'regimental' in his style of leadership than had been Magnus-George. But there was little perceptible difference in spite of the introduction of an amendment to the Industrial Relations Act in May 1965 which, Ampah claimed, aimed at 'the complete removal of all control exercised over workers' organisation by the Government or other bodies'.[5] He suggested that the reason for this amendment was that 'The Party feels sufficiently convinced that the working people of this country would not misuse their freedom of action to disrupt the speedy implementation of the nation's industrialisation programme.'[6] But a rather different rationale was provided by the Minister of Labour in his speech to the Legislative Assembly. The amendment was intended

> to enable Ghana to conform to the code of international labour standards adopted by the International Labour Organisation – It is

my well-considered view that the success of the organisation of the All-African Trade Union Federation is dependent largely on the prestige of the Ghana TUC. This means the Ghana TUC has to do everything possible to attract as much following and support throughout Africa, and its organisational machinery built up as a model to be followed by other trades union movements in Africa. The Ghana TUC must therefore be free from criticisms internationally, and the draft Bill is aimed at achieving this.[7]

The alterations embodied in the Bill were the minimum necessary to serve this purpose. The TUC technically became more independent through removal of the provisions for state control of TUC activities and finance embodied in the 1958 Act. But all the provisions of the existing law were retained with respect to compulsory arbitration, the illegality of strikes in the public sector and TUC authority over the national unions. Indeed, the centralisation of the structure of the trade union movement was carried even further by a reduction in the number of national unions from sixteen to ten. And given the party's continuing control over the appointment of TUC officials, the supposed independence of the labour movement remained purely technical.

There was considerable variation in the extent to which police-state techniques of control were, or could be, effectively implemented in the various unions and branches. This depended largely on the degree of corporate resistance encountered. In the majority of unions, officials could resist the pressure to report on fellow officials only at their own peril. A branch secretary of the Industrial and Commercial Workers' Union confessed:

> Oh, there was a great deal of bitterness, but we were too afraid to oppose the party line. After some of our officials were dismissed from their jobs and one was detained, we realised that certain people were acting as spies. But later it was not so much that they had special spies, we all became spies. Even I was prepared to be a stooge, I must admit it. What else could one do to look after oneself? [8]

In the Sekondi-Takoradi branches of the Railway Union, in contrast, TUC leaders found it impossible to control the rank and file's middle-level representatives by such techniques and were therefore driven to abolish the Working Committee. Later, in 1965, the holding of mass meetings was prohibited.[9] An example of Railway Union resistance to outside control was recounted by Joe-fio N. Meyer, chairman of the TUC Executive Board at the time of the incident (1962):

> I went down to Sekondi with the Minister [of Labour] to talk to the

106

railway workers – we wanted to explain our development plans to them and to warn them against agitators on the union executive – and we told the 'announcer' to beat gong-gong to assemble them together. But he claimed to have misplaced it, and we couldn't persuade him to rediscover it until he was sure that the executive knew about our being there.[10]

More generally, as one railway unionist remarked, 'You wouldn't find anyone willing to spy for the government here. The sense of solidarity is far too strong. And anyway they wouldn't last long.' [11] Nevertheless, the general atmosphere of repression which prevailed during this period, together with the prohibition on mass meetings, presented formidable obstacles to any attempt at concerted opposition. Subsequent claims that, when the army intervened to displace Nkrumah, preparations were already in train for an unofficial strike, must be treated with a certain scepticism.

It is important to stress the depth of feeling in the unions against CPP authoritarianism because of its influence on worker attitudes to the National Liberation Council and Progress Party regimes. Generally speaking, Ghanaian workers were initially favourably disposed to these regimes, in spite of their obvious elitist character, because (or in as far as) they were relatively liberal regimes, willing to tolerate a certain measure of trade union democracy and independence. As workers frequently remarked even in the summer of 1971 (when government –union relations were extremely strained), 'At least one can speak one's mind'. It is worth pointing out that there was, potentially at least, a negative aspect to this belief in 'free, independent trade unionism', a lack of any more positive sense of unity and purpose. In reacting against the compulsory controls of the CPP regime, there was a tendency amongst some unionists to regress to a fragmented 'bread-and-butter' style of trade unionism, displaying little appreciation of the advantages or prerequisites of labour movement unity. The fact that the Ghanaian labour movement gradually developed a broader sense of unity in 1966–71, and a positive conception of its role, at once more responsible and more radical than that of 'bread-and-butter' unionism, was due in large measure to the leadership of Benjamin Bentum (TUC secretary-general, February 1966–September 1971).

Benjamin Bentum's political background and orientation

In three main respects, Bentum's leadership was crucial to the development of the Ghanaian trade union movement in 1966–71. In the first place, it was on his initiative rather than the government's that the structure of the TUC underwent a significant measure of decentralisation and democratisation. To effect this shift in the orientation and structure of power of the labour movement without provoking a government clamp-down required very considerable political and diplomatic skills on his part. Secondly, he at the same time (and on the whole successfully) checked those centrifugal tendencies in the movement noted above, convincing member unions of the need to act as a united political force, exerting influence on governmental decision-making, in order effectively to advance the interests of labour. Thirdly, while the 'new model' developed under Bentum's leadership was in a real sense democratic, he personally remained very much the leading formulator and spokesman of TUC policy and ideology, possessed of something of the valued 'strong man' image. Bentum's personal popularity, together with his convincing articulation of labour's rights and responsibilities, was a major unifying force. As the Progress Party Minister of Labour, Dr W. G. Bruce-Konuah, was to lament: 'You ask a worker which union he belongs to, and nine times out of ten he replies simply, " Bentum's TUC".' [12]

Since Bentum's role in the events of 1966–71 was so crucial, it is worth taking a brief look at his personal background and political career prior to the military coup of February 1966.[13] He was born on 29 April 1931, at Elmina in the Central Province of Ghana, the son of a clergyman of the Methodist Church Mission. He was educated at the Catholic Mission School at Berekum, and later at the Methodist School in Agona-Swedru; his hopes of attending secondary school were dashed by the death of his parents in a car crash, but he continued his studies at his uncle's home and managed to gain several O-level GCE passes. On this basis, he was awarded a scholarship to take an agricultural science course at the Agricultural Training Centre in Kumasi and later at the Kumasi College of Science and Technology. From there he went to the West African Cocoa Research Institute at Tafo where he formed the first trade union for agricultural workers within a year of his arrival in 1950. When, in 1959, this was merged into the Agricultural Workers' Union of Ghana, Bentum was elected the national organiser of the new body. Three years later he was elected the union's general secretary, a post which he occupied until becoming chairman of the TUC Executive Board in 1964. (The fact that he was also the youngest member of the board testifies to his possession of impressive personal qualities and political skills.)

As chairman of the executive board he rapidly came into conflict with Ampah and other TUC leaders, and in February 1965 Ampah secured his dismissal from the chairmanship by authority of the Central Committee of the CPP.[14] Contradictory accounts of the sources of this conflict are given by former CPP–TUC officials on the one hand, and Bentum's friends and admirers on the other. According to the latter, Bentum objected to the manner in which major decisions concerning the running of the TUC were taken by the CPP Central Committee and simply handed down to the executive board for implementation. He also criticised the degree of detachment which had developed between TUC leaders and the rank and file of the movement, and accordingly pressed for the inclusion of more far-reaching reforms in the 1965 amendment to the Industrial Relations Act. According to the former, the source of friction lay simply in Bentum's manoeuvres to discredit Ampah and displace him as secretary-general.[15] It seems probable that there are elements of truth in both interpretations; that Bentum was ambitious to displace Ampah and played on the themes of the latter's (undoubted) weaknesses and inexperience in his attempt to rally support, but that his sincerity in pointing also to the dangers of excessive centralisation was far greater than former CPP–TUC officials, outraged at his subsequent betrayal of themselves and the party, would ever be prepared to allow.

It is not the intention here to portray Bentum as a staunchly dedicated labour leader of unwavering principles. The course of his career under the CPP regime and, even more clearly, his conduct of the leadership of the TUC under the NLC and Progress Party governments, rather suggest a highly skilful and pragmatic politician, an extremely agile survivor, reacting with fine sensitivity to pressures from both above and below. But the Ghanaian trade union movement needed skilful, compromising leadership of this kind if it was to hold together as an independent movement in the political and economic circumstances of 1966–71. And it is simplistic to equate a well-developed sense of political pragmatism with a lack of any sense of principle or social purpose. Within the limits imposed on his freedom of action, Bentum's TUC leadership can be seen as consistently directed toward the development of the labour movement as a self-conscious force for greater social justice and political democracy in Ghana.

Bentum's 'new model'

Bentum summarised the orientation of his 'new model' as 'independent and democratic, but responsible trade unionism'.[16] The TUC was to be independent of the government, and strictly non-partisan with respect to party politics. It was to be relatively decentralised in structure and committed primarily to representing the interests and grievances of the union rank and file, rather than simply to controlling or restraining them. It was also to be 'responsible', in the sense of acknowledging the damaging effects of strike actions on the fragile national economy, and seeking to educate the rank and file in this reality. Strikes were to be officially condemned except where they were the workers' last resort in the face of the management's refusal to negotiate or implement agreements. Nevertheless, while maintaining impartiality with respect to party politics, the TUC was to lay claim to a major voice in national decision-making, pressing for egalitarian reform of the national wage and salary structure, and articulating policy alternatives on virtually the entire range of governmental issues. The basis for this claim was partly the idea that workers could be expected to forgo strike action only if they had other means of securing the effective representation of their interests. In practice, the TUC leadership did tend to adapt its policy on strikes to the government's sensitivity to the lower-paid workers' situation and its responsiveness to the demands of the TUC. But there was also a strain of populist ideology informing the TUC's drive to political self-assertion. This became increasingly pronounced during the Progress Party regime of Dr Busia (October 1969–January 1972). The workers were to see themselves as the 'watchdogs' or the 'eyes and ears' of society.[17] The creation of a real democracy in Ghana depended on their fulfilling, and being allowed to perform, this role. It was tacitly assumed that the government tended to be elitist, authoritarian and corrupt, and that the 'official' parliamentary opposition provided no direct or effective representation for the 'common people'. The unions were the only genuine mass organisations, and, in consequence, the TUC felt justified in aspiring to the checking, counter-balancing role of a kind of official, but radical, opposition.

This was, in a sense, a spontaneous development, reflecting a general reaction against the experience of CPP party control; the impulse to political self-assertion of a relatively well-educated and informed class of skilled workers, geographically and structurally close to the national political centre; and the radicalising effects of a steady widening of the elite–mass gap in Ghanaian society during the 1960s, involving a strong downward pressure on the socio-economic position of the skilled workers which forced them more clearly than ever before down toward the ranks of the urban poor.[18] Yet the actual process of political development was more complex than such generalisations suggest. One must take cognisance, firstly, of the institutional and political prerequisites for the democratisation of the trade union movement and, in this connection, of the importance not only of the ousting of the CPP regime in February 1966 but also of the initiative and diplomatic skill, mentioned earlier, of Benjamin Bentum. Secondly, although the development of the policy and ideology of the Ghana TUC in 1966–71 was, viewed in retrospect, consistent, there was an important shift of emphasis, and change of tone, in this ideology between the National Liberation Council regime (February 1966– October 1969) and the Progress Party Government (October 1969–

January 1972). Under the NLC, the TUC generally appeared willing to settle for relatively minor incremental gains and official acknowledgement of its claim to a major advisory role in governmental decision-making. When this moderate 'responsible' strategy proved ineffective under the PP regime, however, it sought to lead popular criticism of the status quo and to attract the support of a wider urban mass constituency for a radical political programme.

This did, it should be stressed, represent a shift of emphasis, not a sudden or complete change in policy. Bentum was concerned both to restrain the tendency to resort to illegal strike actions *and* to voice his criticism of conservative economic policies under each of these regimes. Moreover, it was a shift of emphasis which, while motivated in part by growing personal antipathy to the PP leaders, was also a consistent response to the growing socio-economic elitism and authoritarianism of that regime.

Bentum's TUC and the NLC regime

Bentum was appointed secretary-general of the Ghana TUC within forty-eight hours of the military coup d'état of 24 February 1966, and he immediately led a demonstration of workers in Accra in support of the intervention by the army and the police.[19] He alone of the former CPP Ministers was retained in senior office by the National Liberation Council,[20] and several groups of workers, including most prominently the Sekondi-Takoradi railway workers, protested against his appointment and requested that a new, more trustworthy secretary-general be elected. But a Railway Union delegation was assured by NLC leaders that they had every reason to believe Bentum would prove a capable and dependable leader of the TUC.[21]

From the point of view of the NLC leaders, Bentum's (initial) dependence on their favour for his political survival was one of the attractions of his appointment as secretary-general. Ideologically and politically they were committed to a liberalisation of the nation's political structures, yet it was crucially important that such liberalisation did not go so far as to jeopardise their administrative control. Their ousting of Nkrumah had been rationalised in terms of liberating the nation from tyranny, and an upsurge of popular pressure for the restoration of civil freedoms was naturally to be expected. They were happy to accede to this pressure up to a point. Mostly educated in British police and military training schools, the NLC leaders were liberals of a somewhat Whiggish variety. Conscious of their own inadequacies and inexperience as policy formulators and administrators, they were prepared to rule very largely according to the advice of various committees and commissions. These consisted in

111

the main of civil service experts in various fields and representatives of the country's major pressure groups.[22]

As far as the trade union movement was concerned, 'liberalisation' meant that there would be little overt interference in the affairs of the TUC, that the legal provisions against strike actions, although formally retained, would be less severely administered, and that the secretary-general of the TUC would be accepted as the government's leading adviser on industrial relations. But to the surprise of many who, like the editor of the *Ghanaian Times*, called on the NLC leaders to 'give the TUC a fresh charter',[23] the NLC leaders proved unwilling to dismantle the centralised control structure inherited from the CPP regime. They clearly did not envisage securing voluntary industrial peace by meeting the demand of unionised workers for substantial wage increases. There were several considerations involved here. In the first place, the immediate need was obviously for a period of economic retrenchment rather than of additional government expenditure. In the second place, what development funds did become available were to be directed toward rural development. Thirdly, the NLC leaders were in no sense social radicals, and did not feel committed to any major reform of the national wage and salary structure. The requisites of economic reconstruction and political stability clearly argued, then, for strict limits to union democratisation, and, with a reliable acolyte in charge, the inherited TUC structure and anti-strike provisions suited NLC requirements perfectly.

They did not entirely suit Bentum however, and the NLC leaders had seriously underestimated his determination and ability to pursue an independent course. After weeding out CPP militants in the TUC secretariat (and retaining other officials he thought reliable in order to utilise their expertise), he arranged for the election of new general secretaries for the national unions and set about introducing reforms in the structure of the TUC, which would lend some substance to the rhetoric of democratisation. Authority for conducting collective bargaining and settling industrial disputes was returned from the TUC Executive to the national unions. The right of the TUC to intervene in disputes was restricted to instances where an impasse had clearly been reached, or where TUC intervention was formally requested by the union concerned.[24] A further provision declared that 'A vote of non-confidence by a two-thirds majority of delegates shall be required to demand the resignation of the Secretary-General'.[25] This was an important innovation, since there had been no such provision for democratic accountability of the secretary-general in the CPP–TUC Constitution. Early in 1968 it was announced that free elections would be held for the post of secretary-general at a special delegates' conference to be held in the summer.

Bentum was attempting, then, to establish himself as the elected leader of a genuinely independent and democratic TUC, and the NLC leaders naturally looked on this move with considerable suspicion and disfavour. At the 1968 Congress, held in Tamale, John Alex Hamah's candidature for the secretary-generalship received the backing of several NLC leaders. The final voting, however, provided eloquent proof of Bentum's success in winning over to his support even those unionists who had originally protested at his appointment. Bentum received eighty-eight votes, Hamah thirteen.[26] That the NLC refrained from taking more forceful action to remove or discipline Bentum was due to several factors. Police-Inspector Harlley, the NLC leader with the closest personal association with Bentum, was convinced of his continuing dependability. Those who were less certain had no wish for a confrontation with labour, partly because they did not feel their position to be sufficiently stable, partly because they were concerned to maintain a liberal image abroad (especially in Britain). Moreover, Bentum did appear to be genuinely committed to restraining workers from abusing their new-found freedom through unnecessary illegal strike actions, and to keeping his criticisms of the regime within the bounds of the non-subversive. They were therefore prepared to tolerate him.

In fact, Bentum maintained a censorious attitude to illegal strikes for as long as there seemed some chance of gaining concessions to the demand for increased social justice or, as he put it, for 'a bridging of the wages gap between the lower and higher income groups'.[27] Early in 1967 the Mills–Odoi Commission was appointed to make recommendations on the structure and remuneration of the public services, and although its report proved extremely disappointing to the lower-paid workers, Bentum was appointed to the Mensah Commission to consider this report and formulate a government incomes policy for the future. Until the beginning of 1969 Bentum retained some hope of gaining special concessions for the lower income group (i.e. the skilled and unskilled manual workers), and during this period he went along with the government in condemning strikes, and concurred with the imposition of fines on the leaders of illegal strikes. In response to the Railway Permanent Waymen's strike of September 1968, one of the most serious the NLC regime had to deal with, he took an extremely tough line. He expressed his support for the government's arrest of the ringleaders, announced a new disciplinary code to be operated against unofficial strike leaders, and warned the National Executive of the Railway Union that unless they took steps 'to dismiss the undesirables [from the union] I will be compelled to recommend to the Executive Board of the TUC to review your affiliation with the Congress'.[28] He concluded, rather sadly, 'I do not want to be a Secretary-General who only breaks strikes.'[29]

Bentum's attempt to reduce the incidence of strikes by persuasion (and, occasionally, threats) rather than actual repression could, however, hardly be said to have succeeded by the end of 1968. In the two-and-a-half-year period preceding the 1966 coup d'état, the Ministry of Labour recorded a total of 22 strikes, involving some 10,000 workers, and a loss of 68,000 man-days (see Table 6.2). This was probably an inaccurate, understated figure, but not so inaccurate as to invalidate the reality of the contrast with the immediate post-coup period. From April 1966 to December 1968 there were 108 strikes, involving 66,133 men and a total loss of 166,005 man-days. The NLC's reaction was to become increasingly impatient with strike participants, and to resort to lock-outs and dismissal of striking workers.

This policy provoked a public protest from Bentum, who increasingly took the position that strikes could only properly be condemned if the government recognised the deplorable financial situation of the lower income group and took effective measures to 'bridge the gap'.[30] There appeared to be little hope of this by the beginning of 1969. The Mensah Commission had approved the recommendation of the Mills–Odoi Commission for an across-the-board increase of 5 per cent in wages, the only special concession to the lower-paid workers being the introduction of incremental scales for the daily-rated which would give them, on average, an effective increase of 7–8 per cent per annum over the following three years. This barely compensated the lower-paid for the impact of inflation on their real incomes since the 1966 coup, and did nothing to redress the impoverishment they had suffered in the first half of the decade (see Table 6.1). Moreover, the Mensah Commission was now advocating a government wages policy which would restrict the wage growth rate to a maximum of 5 per cent per annum, again without distinguishing between the lower and high income groups.[31]

Angered by the insensitivity of these proposals, Bentum tendered his resignation from the Incomes Commission in March 1969, and published a scathing critique of government policy. This first referred back to the TUC's criticism of the Mills–Odoi Commission's report in May 1968:

We do not accept the conservative and biased economic arguments advanced by the Commission in arriving at its conclusions . . . The Commission has not recommended a living wage for lowest paid workers, and at the same time has been most generous in its treatment of the more highly paid employees . . . By its report the Commission recognises that 88 per cent of the total employed labour force was earning less than N₵50.00 per month. By the use of the Government's own figures [on minimal nutritional requirements] this means that

114

Table 6.2. *Recorded labour strikes, workers involved, and man-days lost in Ghana, 1944-71*

Year	No. of strikes	Workers involved	Man-days lost	
1944–5	2	700	n.d.	
1945–6	3	7,750	n.d.	
1946–7	7	946	n.d.	
1947–8	37	48,865	n.d.	(inc. 37-day strike by mineworkers)
1948–9	27	7,650	n.d.	
1949–50	54	38,557	123,311	(not including 'Positive Action' general strike)
1950–1	19	5,482	11,017	
1951–2	39	15,404	38,185	
1952–3	83	32,548	129,676	
1953–4	65	25,529	125,927	
1954–5	35	7,263	29,107	
1955–6	23	1,039	13,191	
	+ 2	29,216	2,479,224	(mineworkers' strikes)
1956–7	45	11,858	33,005	
1957–8	64	18,964	41,020	
1958–9	49	8,875	21,673	
1959–60	50	10,101	12,788	
1960–1	26	4,404	6,459	(excludes 1-day commercial workers' strike)
1961–2	10	3,240	6,482	(excludes Sekondi-Takoradi strike)
1962–3	7	820	1,390	(understated)
1963–4	9	3,033	1,477	(understated)
1965–3/66	13	6,802	66,508	
3/66–6/66	17	5,685	4,208	(CPP ousted by NLC 2/66)
7/66–7/67	26	11,228	15,854	
7/67–7/68	52	40,441	113,104	
7/68–12/68	13	8,784	32,839	
1969	51	28,369	148,404	(Busia regime 9/69)
1970	55	21,376	123,000	
1/71–7/71	46	25,169	49,115	

Source: All data are as recorded by the Department of Labour, which, after 1961 during the Nkrumah regime, excluded reports on certain (illegal) strikes. The data are to be found in: Roper, *Labour Problems in West Africa*, p. 108 (for 1944–50), Ghana, Labour Department, *Annual Reports, 1950–68* (Accra) and Ghana, *Parliamentary Debates: Official Reports*, 8, 29, col. 1604 (for 1969–71).

88 per cent of the total employed labour force cannot afford a balanced diet even if they spend their entire income on food alone. They have been asked to wait even though the main cause of low productivity in Ghana is poor management . . . We strongly wish to state that we expect the man at the top to bear more of the national burden and not the labourer who is already carrying too much.[32]

To this Bentum now added the further charge that a rigid incomes policy restricting wage increases to 5 per cent per annum could not possibly be acceptable unless it also covered all members of Ghana's socio-economic elite, such as lawyers, judges and doctors: 'The NLC or any civilian government should consider whether it is social justice for the ordinary worker to be controlled in the sharing of the national cake whereas the "big shots" and other sections of the society are not similarly controlled.'[33]

This growing friction between the TUC and the NLC regime was further aggravated in the summer of 1969 by two strike incidents. In the first, a strike of mineworkers at Obuasi, police opened fire on a crowd of demonstrators, killing several people.[34] In the second, a strike of dock-workers at Tema, all 2,000 strikers were dismissed from their jobs. Bentum demanded an official enquiry into the first incident, and led a delegation to the International Labour Organisation to protest at the second. It was clearly only the prospect of a change of government in the near future – general elections for a return to civilian rule were scheduled for September 1969 – that prevented the development of a more serious confrontation between the TUC and the NLC regime at this time.

The 1969 election and the victory of the Progress Party

With a general election scheduled for September, the issue of the labour movement's stand in relation to party politics was again raised at the June 1969 Congress of the TUC. The suggestion was made that the TUC might form or sponsor a labour party, possibly in alliance with the Labour Party of Frank Wudu (formerly Frank Woode, general secretary of the Railway Union 1947–9), but this proposal received little support from the leadership or the assembled delegates, and the policy of strict neutrality in party politics was reaffirmed.[35]

While there are no means of determining the voting pattern of unionised workers in the 1969 elections with any precision, interviews conducted in 1971 suggested that the large majority of rank-and-file members and union officials in Sekondi-Takoradi had voted for the victorious Progress Party, led by Dr Kofi Busia.[36] It would seem likely that a similar pattern occurred throughout the country, except possibly in towns in the Volta Region, and in Accra, where the Progress Party won only three out

116

of eight seats. In the country as a whole the Progress Party won 105 out of 140 seats in the new Legislative Assembly, with twenty-nine going to the National Alliance of Liberals, led by Komla Gbedemah. The Progress Party also carried all the regions, in most cases with an overwhelming majority of seats, with the sole exception of the Volta Region, where the Ewe people voted NAL candidates into almost every seat.

Gbedemah was himself an Ewe, as were most of the prominent figures in his party. The final results therefore give the impression of a fairly straight tribal contest between the Ewe people on the one hand, and an Akan alliance of Ashantis, Fantis, Akwapim and other Akan cultural groups on the other. Yet, in many parts of the country, and especially in the southern coastal towns, the differences perceived between the two main parties to the election were more complex and subtle than this suggests, and the seats more closely contested.[37]

The National Alliance of Liberals attracted the support not only of the Ewe people but also of many former CPP enthusiasts and others who, although disillusoned with the Nkrumah regime during the 1960s, had looked favourably on the CPP in its earlier days. Komla Gbedemah had been one of Nkrumah's most senior lieutenants until 1961, and was credited with most of the organisational work that had gone into developing the CPP into so powerful a force in the 1950s. From the more particular point of view of 'labour appeal', Gbedemah could claim personal association with the 1952 Wages and Salary Commission which, disappointing as it was to Biney and the radicals, did more than any other commission, before or since, for Ghana's lower-paid workers. This is not to suggest that the NAL was seen as, in any real sense, a radical alternative to the Progress Party, nor did it attempt to present itself as such. Gbedemah had become closely identified with the right wing of the CPP, and there was little discernible difference between the programmes proffered to the public in 1969 by his National Alliance and the Progress Party. Rather, Gbedemah and his leading followers projected a kind of comfortable entrepreneurial appeal, by comparison with which the Progress Party leadership might appear distinctly over-educated for its capital base. For many, however, an important question-mark hung over the character of Gbedemah. In 1961 he had fled into exile under the threat of imminent detention. According to his own account, this was because he was attempting to right the abuses and check the excesses of the Nkrumah regime from within, but, according to President Nkrumah, it was because he was guilty of embezzlement on a huge scale while he was Minister of Finance. (The Jiagge Commission in fact found him guilty of past financial irregularities and he was debarred from taking up the seat he had won in the Legislative Assembly.)[38]

117

The Progress Party leadership played on the theme of Gbedemah's financial untrustworthiness to considerable effect. At a rally in Takoradi, one PP speaker remarked: 'If Gbedemah offers you money to vote NAL, then accept it and feel free to vote PP. It was your money anyway before he stole it';[39] and the slogan 'Say NAL and Vote Progress' became widely current during the last weeks of the campaign.[40] According to most interviewees in Sekondi-Takoradi, it was this issue, not that of alleged Ewe tribalism, that persuaded them to vote PP rather than NAL.

There were other reasons for the Progress Party's electoral victory, some of them, it must be said, reflecting (strictly speaking) irregular advantages the PP held over other parties. While the NLC as a unit preserved a public stance of neutrality between the contestants and administered the elections with admirable fairness and efficiency of organisation, deviations from the norm of impartiality did occur in more subtle and unofficial forms. Joe Appiah, leader of the United Nationalist Party (which won only two seats), claimed that 'certain persons have been going about the country indulging in vile propaganda that the NLC will not hand over power to civilians if the Progress is not voted into power'.[41] Whether or not this was strictly accurate, it was certainly the case that Brigadier Afrifa openly threw all his prestige as the youthful hero of the 1966 coup behind Dr Busia. According to one newspaper report, he even announced that he owed the inspiration for the coup to Busia and therefore hoped the 'Prof' would some day be taking over from himself and his military colleagues.[42]

In addition, the NLC regime provided Dr Busia with special assistance of an organisational nature by appointing him chairman of the Centre for Civic Education in February 1969. This was supposed to be a non-party political institution, designed to help educate the electorate in their democratic rights and responsibilities, and to stimulate discussion of major national issues on a non-partisan basis. But, in practice, Busia was able to use the CCE, and his trips by state helicopter on CCE business, to lay the foundations of his party, developing political contacts throughout the regions and weaving the threads of local elite support into the fabric of a cohesive national organisation; this at a time when other politicians had no chance of openly soliciting support, since the NLC's ban on party political activity was not lifted until May.

In spite of its possession of these advantages, and the distinctly mediocre quality of its rivals, it would be wrong to suggest that the Progress Party leadership possessed no more positive electoral appeal. In addition to the obvious attraction of self-advancement for its organisers and 'enthusiasts', the Progress Party promised to provide honest, democratic government – a promise lent more credibility than that of other parties by its leadership's record of opposition to the Nkrumah regime. For this leadership consisted essentially of a regrouping of the old United Party leaders, who claimed to be 'the champions of democracy' in Ghana, together with a new crop of professional men and intellectuals who had surfaced in the political vacuum created by the 1966 coup. Dr Busia himself, J. Kwesi-Lamptey, S. D. Dombo, W. Ofori-Atta, R. R. Amponsah, Jatoe Kaleo and Victor Owusu had all suffered preventive detention or exile under the CPP regime for their oppositional activities. It was a well-calculated strategy to emphasise the 'democratic' element, and divert attention from the tribalistic and elitist tendencies in this group's record, by launching the Progress Party in Sekondi-Takoradi (rather than Kumasi, the heart of the old National Liberation Movement). Dr Busia specifically appealed to the railway workers, as natural allies in the fight for democracy, to help vote the party into power: 'Some in Nkrumah's government, I am told, called you "Western Rats" for going on strike. Today we salute you as Western heroes for you rose to resist tyranny . . . We will strive constantly to merit your support and confidence.'[43] This appeal did not go unheard. Some of the railway workers were among the leading Progress Party activists in Sekondi-Takoradi, and the Railway Union Executive had to issue a warning that the union's platform should not be used for party political propaganda.[44]

Beyond the vague commitment to democratic government, and to recognising and protecting the independence of the trade union movement, the Progress Party did not define its community of interest with the lower-paid workers. This was not necessarily because it had already formulated, with any clarity, a policy programme unfavourable to labour. More probably, it was simply because, with the addition of several young intellectuals of varying ideological complexion to an original leadership itself united more by common opposition to the Nkrumah regime than by positive beliefs, the Progress Party high command was something of a hotch-potch of conflicting ideas. Together with some of the most extreme and eccentric of Ghanaian conservatives – men such as Victor Owusu and R. R. Amponsah – were several young welfare-state liberals, such as Dr W. G. Bruce-Konuah, K. G. Osei-Bonsu and Dr Jones Ofori-Atta, and even the former young radical, J. H. Mensah, author of the CPP's Seven Year Development Plan. Such a gathering dictated that the identification of ideological aims be muted, a strategy made the more feasible by the failure of rival parties to engage the Progress Party in a meaningful ideological debate.

Yet, in a sense, this disinclination to present definite programmes itself constituted a distinctive ideological self-projection, that of the rule of experts or 'the best brains in the country'. The Progress Party had succeeded in attracting to its senior ranks the majority of the nation's intellectual figures, including, it seemed, almost the entire indigenous staff of the University of Legon, and, presiding over them, Ghana's most famed academic, Professor K. A. Busia.[45] Were not such men best fitted, even essential, to sort out the economic mess into which the Nkrumah regime had plunged the country, and to find the path to progress? As Dr Busia himself put it: 'The Progress Party has power to overcome – power to overcome the heritage of debt, corruption, inefficiency and poverty. Power to overcome the present unemployment, the low standard of living, disease, and poverty, and the humiliation of our nation and of the Blackman . . . The solution to these problems will be based on carefully collected data'.[46]

This was an argument of some force with the electorate, and one which certainly influenced the Progress Party leadership's image of itself and its actual conduct of government. But it is important to note a certain ambivalence in the reaction of the urban populace to this assertion of an educational right to rule. The intellectual arrogance which led Dr Busia to claim he was the only man fitted to rule Ghana was liable to be interpreted as a gross insult to the abilities and potential political contributions of her ordinary citizens if academic expertise failed to produce the promised economic progress. The development of an open confrontation between the labour movement and the PP regime, within two years of its accession to power, derived from frustration not only of the economic expectations of the union rank and file, but also of that aspiration to an effective and acknowledged political voice which, for union leaders and the skilled worker class more generally, was central to the notion of democratic trade unionism.

Economic policies of the Progress Party regime

The Progress Party, we have seen, came to power without a clearly formulated economic programme. Prior to the budget of 30 July 1971, the regime simply proclaimed its commitment to 'privatisation' of the state sector, appealed for an increase in national discipline and self-help, and made vague avowals of its special concern for the poorest sections of the national community, the rural populace and the unemployed. The regime's economic programme was presented in its most systematic and appealing form in the July 1971 budget. The reactions and objections of the majority of skilled and semi-skilled workers to that budget programme help to clarify to what degree the strikes and demonstrations of September 1971 were motivated by opposition to the budget proposals, and to what degree they arose from other considerations or sources of conflict. More generally they provide some insight into workers' attitudes on the vexed question of urban versus rural imbalance.[47]

120

The first priority and cornerstone of the PP regime's economic strategy was the focusing of resources on rural development.[48] There were really two aspects to the rural development programme, the one of particular concern and benefit to the rural populace, the other conceived rather in terms of the general interest of rural and urban dwellers alike. The former aspect consisted in the provision of pipe-borne water, electricity and medical centres for the rural areas so as to reduce the disparity between urban and rural standards of existence. This was presented by the government as an essentially altruistic, compassionate policy, calling for self-sacrifice on the part of the politico-administrative elite and the urban populace as a whole, though the motivation clearly had an element of electoral interest.[49] The second aspect lay in encouraging the production of sufficient food to sustain Ghana's growing population, thereby to reduce the cost of living in the urban areas and to improve the nation's balance of trade position. The government hoped to stimulate this agricultural revolution by constructing more feeder roads between the rural areas, the towns and the cities, by educating Ghanaian farmers in more advanced agricultural techniques, and by setting the National Service Corps to work to extend the area of land under cultivation.

The government's second major priority was described by the Minister of Finance, J. H. Mensah, as 'the launching of a frontal attack on the problem of unemployment'.[50] This was to be tackled partly through the expansion of rural employment opportunities, but also by embarking on a massive programme of housing and public works construction in the urban areas. This would also have the beneficial effect of 'stemming the rise in rents which is placing such a burden on the finances of the lowest paid workers'.[51] It was by means of reducing the cost of food, housing and transport in the urban areas, rather than by awarding wage increases, that the government aimed to relieve the financial position of the lower-paid workers.

As to whether any wage increases at all could be anticipated the government was somewhat vague and vacillatory. During its first eighteen months in office the PP regime consistently refused to consider raising the minimum wage, in spite of the fact that the financial position of lower-paid workers continued to deteriorate seriously under the impact of inflation. In May 1971, however, the Minister of Labour and Co-operatives, Dr W. G. Bruce-Konuah, declared that the government recognised 'that the gap between lower and higher income groups was becoming too wide and needed bridging', and announced the appointment of the Campbell Commission 'to look into this problem and the conditions of service of employees of the public service with a view, primarily, to bridging this gap'.[52] Workers' hopes were obviously raised. Yet, in his budget speech on 30 July, J. H. Mensah announced that,

121

Upon a careful examination of the information and advice offered by the Commission, government has come to the conclusion that it would require very large proportionate increases in the wages of the lower paid public officers to compensate them for the changes in the cost of living since the last increase in wages, or to bridge the gap between their incomes and those of the higher paid officers. . . In the face of the existing inability of the country to provide more food, housing, transport and any of the other goods and services which the workers would wish to buy, a general increase in money wages would undermine the stability of the whole economy. It would also be self-defeating.[53]

Moreover, the government's decision to embark on an ambitious and expensive rural development programme, in spite of the nation's weak balance of payments position and huge external debt, necessitated the introduction of new tax measures. These included a national development levy 'which will require every employed person to help the development effort'.[54] The imposition of additional taxation on even the lowest-paid workers was justified on the grounds that 'In Ghana there are two classes of people who can be said to be relatively poor: those who live in the big towns and cities but have no work to do, and those who live in the villages and can only afford the bare necessities of life. By comparison to these groups, anyone with a regular job, even at the minimum wage, is well off.'[55] Many lower-paid workers no doubt found it difficult to accept this assessment of their situation: but the government later qualified its position by announcing that those earning less than N₵34 per month would be exempt from the levy. Furthermore, the levy was to be scaled according to income level, rising from a 1 per cent tax on incomes below N₵1,000 per annum to 5 per cent on the chargeable incomes of corporations. This was hardly as steep a scaling, perhaps, as the demands of social justice might require, but then the higher-paid were to make additional sacrifices of various perquisites and allowances. Car and entertainment allowances were to be abolished, and the subsidised rents for government bungalows raised to a more realistic figure. Taken together, these measures could perhaps be interpreted as a negative form of 'bridging the wages gap'.

Labour's reaction to the budget

The equitable character of the budget, taken as a whole, was not lost on Ghana's lower-paid workers. The large majority approved of most of its aspects and its general orientation. But they were concerned, firstly, to

122

question certain items, and, secondly, to distinguish between the theory, or stated objectives, of the budget and what they believed it would mean in practice. The idea of rural development appealed very strongly, partly because they recognised that the rising price of foodstuffs was the major burden on their wage packets, but also because the persistence of strong ties, whether practical or more vaguely emotional, between most workers and their rural (or less urban) homes, inclined them to support plans for improving rural living standards. As one interviewee commented, 'Every man living on the coast has some village people living in wretched conditions. And this will enable them to produce more food and bring it to us'.[56] And another, with a slightly different perspective, remarked, 'Up in those rural areas, they're still living very darkly and savagely. Therefore, they should deduct just a bit of our pay to polish them, because they are so dark over there'.[57] Similarly, the idea of temporary sacrifice in order to help create jobs for the unemployed appealed to both altruistic and self-interested motivations, mixed as they generally were. The burden of supporting relatives who could find no work was a major drain on many workers' incomes. Questioned more generally as to the primary objectives which the trade union movement should be pursuing, 70 per cent rated 'helping to solve the unemployment problem' as being of the highest priority.[58]

However, many workers were sceptical as to what would actually materialise from these programmes. As far as the creation of new industries and job opportunities was concerned, the PP regime had so far been all talk and no action. More important perhaps, government aid for rural development seemed so far to have been allocated on a regionally favouritistic basis. Rural development had meant development of the Ashanti and Brong-Ahafo Regions, the home areas of the majority of Progress Party leaders, and, to a lesser extent, of the Volta Region where the party was concerned to win over the Ewe people to its support. As Dr Busia had announced on 21 November 1969, 'The Progress Party Government has within barely two months of assumption of office voted approximately N₵5.6 million for development projects in the Ashanti Region'.[59] It is doubtful whether the Central and Western Regions received as much as this during the first two years of Progress Party rule.[60] Workers who originated from these regions, as did the majority in Sekondi-Takoradi and many in Accra-Tema, were therefore sceptical as to what rural development would mean for their relatives: 'Rural development is good, but not if there is too much concentration in one area. We have yet to see any in Ahanta'.[61] The influence of this communal division on the determination of workers' attitudes to the budget (and to the regime more generally) became apparent when considerable numbers of workers in Kumasi

123

proclaimed their support for the national development levy and dissociated themselves from the TUC's critical stance.[62] (With the exception of the members of the Confederation of Labour, the rival trade union centre, they were the only workers in Ghana to do this.) Nevertheless, this communal dimension was of marginal significance relative to other factors in generating labour opposition to the budget.

More important by far was the government's apparent refusal to make any positive concession to the demand for an increase in wages, or to the idea of reducing the differential between lower and higher income groups. The need for sacrifice was generally recognised, the argument that wage increases tended to be self-defeating without a concomitant increase in food production widely appreciated. But, as the government itself admitted, it would be some years before the agricultural revolution was sufficiently advanced to produce a fall in prices or before the problem of unemployment could be significantly reduced. In the meantime, the lower-paid workers were having to provide for the unemployed, and, with basic foodstuffs costing at least 50 per cent more by the summer of 1971 than at the time of the Progress Party's accession to power, many were finding it quite impossible to make ends meet.[63] They survived only by further reducing their consumption of staple foods, such as yam or fu-fu, or else turning to gari, a food 'formerly considered fit only for pigs',[64] according to one elderly Fanti, and certainly of very low nutritional value. Whether considered in terms of social justice or regarded as a precondition for raising productivity, some increase in the minimum wage was surely justified, even if it offered only relatively temporary relief. It could be financed by severe cuts in the salaries of higher-paid wage-earners and the political elite. As one speaker argued at a Railway Union mass meeting, 'We want to take at least N₡200 off all those rich men. How can one man possibly eat thirty-nine times as much as another?'[65] – a perspective of distinctly radical implications. Certainly, to raise workers' hopes of some concession by appointing the Campbell Commission only to dash them three months later, was politically inept in the extreme.

This served to bring to the surface a great deal of simmering resentment at the wealth and insensitivity of the Progress Party elite: 'Why should we shoulder more of the burden when they are not attempting to sacrifice at all?'[66] This was perhaps not strictly accurate, since in August 1971 Prime Minister Busia announced that, in order to 'set an example of making sacrifice', his salary was to be cut by NC6,000, those of Cabinet Ministers by N₡4,000 and those of ministerial secretaries and regional chief executives by N₡2,000.[67] But such a lead was long, perhaps too long, overdue. On its assumption of office, the PP regime had set the salaries and allowances of its Ministers and regional chief executives at levels

124

almost twice as high as those enjoyed by their equivalents in the CPP regime.[68] The Prime Minister was to receive N₵18,000, Cabinet Ministers N₵14,000 and ministerial secretaries and regional chief executives N₵10,000, while the allowances for which they were eligible raised their total emoluments several thousand cedis above these figures.[69] These awards provoked jealousy among ordinary MPs who began pressing in May 1970 for substantial increases in their allowances, and in July most of their demands were granted, giving them total emoluments of some N₵7,000 per annum. It was clearly hypocritical to the point of being ludicrous, therefore, to characterise Bentum's demand for an increase in the minimum wage from N₵0.75 to N₵1.00 per day as 'a very high level to set workers' demands' and 'calculated to incite workers against the government by making demands which Mr Bentum knew were impossible'.[70] Rather, these early measures of the PP Government had made it extremely difficult for Bentum to restrain workers' demands at that level.

There were further examples of such insensitive behaviour during the following twelve months. Mention will here be restricted to those instances to which workers specifically referred in interviews in August 1971. It rapidly became obvious during 1970 that many Progress Party leaders were building up very considerable commercial empires for themselves. In December, Lt.-General A. K. Ocran, a leader of the 1966 coup who retained a great deal of popular respect, especially in the Western and Central Regions of Ghana, wrote to the Speaker of the Legislative Assembly and the presidential secretary expressing his disappointment that many members of the legislature had not yet declared their assets as they were required to do under articles 67 and 80 of the constitution. Instead of meeting this criticism squarely, the Progress Party's general secretary accused Lt-General Ocran of being 'only concerned with creating sensation and publicity for himself'.[71] In consequence, according to one newspaper report, 'Both at Cape Coast and Takoradi party officials were admitting that they are going to have a tough time overcoming the effect of "Mr da Rocha's tactless and arrogant statement".' [72]

Then, in March 1971, there was further disquiet over the government's announcement that, in spite of the continuing economic crisis, it had been spending N₵2.8 million on the construction of rest-houses in the regions for members of the government. A month later, it was decided to allow judges to retire on full salary. And shortly afterwards the government's image was hardly improved by Dr Busia's admission that (himself excluded, of course) 'There is not a single honest person in my Cabinet'.[73]

It was hardly surprising then, that the lower-paid workers were reluctant to heed the Progress Party Government's call for national discipline and voluntary sacrifice, or to refrain from strike action in support of their

125

demands; or that by July–August 1971 they were inclined to view Mensah's austerity budget with scepticism, although admitting to approval of most of its stated objectives. Bentum could therefore legitimately claim to be representing general rank-and-file opinion when he began criticising the government's failure to do more to bridge the wages gap in the first week of September. But there was more to the TUC's confrontation with the government than this, in the view of rank and file as well as leadership.

In the first week of September Bentum toured the district labour councils, criticising the budget on various particular points and more generally the government's refusal to listen to the TUC's objections. Government leaders saw this, quite correctly, as an incitement to direct action for other than strictly economic aims; yet, within the broader context of government–TUC relations, it was a defensive rather than aggressive move, a last determined protest against the regime's known intention to amend the Industrial Relations Act so as to emasculate the TUC. This was the culmination of a progressive deterioration of relations between the TUC and the Progress Party regime since October 1969, a process which derived from several sources and levels of conflict.

The strike-incidence issue

At one level, conflict centred on the continuing high level of strike actions, and the issue of whether or not the TUC could, or could properly, do more to prevent them. Relations with the PP regime, and particularly Dr Busia himself, were initially cordial, the government agreeing to find jobs for the 2,000 Tema dockworkers dismissed by the NLC regime.[74] But friction developed as the TUC leadership proved unable to lower the level of strike incidence. In 1970 there were fifty-five strikes, involving a loss of 123,000 man-days, a level showing no improvement on that occurring under the NLC regime, and quite unacceptable to the new government (see Table 6.2). The TUC's official position on strikes remained essentially unaltered from that adopted under the NLC regime. At district labour council meetings and seminars organised by the TUC, local officials were consistently admonished to follow the official procedures for settlement of disputes, and impressed with the need for harmonious industrial relations in the cause of national economic reconstruction. At the same time, however, Bentum made public his view that the dilatory and inadequate procedures for settling disputes, often deliberately exploited by the management, together with the widening income gap between lower-paid manual workers and the top-level salariat, were primarily responsible for the high level of strike actions. Until these basic sources of conflict were

126

remedied, he suggested, it would be useless and improper for the TUC to take a sterner line against strikers. And as the real incomes of lower-paid workers continued to decline in 1970-1, and the PP regime failed to respond to the demand for a reduction of differentials, there was a shift of emphasis by the TUC from condemnation of strike actions to criticism of the government's inaction.

The government's position, as enunciated by Dr Busia in August 1970, was that 'the unions have the greatest responsibility to raise our product-ivity', that strikes served no purpose except to hurt the whole community, including the workers themselves, and that virtually all recent strikes had been unnecessary and illegal: 'In all these strikes the procedure laid down for settling disputes was not used . . . some of the reasons for the strikes could hardly bear examination.' [75] The regime was not, however, united on the issue of how to deal with this problem. There was mounting pres-sure from the right wing of the Progress Party to introduce amendments to the Industrial Relations Act so as to stiffen the anti-strike provisions. But until June 1971 this was resisted by the first PP Minister of Labour, Jatoe Kaleo (later Minister of Transport and Communications), who insisted that 'strikes are human problems and they can't be solved by legislation';[76] and also by his successor, Dr W. G. Bruce-Konuah, who, while often critical of the inability of union leaders to control their rank and file, displayed considerable appreciation of the difficulties involved, and a desire to appease rather than confront the unions. Accordingly, Dr Konuah established a commission on May 1971 to recommend solu-tions of the problem of 'the gap between the lower and higher income groups becoming too wide'.[77]

But this show of action came too late to avert a series of major strikes which disturbed the country in June–August 1971. The sanitary workers and Public Works Department employees in Accra, dockworkers in Tema and the railway enginemen in Accra and Sekondi-Takoradi all went on strike.[78] They coincided with, and reinforced, growing pressure from the party's right wing to take a stiffer line against strikers. Some of these extremists went so far as to promise that all participants in illegal strikes would be dismissed and replaced by party supporters amongst the un-employed.[79] Partly, no doubt, in deference to this pressure, Dr Bruce-Konuah ordered the dismissal of 400 striking dockworkers when they failed to respond to a government ultimatum to return to work, supported the laying off of 150 striking Public Works Department workers, and issued a similar return-or-be-fired ultimatum to the railway enginemen.

The leadership of the TUC condemned these dismissals and threats of dismissal as 'arbitrary, wicked, degrading and indeed a flagrant violation of the Industrial Relations Act', and demanded that they be rescinded or

127

else 'the co-operation which the TUC has given to the Ministry of Labour and Co-operatives will have to be reconsidered'.[80] The government was warned that, by intervening directly and arbitrarily in disputes which should be settled by unions and management, it ran the risk of being 'drawn into head-on collision with the workers'.[81] Yet Bentum clearly did not relish the prospect of a destructive confrontation with the government, and accordingly put out peace-feelers. Early in July, he wrote to the Minister of Transport and Communications, Jatoe Kaleo, expressing his 'dismay at the way the labour situation in the country is deteriorating as a result of recent methods of handling strike actions', assuring him of 'the assistance of the Congress and its affiliated unions in bringing about peace and harmony' and requesting the Minister's intervention as an impartial authority in the railway enginemen's and other disputes, 'using your good offices to invite the managements and the unions to settle the issues amicably'.[82] This resulted in talks between the Minister, the Railway Enginemen's Union Executive and a TUC delegation, which succeeded in resolving the dispute and getting the strikers back to work a few hours before the government's ultimatum expired. Yet, instead of building on this successful initiative in the improvement of government–labour relations, Minister Kaleo immediately returned to the attack, accusing union leaders of being primarily responsible for 'the issuance of ultimatums and threats that have crept into our industrial relations', and expressing bafflement at Bentum's 'apparent silence and seeming indifference' with regard to many recent strike actions.[83] There were to be further indications during the following months of the ascendant influence of the right-wingers over the PP regime's labour policy.

Trade unionism and party politics

The industrial disturbances of June–August 1971 played into the hands of those elements in the Progress Party who wished to curtail the independence and undermine the strength of the Ghanaian trade union movement. Yet the pressure for such measures did not originate with these disturbances but dated back to the earliest days of the regime and derived from other sources. At the first Congress of the TUC to be held under the Progress Party regime, certain PP Ministers, most prominently R. R. Amponsah, backed a bid by K. A. Ossei-Mensah, general secretary of the Petroleum and General Transport Workers' Union, to displace Bentum as secretary-general of the TUC. Ossei-Mensah, it was felt, would prove more easily controllable than Bentum since he originated from Dr Busia's home area and had close links with the party leadership. In the event, Bentum defeated Ossei-Mensah by ninety-four votes to seventeen, and gained a public assurance from Dr Busia that he dissociated himself from any attempts to intrude party politics into trade unionism or to check the freedom of trade unions.[84] Government support was nevertheless forthcoming for the attempt to develop an alternative trade union centre, the Confederation of Labour, during the first half of 1971.[85] And in July–August of that year, Amponsah, Owusu, Kwow Richardson and other right-wingers succeeded in fuelling the conflict between the government and the TUC with inflammatory public statements, and in winning over a majority of Progress Party leaders to a policy of confrontation and repression.[86]

The hostility of these right-wingers to Bentum seems to have derived partly from the (somewhat irrational) fear of a possible recrudescence of support for the former president, Dr Nkrumah. Bentum, they believed, was still secretly an Nkrumah supporter, or at least a Soviet-trained communist who would take every opportunity to exploit labour unrest for subversive political purposes. This was in spite of the fact, obvious to virtually everyone in the labour movement, that as far as strikes and wage demands were concerned, Bentum had consistently played a moderate, restraining role. At the July 1970 Congress, for instance, the delegates' decision to press for a rise in the minumum wage from N₵0.75 to N₵1.50 per day entailed their rejecting the recommendation of the Committee on Resolutions, and a passionate appeal by Bentum himself, to retain the N₵1.00 demand.[87] Bentum later came round to supporting the N₵1.50 demand as the impact of inflation further undermined the real value of wages in 1970–1, and, in his proposals to the Campbell Commission, he pointed out that N₵2.50 would be a more realistic figure according to the government's own statistics.[88] (Allowing for the ideal character of the Ministry of Health statistics, and possibly a slight exaggeration in the food prices used by the TUC in its calculations, the finding that a balanced diet for a family of a man, wife and two children, would cost N₵3.30 per day was strikingly indicative of the inadequacy of the existing minimum wage of N₵0.75.) But, in setting the TUC's demands at steadily higher levels, he was continually resisting pressure from middle-level unionists to raise them even higher. It is worth noting, moreover, that whatever Bentum's personal feelings about the Progress Party, the large majority of both top- and middle-level unionists were PP supporters (at least in the sense of having voted PP in the 1969 elections), and certainly held no lingering affection for the CPP regime. Richard Baiden, for instance, general secretary of the Maritime and Dockworkers Union, and acting secretary-general of the TUC during Bentum's absences, had ties with the Progress Party leadership extending back to his role as a United Party agent provocateur in the 1961 Sekondi-Takoradi strike, yet he became more scathing even than Bentum in his criticisms of the regime's economic and labour policies in the summer of 1971.[89]

As far as strike actions were concerned, Bentum had a remarkably successful record of intervention in labour disputes to negotiate compromise agreements between unions and management, and so persuade strikers to return to work. The Obuasi mineworkers' and railway enginemen's strikes were perhaps the most notable instances, in that either might have developed into major political crises had not Bentum intervened. Admittedly, he generally delayed until strike action had actually commenced and an impasse between union and management had clearly been reached, so provoking the government to accuse him of dilatoriness. But this was the course of action required by the new constitutional provisions of the TUC. And it was largely because he faithfully observed these provisions for protecting the powers of individual unions, and made apparent his sympathy with workers' grievances, that he was able to perform the role of conciliator so effectively.

The Progress Party right-wingers' hostility to Bentum was, in this sense then, irrational. But, in seeking to displace him, they were also representing a strong pressure from within the ranks of the party, like all winning or victorious parties something of a bandwagon, to maximise the advantages that being in power might give it. Many of the party's core-following, and especially those with a personal interest involved, resented the fact that avowedly pro-PP unionists, such as Quist and Quartey of the Railway Union (i.e. the leaders of the splinter Railway Union and of the Confederation of Labour), had not succeeded to the positions of TUC leadership they were thought to deserve. More generally, they disliked the fact that a major centre of power should remain outside the party's grasp. It is unlikely, however, that Dr Busia would have given in to this pressure had it not been for the emergence of more genuine grounds for anxiety as to the likely political consequences of Bentum's leadership of the TUC. After all, the Prime Minister had largely resisted similar pressure to intrude the party into the civil service.[90] But in the summer of 1971 he united with the right wing over the issue of the TUC's claim to a larger voice in national decision-making, and supported, not a party take-over of the TUC, but its statutory dissolution.

The TUC's concept of 'democratic participation'

Benjamin Bentum was ideologically committed to an extremely assertive, participatory conception of political democracy, and more particularly of the role of the trade union movement within such a democracy. Progress Party Ministers preferred to suggest that he had an exaggerated sense of his own wisdom and self-importance. Yet since his personal drive to political influence was so closely geared to the interests and opinions of the union rank and file, the two amounted, in practice, to very much the same thing. Bentum's leadership of the TUC was not an especially radical political force, and certainly not intentionally subversive. It could perhaps have been quite easily accommodated, and even constructively utilised, by a regime more genuinely democratic in spirit, or simply more sensitive in its handling of criticism. Unfortunately, the leadership of the Progress Party regime was characterised by an extreme intellectual arrogance which made it unwilling to compromise its expertly formulated programmes, and intolerant of the criticisms of its policy voiced by Bentum and encouraged by him in the local forums of the TUC. It was, moreover, undoubtedly the case that, confronted with this intolerant and intransigent attitude, Bentum was inclined to mount increasingly radical and open attacks on the policies of the regime. The prevalence of urban unrest at these policies, and Bentum's immense prestige with the rank and file of the labour movement, made him capable of transforming the TUC into what was less a pluralist pressure group than a powerful oppositional party or movement. Certainly this tendency in the TUC presented a far more serious challenge to the standing of the regime than that posed by the official parliamentary opposition, the Justice Party (an amalgam of NAL and the other minority parties), whose leaders were generally as detached from the urban masses as those of the Progress Party.[91] Indeed, it was partly because of the lack of an effective, responsive opposition party that many urban dwellers looked to the TUC to perform the function of expressing 'mass' grievances. The populist tendency in TUC ideology reflected sensitivity to this pressure as much as Bentum's personal political ambitions.

During the first twelve months of the Progress Party regime, Bentum had announced various measures to decentralise the TUC further and, at the same time, extend the effective reach of the TUC's educational programme beyond middle-level officials to local officials and the union rank and file. The district labour councils were to be strengthened both financially and in terms of personnel so that they could organise regular educational programmes and seminars for the workers in their areas.[92] These seminars did in fact materialise, unlike most of the schemes of the CPP–TUC, and proved to be remarkably active and well attended. They were designed partly to instruct the rank and file and inexperienced local officials in the proper procedures to be followed in labour disputes, and in the advantages of peaceful negotiation over direct, disruptive action. But they also provided for discussion of national political and economic issues along lines which were often extremely critical of the status quo and the government's inaction. The workers, as speakers from TUC

131

headquarters repeatedly stressed, must act as the 'eyes and ears of society', speaking out against injustices and abuses. An extract form an introductory lecture given by Richard Baiden to the Sekondi-Takoradi District Council of Labour will serve to illustrate this theme:

> We must challenge the economy as presently structured and administered . . . We are still operating an obsolete colonial work structure and educational system, geared toward the production of administrative personnel, when the need is rather for providing incentives and training opportunities for technicians and skilled workers. It is the duty of workers to speak out against this and against other stupidities and injustices. A labour movement must be bold and free to express our views, make our criticisms. It is only the trade unions which can check these things – corruption, waste of public money, the irresponsibility of those in authority. The labour movement should participate in economic development not only through hard work, but through contributing to the necessary rethinking of our national priorities. We must concern ourselves not only with the worker but with everything in our community life, for bad men can only prosper while good men do nothing.[93]

Such calls to political participation met with an enthusiastic response from the type of person who generally took an especial interest in union affairs, became a local official and attended these TUC seminars. These were mostly young people (in their twenties or early thirties), and extremely activist. Many were leaders in several other organisations apart from their trade unions. Generally educated to middle-school level, many had taken, or were taking, correspondence courses to further their education.[94] For such people trade union participation was motivated by something more than a desire to protect a particular group of workers: by a desire for self-improvement certainly, but also by the ideal of actively contributing to the creation of a progressive and more just society.

At the national level too, Bentum pursued the line that 'nation building is not the responsibility of Government alone but also that of the citizens . . . politicians should consult the workers on all matters affecting them before a decision is taken'.[95] In addition to pressing the demand for a radical restructuring of the national wage and salary structure, he was continually tendering his advice to the government, through the national press and the TUC's own organs as well as in private, on virtually the entire range of national policy issues: unemployment, the external debts problem, reform of the educational system, the siting of new industries, assistance for the fishing industry etc. Most crucially, he claimed that the TUC had a right to be consulted in the formulation of the budget: 'The

Congress cannot accept the principle that the destiny of the country should be determined only by a chosen few, neither can we accept that wisdom and knowledge is with a few'.[96]

The Progress Party regime did not take kindly to such criticisms and claims. A relatively moderate statement of the government's objections was provided by Dr Bruce-Konuah in a private interview: 'The idea that we should practise democracy like America today is absolute nonsense. Did America have developed trade unions when she was fifteen years old? No, she had slave labour ... What is the proportion of workers to the rest of the population? They are just a minority. It's all wrong for them to say, "The government must consult us." ' [97] During the summer of 1971, several Ministers, in conjunction with the editorials of the *Daily Graphic* (to all intents and purposes the government's mouthpiece), made ever more frequent and hostile attacks on 'the impudent claim of the trade union leaders to represent the people in matters which do not concern them'.[98] This only served to incline Bentum to more vociferous criticism of the regime's policies and to swing the rank and file more solidly behind him. To describe Bentum's demand for a rise in the minimum wage from N¢ 0.75 to N¢1.50 as 'outrageous and politically instigated',[99] for instance, carried no conviction with union members who were well aware that he was doing no more than pressing the minimal demands of their own delegates, and that 'it is an old trick of governments to charge the unions with playing politics as soon as they stand up for their rights'.[100] During July and August, several of the district labour councils passed resolutions calling on the Prime Minister 'to advise his Ministers and Ministerial secretaries from attacking the TUC unnecessarily on political platforms'.[101]

The confrontation of September 1971

These various sources and levels of conflict came to a head in mid-August when Dr Bruce-Konuah alleged that the TUC contained too many politicians 'who had identified themselves with trade unions in order to use them for their political ends'.[102] He announced that the Industrial Relations Act was to be amended in the current session of parliament so as 'to remove anomalies in the Act and bring it in line with the provisions and spirit of the constitution'.[103] This was interpreted by TUC leaders, quite correctly as it proved, as a reference to the demand of Victor Owusu and Oheneba Kwow Richardson for the abolition of the check-off system, which they claimed 'smacked of Communism'.[104] The compulsory check-off system, introduced by the 1958 Industrial Relations Act, was an arrangement by which union dues were deducted at source from workers' wage-packets and distributed, according to the stipulated proportions, to

133

the TUC, national union and local branches. In some industries, but not all, workers could contract out of this arrangement if they wished. The check-off was certainly a major source of strength and unity for the Ghanaian trade union movement, assuring the unions of financial viability, and freeing officials from the arduous task of collecting dues. It also reduced the opportunity for, and occurrence of, fraudulent practices at the level of local officialdom, and thereby contributed to an improvement in the quality of that officialdom. Some Progress Party Ministers, together with the leaders of the Confederation of Labour, claimed that the system gave too much power to the TUC and national union leadership, and freed them from the necessity of regular contact with, and accountability to, the rank and file. While there was doubtless some validity to this argument (as the CPP experience had shown), it is difficult to see how good communications between union leadership and rank and file could be fostered better by a continuous preoccupation on the part of the union officials with the business of collecting dues than by directing their time and energy to grievance-handling and other more positive functions.

Confronted with this threat of legislative action to undermine the strength of the Ghanaian labour movement, Bentum moved onto the offensive. He described the government's charge that union leaders were 'playing politics' as 'a mere cover for you to escape from facing the realities and challenges of an independent labour movement in our present-day democracy'.[105] In mid-August he had written privately to the Minister of Finance requesting a meeting to make known the TUC's views on the budget. When, two weeks later, no reply was forthcoming, he began a tour of the district labour councils, declaring that 'the TUC will not be disturbed by threats or intimidations from continuing to fight for the rights of the workers . . . the TUC will not be a rubber-stamp to the Government . . . No Government in the world can succeed without the workers'.[106] He still refrained from calling an official general strike, but, early in September, declared his support for proposals to stage demonstrations against the national development levy.

The government reacted by warning workers that any strike against the levy would be regarded as a political strike and 'treated in a way different from the way in which we treat genuine strikes'.[107] It claimed to be aware 'that for two years some people have tried to use the labour movement for political purposes'.[108] On 8 September the Minister of Internal Affairs, N. Y. B. Adade, announced, 'We'll stop Bentum', and issued a notice freezing the assets of the TUC.[109] Within two days, an Industrial Relations (Amendment) Bill was rushed through the Legislative Assembly, abolishing the check-off system and the legal status of the TUC, and stipulating that a ninety-day cooling-off period be observed in the event of

134

threats of strike action.[110] By the end of the week 8,000 workers in Sekondi-Takoradi were out on strike.

Demonstrations of opposition to the levy and support for Bentum were staged in Accra, Tema and other industrial centres, and it looked as though the Sekondi-Takoradi strikers would be joined by workers throughout the country. There were a number of reasons why this general support failed to materialise. In the first place, the government instantly dismissed 500 State Transport Corporation workers for stopping work, and this deterred other groups from risking a similar fate.[111] But it was possible for the government to pick off strikers in this manner only because they did not come out simultaneously in solid, concerted action. Bentum's failure to call and co-ordinate an official general strike must therefore be considered a major blunder. As it was, his declaration of support for demonstrations against the government's policies threw the responsibility for taking strike action onto the leaders of the individual unions, most of whom, having earlier been informed of Bentum's opposition to the idea of a general strike, were now found surprised and unprepared.[112] In addition, although he had very good relations with most of the general secretaries of the national unions, several had recently become piqued at what they regarded as a lack of adequate consultation in the determination of TUC policy. In some cases, there was perhaps also an element of jealousy at the extent of Bentum's personal popularity with their own rank and file.[113]

Nevertheless, the near universality of labour support for Bentum's stand was indicated by the immediate resolution of all the national unions, with the exception of the Seamen's Union, to join in forming another trade union centre with Bentum as leader.[114] The only instances of dissent from this stance were the National Seamen's Union, whose general secretary, J. K. Smith-Mensah, had recently been involved in a bitter dispute with Bentum and Baiden over the jurisdiction of his union; a group of some 700 railway workers in Kumasi, almost half the railway labour force in that city, who expressed their support for the budget measures and agreed with the government in seeing Bentum's opposition as politically moti-vated (presumably in the sense of being designed to topple the PP regime);[115] and, the leaders of the Ghana Confederation of Labour, the rival trade union centre, who were also the leaders of a splinter-group of Sekondi-Takoradi railway workers, now formed into the Railway and Harbour Employees' Union. (The Ghana Confederation of Labour con-sisted at this time of the Railway and Harbour Employees' Union and the Manufacturing and Commercial Allied Workers' Union, a small Takoradi-based splinter group from the Industrial and Commercial Workers' Union.)

But, although support for Bentum was so widespread, and the Ghana Confederation of Labour failed to make any significant inroads among the TUC's membership, the Sekondi-Takoradi workers were again alone in being prepared to maintain physical opposition to the government. 8,000 workers in that city stayed out on strike from 12 to 17 September. The strikers' placards suggested (and interviews confirmed) that so far as they were concerned the issues were twofold: 'Suspend development levy, it is unjust' and 'We still recognise Mr Bentum as TUC boss'.[116] A further placard slogan provided deeper insight into these grievances: 'An end to PP false aristocracy'. The interrelation was clearly articulated by one railway unionist: 'We must stand by Mr Bentum's effort to speak up for us poor people and tell these big men what sacrifices they should be making.'[117] Interviews conducted during the strike also indicated a great deal of sympathy from other groups for Bentum and the strikers' stance, though this was most apparent among middle- and lower-middle-class groups such as the market-women, middle-ranking executives and teachers, who stood to be directly affected by the levy and other budget provisions.

For most participants, the aim of the strike was simply to impress on the government their opposition to the levy exactions and their confidence in the TUC leadership and its stated objectives. Some certainly hoped to displace the regime. In the outspoken atmosphere of the Sekondi akpeteshie bars, workers could sometimes be heard speculating that 'We'll show this government and its development levy. If the military are sent to stop the strike, it could bring the government down.'[118] But, in general, the whole point of the strike was rather to refute the suggestion that they had been misled by a politically subversive union leadership, while standing by the TUC's demand for reform of the wage structure and the view that popular criticism of the regime's policies was an essential element in real democracy. The majority of strikers and their leaders were PP voters (some indeed were officials of the party's ward committees) and it was precisely such 'real democracy' that, in their eyes, the Progress Party had stood for in the 1969 election.

It was partly the concern to make this position clear that led the strikers to return to work after five days. Robert Mensah, chairman of the Takoradi Branch of the Railway Union, expressed the views of many when he observed,

> I tell you, the workers are the eyes of the country, they know what is going on, and you should not try to treat them like trees. If only the government had co-operated with the TUC in educating them, it would have been good for Ghana. But this attack on the TUC does not make for stable government. We want to impress this on the government, but we also want to make it clear we are not after political ends. So it is best to cool the situation now we have made our point.[119]

136

The strike leaders' decision to return to work was greeted with hisses and boos when it was first put to the assembled strikers on Thursday, 16 September. But Mensah eventually convinced them with the promise that 'We will never let you down. The struggle has reached a new phase and we must react accordingly. But if those of our leaders who have been arrested are not released by next Monday, then we will resume the strike.'[120]

The arrest of these union leaders had resulted from violent confrontations with members of the splinter Railway and Harbour Employees' Union who insisted on attending duty. This was the second reason for abandoning the strike action. Some wished to take it to a more decisive conclusion, but the railway workers' front was far from solid and, with such division in their ranks, the morale of the strikers was relatively low. Approximately one third of the railway and harbour workers were members of the breakaway union, and nearly all of these abided by their leaders' decision not to strike against the levy. An analysis of the reasons for this decision, and of the sources of division within the Railway Union rank and file, will be presented in the following chapter. The important point to note here is the practical significance of this conflict in the situation of September 1971 as an instance of atypically astute, successful 'divide and rule' tactics on the part of the Progress Party regime, and one which illustrated government leaders' appreciation of the crucial importance of control of the Sekondi-Takoradi workers in the politics of government–labour relations.

Finally, it is worth remarking on the close similarities, and also certain differences, between the Sekondi-Takoradi strikes of 1961 and 1971. In both instances, the respective regimes faced what were perhaps the most serious (civilian) challenges they were to experience from any quarter; and this from a group of workers who had been amongst the most enthusiastic and politically influential supporters of these regimes at the beginning of their periods in office. The 1971 strike proved to be not so protracted a challenge as that of 1961, though it might have been so had not poor planning and internal divisions amongst the railway workers undermined the strikers' morale. In any case, its implications were equally serious. Indeed, perhaps more clearly than that of 1961, it heralded the imminent downfall of the existing regime. Just four months later, in January 1972, with the economic situation deteriorating even further, and the disillusionment of many farmers added to that of the workers, the army intervened to displace the Progress Party Government.

In each case, the objectives of strike action were very similar: to protest at the imposition of additional taxation which seemed unfair in view of the excessive wealth and high living of the politico-administrative elite, and which lacked credibility as a genuine developmental measure. For some

137

at least, the aim was consciously conceived as protest against the growth of gross socio-economic inequalities in Ghanaian society, and the authoritarian style of government to which each regime increasingly resorted, partly in consequence of popular unrest at these inequalities. In more positive terms, the strikers asserted the claim of the trade union movement to a regular and major voice in national decision-making in order to impress on the government the demand for greater social justice. The majority of strikers and their leaders were concerned to distinguish these objectives from 'mere party politics' or 'subversive motivations', not only for the benefit of the government, but also out of the desire to act consistently with their purpose – i.e., to demonstrate the legitimacy and political viability of a certain type of trade union movement (democratic–reformist) and thereby to establish it on a permanent footing (or defend it, once established).

In 1971, as in 1961, the government characterised the strikers as a relatively privileged labour elite pursuing selfish interests to the detriment of the real poor, the unemployed and the rural populace. There was perhaps some validity to this accusation in the sense that the additional taxation which the strikers protested at was, theoretically, to be used for the benefit of these groups. And the skilled workers who led the strike were, of course, better off than the unemployed and some, though certainly not all, of the rural populace. Yet it is readily understandable that such an emphasis on the relatively slight differentiation within the ranks of the poor should be interpreted by the strikers as a calculated attempt to divert attention from the primary and immense gap between the masses and the elite.[121] There was greater validity to the workers' claim to be acting as the 'spokesmen of the people', since, with the suppression or buying off of opposition parties, the unions represented the only institutional means for the expression of popular discontent. It was difficult to assess the extent or group-location of public sympathy for the 1971 strikers with any precision. But, in addition to the impressionistic evidence of interviews, it was significant that during the last quarter of the year there was much talk amongst aspirant politicans in the Central and Western Regions of forming a Labour Party, with Bentum in its leadership, aiming to attract the support of the unionised workers and the urban poor more generally. This was at least indicative of the judgment of men with their fingers on the pulse of public opinion that sympathy for the aims and stance of Bentum's TUC had been widespread.

The fact that such ideas were most prevalent in the Central and Western Regions of Ghana was again significant. In 1971, as in 1961, there was a communal dimension to the anti-government feeling of Sekondi-Takoradi workers. The Progress Party regime was regarded as favouring Ashanti and Brong-Ahafo. Workers from the Central and Western regions, like the majority in Sekondi-Takoradi, were the less willing to make sacrifices for rural development since they doubted that their home areas would receive an equal share of such development. Workers in Kumasi, in contrast, had good reason to expect very real benefits for themselves and their relatives from the budget proposals. The years 1970–1 witnessed the disintegration of the Akan (Ashanti–Fanti) alliance which Dr Busia had cultivated during 1969, and the re-emergence of that Ashanti–Coastal Town conflict, dating back several centuries, which had informed the struggle between the CPP and the opposition (i.e. the Congress Party and later the National Liberation Movement) during the 1950s.

Too much emphasis on this communal dimension to the September 1971 confrontation would nevertheless be misplaced. The major issues were the national ones of the elitism of the Progress Party regime and the legitimacy of the role which Bentum had attempted to develop for the TUC. On this occasion, unlike 1961 (or certainly more clearly than then) the Sekondi-Takoradi strikers were ideologically at one with the TUC and with the vast majority of workers throughout the country. It is this unity and sense of solidarity of Ghanaian workers during 1971 which deserves emphasis. In this (admittedly limited) sense one could almost speak of the emergence of a sense of national working-class identity at this time. Certainly, the government–TUC confrontation in September, though unsought and undesired, served to strengthen rather than undermine rank-and-file confidence in the legitimacy of Bentum's 'independent and democratic' style of trade union movement.

7

The railway workers divided: the sources and structure of political conflict in the Railway Union

At a mass meeting of the Sekondi Location Branch of the Railway and Ports Workers' Union on 21 January 1970, a majority of the assembled workers resolved to secede and to form themselves into a new union. This splinter group, officially terming itself the Railway and Harbour Employees' Union, but known in local parlance as the 'Biafrans' (in distinction from the 'Federalists'), explained its action in terms of the fact that 'There has been no improvement whatsoever in the administration of our former union since we passed a vote of no confidence in the national officers in May 1967'. [1] Almost two-thirds of the Location manual workers (i.e. some 900 out of a total of 1,580) became members of the new union, and they were soon joined by approximately a quarter of the workers employed at Takoradi harbour (i.e. some 1,100 out of a total labour force of nearly 5,000), together with small groups in Tema and Kumasi.

The leadership of the new union (hereafter referred to as the 'splinter union' in distinction from the 'mother union' – terms also used by the railway workers themselves) then proceeded to extend the object of its criticisms to the leadership and structure of the Ghana TUC. In June its general secretary, K. G. Quartey, called on the government to repeal the Industrial Relations Act (inherited from the CPP regime) and to proscribe the TUC. [2] In September 1970 the union was granted official registration, and in August of the following year its leaders launched a new national trade union centre, the Ghana Confederation of Labour. The other affiliates of the GCL consisted of the Manufacturing and Commercial Allied Workers' Union (a small splinter group from the Industrial and Commercial Workers' Union) and the Co-operative Distillers' Union. [3] These developments clearly enjoyed the tacit backing of the Progress Party Government, without whose special assistance the RHEU could not even have gained official registration. In September 1971 the government reaped the reward of its sponsorship when the splinter unionists proclaimed their opposition to the strike of mother-union members

140

and remained on duty, so undermining the aims and morale of the strikers.

Apart from its practical significance in the political situation of September 1971, this major division in the ranks of the Sekondi-Takoradi railway workers raises serious questions as to the validity of the argument developed in previous chapters of this study. Bentum's leadership of the TUC, it has been argued, succeeded in developing an unprecedented level of unity and sense of solidarity in the Ghanaian trade union movement. The appeal of its programme and ideology was especially powerful for many of the railway and harbour workers of Sekondi-Takoradi, strongly attached as they were to the norms of trade union solidarity, independence from government and opposition to elitist tendencies in Ghanaian society. But what degree of support, one must ask, did Bentum's TUC really attract in view of the secession and criticisms of this group of railway workers? How accurate is the depiction of the railway workers as subscribing, with remarkable consistency over time, to a unifying political culture? This alleged ideological continuity, and, more particularly, the idea that Bentum's TUC represented the approximate realisation of an ideal model of trade unionism for which the railway workers had long been fighting, surely requires substantial qualification. One's reservations can only be strengthened by the knowledge that the leaders of the splinter union were precisely those people who had led the 1961 strike action.

In response, we should first admit that the general interpretation thus far propounded does constitute a simplified presentation of a far more complex reality. For example, Bentum's leadership, as has already been emphasised, was extremely popular with the supporters of the mother railway union, the criticisms of the splinter-union leaders (which were far from universally shared by their own supporters) notwithstanding. But Bentum's popularity, and the relatively high degree of unity he brought to the Ghanaian trade union movement, derived from, and depended on, a more complex set of factors than mere ideological rapport. For instance, he was generally adept in his handling of relations with both the general secretaries and middle-level leaders (branch and association officials) of the national unions, satisfying their aspiration to a certain autonomous status within the reformed and rejuvenated TUC. This was a crucial factor in labour movement unity since these middle-level unionists, acting as communicators and interpreters to their rank and file, generally possessed a great measure of control over the views and behaviour of their constituencies. But, in the case of the Railway Union, it proved impossible to accommodate the ambitions of all the union's middle-level leaders, partly because there were simply too many aspirants for the available positions, partly because the ambitions of certain of these leaders were so grandiose, extending to leadership of the national trade union movement as a whole. This situation, of a superabundance of men experienced in union officialdom and determined to retain or accede to the limited number of positions available, was expecially likely to occur in a union, such as the Railway Union, where leadership was highly valued; but it was exacerbated in this particular instance by singular historical circumstances (shortly to be described).

Further, the relative unity of the trade union movement in 1966–71, while reflecting the rank and file's common experience of seriously declining living standards, was greatly facilitated by the government's general failure to exploit potential sources of division within the working class. But here again the railway workers were an exception to the general rule. The depressed financial situation of the lower-paid workers during these years exerted a double-edged effect, increasing the potential for labour solidarity and radicalism under a sufficiently united and responsive leadership, but at the same time intensifying rank-and-file desperation for whatever benefits it seemed possible to gain, and consequently their susceptibility to the manipulation of sectionalist differences. The Progress Party regime exploited this susceptibility with uncharacteristic skill in the case of the railway Location 'tradesmen' through the agency of malcontents among their leadership.

Thirdly, ideological differences as to the degree of co-operation which should be extended to the government's economic policies constituted an additional dimension of the Railway Union split. It is worth pointing out here that there was ample room for genuine differences in this regard within a common commitment to independent, reformist trade unionism. Progress Party government was a strange mixture of elitist and populist, liberal and authoritarian tendencies. This gave considerable scope for differences of interpretation and opinion among union leaders as to the merits of Progress Party rule, slight in themselves perhaps, but of potentially serious political consequence.

Nevertheless, one is bound to ask, did not the Railway Union split of 1970–1 illustrate the relative weakness, or certainly a weakening, of the norm of solidarity amongst this, historically the most solidary, group of Ghanaian workers? To some degree this was certainly so. But the fact is that the railway workers' history of solidarity in action has always been achieved through subsuming potentially serious sources of division. Indeed, the very activism of railway unionism has made for strong divisive tendencies. We have seen how the railway enginemen, for instance, determined to ensure the best possible representation of their grievances, have several times broken away from the main Railway Union. Furthermore, in so powerful a union and so active a union culture, positions of leadership,

142

being highly prestigious, have naturally been keenly fought over. Consequently, leadership factionalism, too, has frequently proved divisive. The ideological consistency which, it has been argued, the railway workers have displayed from the era of Pobee Biney to that of Benjamin Bentum is admittedly only the dominant tendency in Railway Union politics, that which has generally won out in the end (and become, in a sense, the 'official' interpretation of the historical principles of railway unionism). A divergent tendency for some railway workers and union leaders to seek to involve the union in party politics – whether the control-orientated politics of the governing party or the subversive aims of the opposition parties – has been a common feature of the Railway Union political arena. Biney and his followers had to battle to overcome the influence of CPP loyalists in the union in 1954–61. And, in the course of the 1961 strike action itself, a conflict developed between those leaders allied with the United Party interest and those seeking to limit the objectives of the strike action to a non-partisan reformist protest. In 1970–1 these several sources of division – leadership factionalism, economic sectionalism and ideological differences over the issue of union–government relations – all coincided to undermine the solidarity of the railway workers to a degree unprecedented, if not entirely unprefigured, in previous experience. An analysis of the sources and levels of this division will serve to illuminate the complex reality of Railway Union politics, the mediation of general ideological tendencies and issues through particular structures of power and communication, and so provide a necessary corrective to the simplified presentation of previous chapters.

It remains, nevertheless, appropriate to conceive of Railway Union history in terms of the directing and unifying influence of a strong proletarian/populist political culture, and to interpret the 1970–1 splinter union as an exceptional (and temporary) deviant case. In the first place, many supporters of the splinter union, unlike those of the mother union, tended in interviews to be markedly defensive about the legitimacy of their position, recognising its inconsistency with the Railway Union's historical principles of worker solidarity and strict independence of party political ties. Some of these in fact 'crossed the floor' back to the mother union during the crisis of August–September 1971. Moreover, in order to retain what support they possessed, the leaders of the splinter union were very much concerned in their speeches at mass meetings to try to justify their stand in terms of the railway workers' historical experience, and to emphasise their independence of government influence (though they were equally concerned to emphasise their influence *with* the government). In other words, the dominant culture of railway unionism continued to exert a significant reunifying influence on the rank and file, and imposed severe

143

limitations on the position which it was politic for the leaders of the splinter union to take.

Secondly, this split in the ranks of the railway workers resulted and, it might well be argued, could only have resulted, from a historical situation in which the various issues and lines of division were of quite exceptional intensity and, in consequence of a tendency to coincide with (rather than cross-cut) each other, proved mutually reinforcing. Indeed, this close interrelation of divisive factors makes it extremely difficult to clearly separate and weigh their respective influence in the determination of allegiances. This is especially the case with respect to the important question of the relative significance of sectional economic interests on the one hand, and ideological differences (including here differences of opinion as to the sincerity and wisdom of particular union leaders) on the other. The majority of supporters of both unions appeared, in July–September 1971, to attach great importance to the differences in the stances of the rival unions, and to believe sincerely in the positions taken by their own leaders. Yet, again in the majority of cases, union allegiance followed the lines of sectional economic interest very closely. It is necessary to recognise that the ideological issues must have exerted a significant influence on behaviour in order to account for the quite numerous instances of deviation from this dominant pattern. But, generally speaking, they should doubtless be seen as rationalisations of positions essentially dictated by considerations of practical (economic and political) self-interest. This is not to deny them importance. It was precisely the ability to develop tenable ideological justifications of divergent interpretations of economic interest (and of different approaches to their promotion) which served to weld the two groups into relatively solid, opposing camps.[4]

Leadership factionalism in the Railway Union

The rewards, motivations and norms of leadership W. N. Grant, a prominent leader of the 1961 strike and an interested observer of the Railway Union split of 1970–1, considered that 'The cause of all this trouble is a mad scramble for leadership'.[5] Many others held a similar view, including the Progress Party Minister of Labour, Dr W. G. Bruce-Konuah, who remarked that 'This division seems to me to be the only solution, since all those railway people are determined to be leaders'.[6] Before proceeding to an analysis of this 'mad scramble', it is worth considering, in general terms, just why positions of leadership in the Railway Union should be, and were, so keenly sought.

There were several possible reasons, and the motivations of different aspirants varied considerably. But, generally speaking, leadership of the railway workers was highly valued in itself rather than as a stepping-stone to positions in other (e.g. professional or party) hierarchies. Historical experience had shown that prominent union officials, usually clerical unionists, had sometimes gone on to senior managerial appointments, but such cases were very rare.[7] More commonly, branch and association officials were appointed junior foremen soon after their election to union office. The connecting link between advancement in these two hierarchies seemed, however, to consist of the exceptional organisational talent and intelligence displayed by certain individuals, rather than in any deliberate managerial strategy of buying off 'dangerous' union leaders. As frequently as it led to professional advancement, serving as a union official appeared to prejudice an individual's chances of job promotion beyond a certain level. Certainly, it was almost unheard of for an active unionist to be appointed a foreman.[8] Generally speaking, therefore, prominence in the union tended to constitute an alternative channel of advancement to that of the professional–managerial hierarchy – clearly an important factor in accounting for the strength of corporate solidarity among the railway workers.[9]

As regards the connection between mobility in union and party hierarchies there had, as we have seen, been a close but far from simple or consistent interrelationship under the CPP regime. The party had felt obliged to reward such men as Biney and Woode for their contribution to the nationalist struggle, but had rapidly realised the unsuitability, from the government's point of view, of such relatively committed and radical labour champions. Thereafter, party leaders had looked to more reliable, if less prominent or popular, unionists as possible material for recruitment to administrative positions. These included not a single railway unionist during the whole CPP period (if one excepts the somewhat farcical appointment of Biney as a security agent in 1963–5). The fact that the Railway Union rank and file largely succeeded in maintaining their democratic powers of election, and were increasingly disinclined to vote for known party enthusiasts, meant that extremely few reliable party supporters ever attained official positions in the union, through either election or imposition. Even if, once ensconced in senior positions, railway unionists were tempted towards greater co-operation with the official party line by the prospect of advancement in the interlocking CPP–TUC structures, they faced severe problems, on the one hand of maintaining their control over the rank and file, and on the other of gaining the trust of party leaders. The downfall of General Secretary Inkumsah in 1961 was an obvious case in point.

The ideological complexion of the Progress Party Government hardly inclined it to recruit trade unionists into senior positions in the party or administrative structures. Several railway unionists in fact acted as officers of the party's ward branches, but this was more an onerous duty than a privilege or an opportunity for further promotion. One railway unionist, K. G. Quartey, had, according to his union opponents, sought nomination as Progress Party candidate for the Winneba seat in the 1969 general election to the Legislative Assembly, though he himself denied this and it proved impossible to verify or disprove the allegation conclusively.[10] In any case, as the following account will make clear, K. G. Quartey, together with a group of followers amongst the railway unionists, aspired to take over the leadership of the Railway Union (and even of the national trade union movement) with Progress Party encouragement and assistance. In part at least, their motive seems to have been to strengthen the political control and stability of the PP regime. In return they probably anticipated and received financial tokens of appreciation, and, more important, increased security against the return of the Nkrumah regime, a possibility which, after their experience of detention and professional demise under that regime, they understandably viewed with some hysteria. Yet the evidence of interviews suggests that most of these unionists were also genuinely committed to leadership and, as they saw it, faithful representation of the interests of their railway worker constituency. The point is admittedly debatable, and indeed constituted a major issue of disagreement between supporters of the two unions in 1970–1. But, certainly, the fundamental and vigorously asserted Railway Union ethic of primary commitment to the corporate interests of the rank and file exerted a powerful influence on the attitudes and behaviour of even these 'party political' unionists.

The financial rewards of office-holding, whether official or unofficial, were generally speaking of strictly secondary importance. The general secretaryship of the union had been a well-paid position since CPP days. But the large majority of local and middle-level officials did not seriously entertain any hope of ever succeeding to that position, and, as association or branch officials, received annual honoraria so small as hardly to compensate them for the work and responsibility entailed in such office-holding.[11] Instances of embezzlement of union funds, or other forms of corruption, appear to have been extremely rare in the history of the Railway Union, except perhaps during CPP days at the top level of the union. Only three instances were officially brought to light between 1950 and 1971.[12] A more reliable indication, perhaps, is provided by the fact that rank-and-file interviewees could recall only two additional instances in which they suspected officials of embezzlement or of being bribed by the management. The Railway Union rank and file did not consider corruption to be widespread amongst union officials, or to constitute a significant motivation to office-holding, which was rather regarded in terms of 'fighting for one's brothers' or 'the honour of receiving the trust of one's fellow workers'.[13] Such lack of cynicism as to officials' motives and conduct may be suggestive of a real situation if only in view of its rarity (at least in Ghana, and, it would seem, in Africa more generally).

This is perhaps not so surprising or idealistic as it might seem. Attaining the respect of a close cultural sub-community of some 8,000 workers, a sub-community, moreover, which accords its very highest laurels of prestige to great labour leaders, is no small personal ambition. And the experience of socialisation in Railway Union culture has inclined many to aspire to that goal. Others have noted that Ghanaians typically seek material wealth primarily as a means to the high social status which its dispensation brings.[14] Within Railway Union culture, a culture which automatically associates corruptibility with undependability, to seek personal financial gain through the typical extra-union expedients of corruption would be to prejudice one's chances of attaining the desired high status. In any case, virtually all officials sincerely share the rank and file's repugnance at the closed, corrupt style of extra-union (government) politics, and the corresponding determination to maintain an open, responsive 'clean' system within the Railway Union itself.

A word of clarification is required here, however. Various particular meanings might be attached to the general notion of 'representation of rank-and-file interests', and it is important to define this more clearly than in terms of its distinction from extra-union careerism or party political allegiance. In the first place, such representation does not generally take the form of relations of the patron–client type between particular union leaders and particular groups of workers. An element of patronage (or sponsorship) certainly does play a minor role in the structure of leader–follower relations, and, more importantly, some unionists have tended to identify themselves especially closely with the interests and grievances of particular occupational groups. But, generally speaking, union leaders have not had regular, reliable clientele followings. The extent of their support has depended on their continuing to display their dedication and effectiveness as rank-and-file representatives, and on their being able to present a strong case in support of whatever policies they might advocate.

Secondly, 'representation' does not generally signify the pursuit of immediate economic interests by any means possible, or irrespective of wider considerations. The majority of railway workers are not so naive as to fail to recognise the complexity of considerations affecting their long-term interest. More particularly, they do generally recognise the interrelation of their own interests with those of other groups, the unemployed especially, and even with the national economic interest (conceived of in terms of bettering the lot of the 'common people'); the importance of fighting to create or maintain a democratic political system, and more particularly a democratic trade union movement, through which they can make their grievances heard; and, above all, the importance of maintaining solidarity within their own ranks – 'United we stand, divided we fall', as the union motto has it. Certain situations, however, are likely to entail varying degrees of conflict between these considerations and corresponding difficulties of interpretation as to the wisest course of action. The rank and file therefore tend to look to their union officials, and especially the more experienced amongst them, to act as interpreters and opinion-leaders. Moreover, they expect such interpretation to be informed by a wide political perspective on the issue at hand, and by the lessons of historical experience.

The 'scramble for leadership' in the Railway Union, 1961–71 The origins of the Railway Union split of 1970–1 are ultimately to be found in the political aftermath of the 1961 strike. The strike leaders had then been placed in preventive detention for periods ranging from five months to two years, and their company in the detention camps included several United Party leaders (later to become Ministers in the Progress Party regime), most notably J. Kwesi-Lamptey, Victor Owusu and R. R. Amponsah. However tenuous or opportunistic the ties between these UP leaders and the strike leaders were before detention, they were immeasurably strengthened by the experience of fellowship in imprisonment. V. K. Quist, K. G. Quartey, A. Y. Ankomah, T. B. Ward, T. C. Bentil, J. K. Baaku and Kofi Imbeah were all to become keen Progress Party supporters in 1969–71, though, as we shall see, they were also to diverge in their interpretation of the obligations of this party allegiance.

In the meantime, the Railway Union was placed under the direct supervision of a TUC administrator, J. C. Hansen, and an Interim Management Committee, composed of two representatives from each of the branches. These were not hand-picked CPP men, but rather the existing branch secretaries and chairmen, and, in the case of Sekondi Location and Takoradi, junior officials who stepped into the positions left vacant by the detainees. The Location representatives were A. B. Essuman and A. E. Forson, and there is little reason to doubt the sincerity of their explanation that they co-operated with the new executive simply to keep the union running and press for the early release of the detainees.[15]

Many of the up-country representatives, on the other hand, saw this as their opportunity to accede to positions of leadership in the union, and call a halt to the union's domination by the Sekondi-Takoradi militants. When the TUC Executive Board announced in November 1962 that it

148

was prepared to allow the ex-detainees to stand for election at the forth-coming delegates' conference, the Interim Management Committee voted almost unanimously against the proposal, only Forson and Essuman voting for it.[16] F. C. Separa-Grant, the 'official' CPP candidate, was elected general secretary at the conference, and all the other positions on the Railway Union Executive Council went to up-country men.[17] These new officers then proceeded to concur with various measures introduced by Separa-Grant to reduce the power and stifle the voice of the Sekondi-Takoradi rank and file. The most important of these measures were the abolition of the Working Committee, previously the effective day-to-day decision-making body, and generally dominated by the Sekondi-Takoradi Branch and Association representatives; and a decision to allow voting for the election of national officers by equal representation from all nine branches, rather than, as previously, by proportional representation (i.e. proportionate to the numerical strength of each branch). Since the Sekondi-Takoradi Branches comprised approximately half the total union membership, this decision greatly reduced their influence over the selection of national officers (see Table 7.1.). A. B. Essuman opposed these measures and persisted in calling for the reintroduction of the Working Committee at virtually every executive council meeting up to June 1965 (when he was replaced as branch secretary by Kofi Imbeah), but to no avail. He also led criticism of the executive's failure to gain wage increases for the manual workers at a time when the Railway Administration was making large annual profits, and especially deplored its inaction over the tradesmen's grievances.[18] He was supported in these criticisms by the other Location and Takoradi delegates, and, to a lesser degree, by A. K. A.

Table 7.1. *Railway Union membership, by branches (June 1969)*

Sekondi Location	3,000[a]	
Takoradi	3,200	
Tarkwa	360	
Achiasi	300	
Dunkwa	390	
Kumasi	380	
Nkawkaw	120	
Accra	560	
Tema	1,200	
Total	9,510	

Source: *RUA*, Delegates' Conference Minutes, 17 June 1969.

[a] This figure includes more than 1,000 clerical workers and permanent way-men who were officially attached to the Location Branch although not, strictly speaking, part of the Location labour force.

149

Bello from the Accra Branch and W. A. Thompson from Kumasi. At the October 1963 executive council meeting 'a mob from Location with placards of various inscriptions came and demonstrated for 30 minutes'.[19] They dispersed only after handing in a petition calling for Separa-Grant's resignation and for the reform of the structure and voting procedures of the union 'so as to reflect the true feelings and aspirations of the rank and file'.[20] The national officers refused to consider these requests, and, by the middle of 1965, discontent was running so high at Location that General Secretary Separa-Grant prohibited further mass meetings there, 'because he found the meetings were generating subversive motives'.[21] According to some unionists, preparations for an unofficial strike were in train when the army and police intervened to displace Nkrumah in February 1966.

With startling insensitivity to the feelings of the Sekondi-Takoradi railway workers, representatives of the deposed president attempted to bribe them to stage a strike against the new regime. Their leaders' response was unambiguous: 'We vehemently denounce the vain bluff of the deposed Dictator Kwame Nkrumah calling the railway workers to go on strike, as our Union suffered the most under his wicked and capricious rule, and we are the people from whom he should expect the least support'.[22] But while there was no question of the railway workers' loyalty to the National Liberation Council, they were, initially, less than enthusiastic about Benjamin Bentum's appointment as secretary-general of the TUC. J. A. Ashielfie and Kofi Imbeah, on behalf of the Location workers, petitioned the chairman of the NLC to rescind Bentum's appointment, and were forced to apologise for this indiscretion at the April executive council meeting.[23] Apart from objecting to Bentum's CPP background, the Sekondi-Takoradi workers considered that a new secretary-general should be selected from amongst the 1961 strike leaders, men possessed of far better credentials than Bentum (at this stage, at least) as champions of democracy. In particular, they favoured V. K. Quist, Pobee Biney's successor as the 'strong man' of Location. Ashielfie was regarded as Quist's agent, having acted as personal messenger for him during the 1961 strike action. Imbeah, too, had been closely associated with this most fiery of railway unionists, and had been detained for his supporting role in the strike's organisation. Ashielfie and Imbeah could, it was felt, be relied on to press Quist's candidature for the general secretaryship of the Railway Union, and, more optimistically, for the leadership of the TUC. It was largely for this reason that they had been elected chairman and secretary of the Location Branch in March 1966.

Bentum's appointment had frustrated the more grandiose of these ambitions, but it was still confidently expected that Quist would be elected leader of the Railway Union at the July delegates' conference. This expectation was rudely shattered when the result of a secret ballot was announced as ten votes for W. A. Thompson, five for A. K. A. Bello, two for T. B. Ward and only one vote for Quist.[24] The main reason for Thompson's victory was quite clear. The failure to reconstitute the union's voting procedures before this election meant that the up-country delegates retained control. They obviously felt reluctant to hand over the running of the union to the most militant of Sekondi-Takoradi militants, and preferred to play safe politically with their own man, the more cautious W. A. Thompson. But the most shocking aspect of the result, from the point of view of the Location rank and file, was the fact that only one of the four Sekondi-Takoradi delegates had voted for Quist. T. B. Ward, the Takoradi Branch chairman and an ex-detainee, who had been expected to campaign for Quist, had apparently pressed his own candidature. And, more treacherous still, Ashielfie, it appeared, had done a deal with Thompson in order to secure his own election as deputy chairman.

'From that time on', K. G. Quartey explained, 'we were looking for an opportunity to get rid of Thompson and Ashielfie. It came when Thompson failed to present the workers' grievances to the Mills–Odoi and Quarshie Commissions.'[25] Quartey was himself elected Takoradi Branch secretary in July 1966, and Quist the Location Branch chairman. They were supported in their campaign to displace Thompson by virtually all the Sekondi-Takoradi representatives, most prominently Kofi Imbeah and T. B. Ward, A. Y. Ankomah (another ex-detainee, and secretary of the Electrical Association) and A. B. Essuman and A. O. Wiafe (chairman and secretary of the Carriage and Wagons Association, and sometime of the Location Branch). A. E. Forson (Clerical Association secretary) and A. K. A. Bello (Accra Branch secretary) joined in supporting many of the criticisms of Thompson's leadership, but sought to play a moderating role, so as to prevent this factionalism from disrupting the efficiency and solidarity of the union. Yet, although the Sekondi-Takoradi unionists were united in opposing Thompson's leadership, they were divided amongst themselves as to who would prove the most suitable and capable successor. Only Quartey, Ankomah, Essuman and Wiafe were really solid in their support of Quist. Imbeah, Ward, Forson and others could not be counted dependable allies, either because they aspired to the position of general secretary themselves, or because they entertained genuine doubts as to Quist's possession of the necessary qualities. Moreover, some were already suspicious of the motivations underlying Quist's and Quartey's determined (and at times ruthless) drive to take over leadership of the union. The feeling grew that they were perhaps excessively personally ambitious, and were too closely allied with politicians such as Dr Busia and

J. Kwesi-Lamptey. As Imbeah remarked, 'It seemed to us that Quartey's trade unionism had too much of a political flavour.'[26]

In the 1968 elections, as in 1966, Ward stood against Quartey (who had now assumed Quist's mantle, the latter having been seconded to the Centre for Civic Education) thus again dividing the Sekondi-Takoradi vote and facilitating Thompson's re-election.[27] And in 1970, Quartey's faction, realising that the opposition of Imbeah, Forson, Ward and others was likely to prevent their winning the forthcoming election, determined to establish a breakaway union under their own leadership. At the same time, however, this scramble for leadership was informed by real ideological differences and issues of principle.

In the first place, Quist, Quartey and their followers could make out a very strong case against Thompson for serious negligence in the performance of his responsibilities. The appointment of the Mills–Odoi Commission in 1967 provided the railway workers with their first official opportunity in ten years to argue their case for improved wages and conditions of service. Thompson set about formulating his proposals to the commission without even consulting the union's association officials – i.e. the experts in grievances held by the various categories of employee. He finally produced a document which the latter unanimously considered seriously inadequate, and he was later blamed, with some justification, for the commission's failure to redress the most pressing grievances of the Railway Union rank and file. In particular, the commission formally recognised the justice of the 'tradesmen's' claim for parity of status with the 'artisans', but declared that it felt unable to make definite recommendations owing to the insufficiently systematic nature of its information.[28]

Then, in February 1968, the Quarshie Committee was appointed to make recommendations on the existing system of job categorisation in the civil service. While it was sitting, the committee's terms of reference were widened to include the question of relative wage-scales, but Thompson failed to bring this fact to the attention of the branch and association officials or to submit any memoranda of his own on the matter. Realising that yet another opportunity for presenting their demands had been wasted, the Sekondi-Takoradi unionists accused Thompson of gross negligence of duty, and presented resolutions from the branches calling on him to resign.[29] Thompson refused, arguing that he had been attending the Constituent Assembly (charged with formulating a new constitution for the return to civilian rule) when the communiqué on the committee's revised terms of reference had arrived at union headquarters. The TUC subsequently appointed a committee to investigate this dispute, which found Thompson guilty of minor negligence in having failed to make proper arrangements for the union's administration during his absence, but decided that these were 'inadequate grounds for his dismissal'.[30] The malcontents would therefore have to wait until the next delegates' conference (some nine months away) to secure his replacement by a more capable man.

The Sekondi-Takoradi unionists were unanimous in deploring these examples of Thompson's inefficient and incommunicative running of the union. But several of them refused on principle to support his replacement by Quist or Quartey. It was perfectly obvious that Quist and Quartey had set out to fault Thompson's leadership irrespective of its real merits or demerits, and had tried to stir up rank-and-file feeling against him on what were sometimes quite bogus charges. This unprincipled agitation was partly to blame for the poor quality of communications between Thompson and the Sekondi-Takoradi workers, and the deplorable state of the union's administration. Moreover, it was increasingly apparent that Quist and Quartey were prepared to utilise their ties with national politicians to further their campaign in the Railway Union. Such a strategy, it was suspected, might eventually involve the union in a covert and dangerous manner in the personal manoeuvres of these politicians. Some, for example – both outside and inside the Railway Union – suspected Quist of instigating the permanent waymen's strike of 1968 in order to impress on the NLC the increasing fragility of its control and the advisability of transferring power to the civilians, more particularly Dr Busia. There would seem to be little ground for such allegations. There could be no doubt, however, as to the influence of the Quist–Quartey faction in securing the inclusion of Thompson and Ashielfie in a group of 608 civil servants summarily dismissed from their positions by the new Progress Party Government in December 1969. Quartey proceeded to argue that, since they no longer held jobs in the Railway Administration, they were ineligible to serve as officers of the Railway Union; fresh elections should therefore be held immediately. At last, it seemed, the 1961 strike leaders would accede to their rightful positions as official leaders of the Railway Union. But many of the Sekondi-Takoradi unionists, including some of those detained in 1961, were extremely perturbed at this prospect. Now that the party allies of Quist and Quartey were in power, it seemed inevitable that the Railway Union (and TUC) principle of strict independence of government would be seriously compromised under their leadership. Consequently, although Ward, Forson, Imbeah, Bello and others retained little affection or respect for Thompson personally, they supported an executive council decision to retain him in office until the forthcoming delegates' conference (in June 1970).[31] They argued that the general secretary, as a full-time official, did not have to be a Railway Administration employee, and that the general manager's refusal to recognise, or negotiate with, Thompson constituted 'a gross interference with the internal affairs of the Union'.[32] Eventually, since the general manager stood by his position, it was decided to appoint an interim management committee, headed by Forson and Bello, to carry on the administration of the union. At the June delegates' conference, Forson was elected general secretary by ten votes to Bello's nine.[33]

By this time, Quartey, impatient at the executive council's refusal to hold fresh elections earlier in the year, had decided to establish a break-away union. The leadership of this new union included A. Y. Ankomah, A. B. Essuman and A. O. Wiafe. However, T. C. Bentil and J. K. Baaku, till now strong supporters of Quist and Quartey, refused to go along with the breakaway. Bentil stayed on as an official of the mother union, and Baaku sought to work as an intermediary between the two camps so as to engineer a reunification. As Baaku explained:

> We were trying to overthrow Thompson for the Progress Party and ourselves, and because we thought the PP was best for the workers. When Thompson was dismissed we saw we had our chance, and I thought we would come together to win the next election. But those TUC boys are clever, you know, and saw what we were up to, and started to campaign against us. Quartey and Ankomah thought that because the mother union still had the majority along the line they might lose the elections. So they started their own union and refused all efforts to reunite the two groups. This was when I left Quartey's side. It had become a selfish personal interest. I am very strong PP, but it is not right that the Railway Union should be divided and ruled by two leaders. United we stand, divided we fall. The moment you divide the worker, that moment you give access to management and the government to rule the workers. And if you mix politics with trade unionism too much then that will not make for stable government.[34]

The subsequent development of the splinter union, the RHEU, was outlined at the beginning of this chapter. It is now necessary to proceed to a more detailed analysis of its ideological stance, and the sources and bases of its support.

The RHEU leadership's ideological stance

The new union's policy position, as enunciated by its general secretary, K. G. Quartey, was opposed to that of the TUC and the mother union on two main issues. Firstly, Quartey argued that Bentum's TUC, formally constituted and structured as it was in line with the industrial relations legislation of the CPP regime, was basically undemocratic. In particular, he objected to the order of elections within the trade union movement, by which the secretary-general of the TUC was first elected, then the general secretaries of the national unions, and finally the local branch and association officials. 'Such a practice', he claimed, 'enables the Secretary-General to influence the elections of the national unions, particularly in the choice of General Secretaries.' [35] Bentum, he implied, had been able to maintain Thompson in power against the wishes of the Railway Union rank and file.

In response, the leadership of the mother union pointed out that there had been no interference from Bentum in the Railway Union's elections, unless his refusal to dismiss Thompson in 1969 were to be construed as such; that Bentum had in fact supported the reform of the union along more democratic lines by reinstituting the Working Committee; and that, at the TUC Congress of 1967, Quartey himself had concurred with the majority of delegates that to reverse the order of elections would unfortunately be financially and procedurally impracticable. [36] (If the elections for local officials were held first, and a branch official was subsequently elected as a national officer, fresh elections would have to be held to fill the vacated post.) Nevertheless, Quartey certainly did have a point as regards the failure to reform the procedure for election of national officers. The CPP institution of equal representation for each branch was still official procedure, and this clearly did not provide for adequate representation of the wishes of the Sekondi-Takoradi rank and file who comprised more than half the union's total membership.

Quartey's second major criticism of the TUC leadership was that it often lent its tacit support to strike actions instead of insisting on utilisation of the available procedures for peaceful negotiation. This was not so much a question of supporting the government line, he emphasised, as one of recognising the general failure of strike actions to attain the desired improvements in wages or conditions of service. Truly resourceful and energetic union leaders should be able to secure redress of the workers' most pressing grievances through the existing negotiation machinery. Of course, since the main mechanism for wage adjustment consisted in specially appointed commissions, this assumed a government essentially well-intentioned toward the workers. Quartey and his fellow union leaders admitted to having a great deal of faith in the ability and good intentions of the Progress Party regime. 'But if it doesn't rule very well, if it does nothing good for us, then certainly we will consider strike action and decide to vote for another party at the next elections.' [37] Part of the attraction of Quartey's leadership lay in the fact that he had close ties with Progress Party Ministers, and could, it was hoped, use these to secure redress of outstanding grievances, in particular through pressing for a speedy

155

investigation into 'the tradesmen's case' by the Pay Research Unit. But it was at the same time crucial to the retention of his support to maintain a convincing image of relative independence of the government, and of primary commitment to rank-and-file interests and opinion. A. Y. Ankomah, who tended to speak more passionately and openly of his allegiance to the Progress Party, had sometimes to be hushed up by his colleagues at mass meetings for just this reason. And, as we shall see, Quartey was to experience great difficulty in controlling his rank and file in September 1971, owing to his failure to maintain a consistent line over the budget and the consequent spread of doubts as to the location of his primary allegiance. It was indicative of the bases and the limits of his support that mother-union members generally charged the splinter-union rank and file not with being PP enthusiasts, but rather with being easily misled ('since they are mostly illiterates') by party politicians among their leadership.

The sources and bases of support for the two unions

By the end of 1970, the splinter union could claim the support of almost two-thirds of the Location rank and file, and approximately a third of the workers employed at Takoradi harbour. Thereafter there was little alteration in the situation until, in September–October 1971, some splinter-union supporters started drifting back to the mother union.

Tribal differences, it should first be noted, played no perceptible role in the determination of lines of division and allegiance. The leadership cadres of both unions were tribally heterogeneous but predominantly Fanti, as were their rank-and-file followings (see Table 7.2).

Slightly more than half the splinter-union supporters interviewed claimed to have voted for the Progress Party in the 1969 elections. But this was

Table 7.2. *Tribal composition of rival union followings*[38]

Tribe	RPWU	RHEU
Fanti	25[a]	18
Ahanta	6	7
Nzima	3	1
Ashanti	3	3
Akwapim	3	–
Ewe	–	3
Others	2	–

[a] Absolute numbers of interviewees.

also the case with almost half of the mother-union supporters (see Table 7.3). There was no strong or simple correlation, therefore, between party and union allegiance. Nor, as Table 7.4 makes clear, did members of the two unions differ greatly in their conceptions of union purpose and priorities. The most obvious difference in this respect was between members of both unions on the one hand, and non-members on the other. The latter

Table 7.3. *Electoral affiliations of Location labour force*

Progress Party	44%
Other parties	20%
Non-voters	36%

By union membership:

	RPWU	RHEU	Non-members
Progress Party	41%	56%	31%
Other parties	26%	13%	19%
Non-voters	33%	31%	50%

Table 7.4. *Conceptions of union priorities*[39]

	RPWU members	RHEU members	Non-members
(a) Obtaining improved conditions of service and promotion opportunities	55%[a]	48%	88%
(b) Bridging the wages gap between the lower- and higher-paid	63%	59%	25%
(c) Obtaining more influence in the administration of the industry	10%	15%	25%
(d) Developing more union spirit and solidarity among workers	32%	37%	18%
(e) Improving the education and discipline of the workers	47%	63%	75%
(f) Making workers more politically conscious	6%	4%	0%
(g) Establishing a fuller programme of social activities and facilities	10%	0%	6%
(h) Helping to provide employment for the jobless	77%	74%	63%

[a] Interviewees were asked to select from eight alternative goals the three which they considered of highest priority for the Ghanaian unions. Percentages therefore refer to the number of interviewees selecting, e.g., (a) as one of their three highest priorities.

were far more concerned than union members with promotion opportunities, workers' discipline (or productivity) and education, and far less
concerned with wage-levels as such or with union solidarity. The splinter-
union supporters, also, were more concerned than mother-union members
with productivity and education, but on all other questions were in substantial agreement with the mother-union members. That is to say, they
attached the highest priority to helping reduce the unemployment level,
and bridging the wages gap between higher and lower income groups.

It did appear to be the case, however, that in July 1971 a significantly
higher proportion of splinter-union supporters held favourable views of
the PP regime's character and economic policies. Almost half of those
interviewed considered that the country's politico-administrative elite
were economically capable, reasonably honest, and genuinely attempting
to set an example of self-sacrifice, whereas extremely few mother-union
supporters believed this (see Table 7.5). Moreover, in spite of the fact that
most of the splinter-union members were agreed with the mother-union
members in opposing the introduction of a national development levy,
there was a significant difference in the proportion who granted their
general approval to the July 1971 budget (see Table 7.6). The more favourable attitude adopted by the splinter-union supporters appeared to
derive not from any difference of opinion as to the merits of the rural
development programme (which nearly all agreed to be a good thing),
but from the expectation that they would soon be compensated by the
Campbell Commission or the Pay Research Unit.

It would appear, then, that the leaders of the splinter union had succeeded in presenting the PP regime's policies and future intentions to their
rank and file in a more credible and attractive light than that in which
they were viewed by the majority of mother-union supporters. Whereas
virtually all of the latter, including those who had helped vote the Progress Party into power, had become rapidly disillusioned with the regime,

Table 7.5. *Political attitudes of Location labour force*

| | % giving positive response | |
	RPWU	RHEU
Do you think Ghana's political leaders and senior civil servants are:		
(a) mostly fairly honest	22%	38%
(b) setting an example of sacrifice	11%	36%
(c) improving the country's economic situation	38%	61%

Table 7.6. *Attitudes to the 1971 budget*

Questions	% giving positive responses	
	RPWU	RHEU
(a) Do you generally approve of the recent budget?	38%	61%
(b) Do you think the national development levy is justified?	14%	38%
(c) Do you agree that the government's first priority should be rural development?	91%	93%
(d) Do you expect to gain any wage increase from the Campbell Commission or the Pay Research Unit?	36%	85%

the splinter-union leaders had conducted something of a holding operation with their own supporters by performing their 'interpretative' function. It is important to stress, however, that this was never more than a difference of degree, that the majority of splinter-union members were cynical as to the honesty of the regime, and that for few, if any, did sympathy for the PP regime entail willingness to entertain a close alliance with it.

Support for the splinter-union leaders initially (and primarily) derived from sources other than common party allegiance, or shared general attitudes toward the government's policies. Quist, Quartey and Ankomah had proved themselves champions of labour through their sustained and courageous opposition to the Nkrumah regime, and through their outspoken criticisms of Thompson's inefficiency as general secretary. Quist, in particular, enjoyed immense popularity at Location, and especially among the tradesmen in the Carriage and Wagons Department, whose case for parity of status with the artisans he had insistently pressed. An element of patronage also tied the tradesmen to his support, since he was apparently always willing to help them out with a cedi or two when they were in especially difficult financial straits. A number of illiterate interviewees gave as their main reason for supporting the splinter union the simple fact that they had always followed Quist. Although he was not present in person on the Railway Union scene in 1969–71, Quartey was seen as his chosen successor, and Essuman and Wiafe had taken up his spokesmanship of the tradesmen's case.

As this formulation implies, however, the following of the splinter-union leaders derived from a combination of respect for their general qualities and past records with their identification with the grievances of particular groups of workers. And this identification was generally decisive in

159

influencing workers' attitudes towards the course of action Quartey advocated and pursued in 1970–1. Most of the artisans and apprentices at Location concluded that 'Although Quartey is a strong trade unionist and we would have liked him to be our leader, he became too politically ambitious'.[40] Members of the Quist–Quartey faction retained their credibility as champions of the rank and file primarily amongst those groups of workers who had special reason to trust in their determination and ability to redress particular, sectional grievances. Hence, the large majority of tradesmen at Location supported the splinter union, and indeed most of its support came from workers in this job category (see Table 7.7).

As previously indicated, the tradesmen's case had been a long-standing issue in Railway Union politics, Thompson's greatest 'sin' as general secretary having been his failure to secure government action on the matter through the Mills–Odoi Commission. The main grievance involved here was readily understandable. In accordance with the government's 'artisan structure' instituted in 1963, full artisan status was reserved for those who had successfully completed the Railway and Harbour Administration's own five-year apprenticeship scheme. This automatically entitled its possessors to pensions, vacation allowances and various perquisites such as free travel on the railways. 'Tradesman' status, on the other hand, referred, to the majority of skilled (tradesmen grade I) and semi-skilled (tradesmen grade II) workshop employees who, without taking this official apprenticeship course, had been recruited from outside on the basis of their training in the mines or local craft industries, for example, and had passed a government trade test. Although they performed very much the same type and standard of work, tradesmen (grade I) received marginally lower rates of pay than the artisans, were not entitled to pensions on retirement and received none of the side-benefits of pensionable staff. They were debarred, moreover, from progressing beyond the 'senior tradesmen' level into the ranks of foremen and junior foremen. In consequence, many tradesmen of long service found themselves in the invidious position of being required to help train apprentices who might quite rapidly become their supervisors.

As early as 1963, the strength of feeling over these anomalies was apparent from reports that 'the tradesmen have refused to train the

Table 7.7. *Support for each union by job category*

	Artisans	Tradesmen	Apprentices	Labourers
RPWU	57%	18%	100%	36%
RHEU	23%	65%	–	28%
Neither	20%	17%	–	36%

apprentices, and they [the apprentices] are even debarred from using the tools which belong to the tradesmen'.[41] In spite of persistent pressure from Quist, Essuman and Wiafe, the union's executive had failed by January 1970 to gain more than a vague government assurance that the Pay Research Unit had been detailed to enquire into the matter. The tradesmen hoped that Quartey would be able to use his personal contacts with Jatoe Kaleo, Minister of Transport and Communications, to speed up the PRU's enquiry and secure early government action on the report. This was clearly the main reason why they supported his break-away from the ineffectual mother union. At the same time, however, Quartey's general stance of opposition to strike action and his emphasis on the advantages of peaceful negotiation carried some real conviction with a group of workers whose particular grievances the government had declared itself prepared to consider. A policy of peaceful negotiation offered little prospect of demand-satisfaction for those such as the artisans, in contrast, who were rather concerned to fight for general wage increases for the lower-paid workers in the face of the government's apparent unwillingness to make any such general concessions.

The apprentices, like the artisans, tended to respond enthusiastically to Bentum's call for a major reform of the national wage structure, since, as trainee artisans, they obviously had a keen interest in the future pattern of rewards. It is not to belittle their enthusiasm for Bentum's general position to point out that they also had particular grounds for hostility to the splinter unionists (as their absolutely unanimous support for the mother union might lead one to suspect). Essuman and Wiafe, as branch chairman and secretary at Location in 1968–70, had displayed little sympathy for the apprentices' protest against the threatened introduction of examinations. Rather, they had openly supported the management's plan to make them sit an examination at the end of their five-year course, considering it unfair that only the tradesmen should have to pass some form of trade test. Thompson, Forson and Imbeah, however, successfully opposed this plan, and thereby earned the gratitude and solid support of all the Location apprentices.[42]

To some degree, the pattern of allegiance to the two unions followed similar lines at Takoradi harbour. Although precise figures were impossible to obtain, both sets of union leaders agreed that the splinter union was especially strong amongst workers in the Electrical and Marine Departments. Approximately three-quarters of the Electrical Department workers followed their long-serving association secretary, A. Y. Ankomah, into the breakway group. Ankomah had built up a strong personal following in his association 'constituency', primarily through his record of grievance-handling, but also through the assistance he had given to some of his members in gaining employment in the railways, and in helping them to pass their trade tests. Nevertheless, the fact that some of the Electrical Department workers stayed with the RPWU demonstrated that even Ankomah could not claim to possess a totally reliable bloc of personal followers.

In the Marine Department, some two-thirds of the 300 workers employed there left the mother union out of anger at its leadership's inability (or refusal) to redress their grievance over the 'salvage case'. In 1968, a Nigerian ship had run aground just off Takoradi harbour, and the Marine Department's tug and launch crews had been called out on a salvage operation. The tug crews played the largest part in this operation, but the launch crews involved were understandably aggrieved when only the former received the special salvage allowance, their own efforts going completely unrewarded. B. T. Nahr, the Marine Association secretary, was (quite unfairly) suspected of favouritism in his handling of this matter since he was himself a tug crewman. All the launch crews joined the splinter union when Quartey assured them that he would intervene with the attorney-general, Victor Owusu, to secure a more just settlement.[43]

Yet these two groups of workers in the Electrical and Marine Departments accounted for only a minority of the splinter union's total support at Takoradi harbour (approximately 300 out of 1,110 members). Quartey enjoyed the support of a number (though generally a minority) of workers in all of the departments there, most of which were very much larger than the Electrical and Marine Departments. There was no indication that sectional economic grievances or patron–client links played a major role in determining the allegiance of these workers. In the opinion of virtually all interviewees at Takoradi, the division centred on the issue of whether or not Quartey (whose past record as Takoradi Branch secretary was universally respected) was seeking to intrude party politics into trade unionism, and, related to this, whether it could possibly be justified to secede from the main Railway Union and so divide the railway and harbour workers. In addition, the majority of mother-union members expressed great admiration for Bentum and found Quartey's criticisms of the TUC quite unjustified. There seems no reason to doubt that these ideological differences constituted the real determinants of allegiance in the case of the majority of workers at Takoradi harbour.

It is worth noting, however, that mother-union supporters frequently explained their opponents' apparent blindness to the merits of Bentum and to the dangers of Quartey's brand of political unionism in terms of their illiteracy. Although precise figures on the proportion in each following were not obtained, it was indicative that many splinter-union members acknowledged the existence of this 'educated–illiterate' division, even if they interpreted its significance rather differently from the mother unionists: 'We illiterates must stick together since those tricky people [Bentum, Nahr and Thompson] did nothing for us.' [44] It was also significant in this respect that Quartey deliberately recruited several illiterates to official positions in his union. Mother-union officials, in contrast, were often to be heard complaining, 'Most of our rivals are uneducated, and we find great difficulty in reaching them since those illiterates are so stubborn.'[45] More generally, illiteracy did perhaps constitute an obstacle to the communication of Bentum's views and activities, and thereby contributed to his relative lack of popularity with RHEU members.

The significance of the 'educated–illiterate' division was also frequently remarked upon at Sekondi Location, but there its importance as an independent variable was difficult to assess since it largely coincided with job category divisions (see Table 7.8).

Far more clearly than at Takoradi harbour, the basic pattern of allegiance at Location followed the lines of sectional economic differences. Yet attitudinal differences (or differences of opinion and of degrees of confidence in particular union leaders) did constitute an additional dimension of some importance, and sometimes led individuals to act at variance with the general pattern. Of the artisans interviewed at Location, for instance, 23 per cent supported the splinter union, generally out of personal admiration for Quist and Quartey. As one of these explained, 'They [Quist and Quartey] have always talked straight with us and said things boldly. If it's no good, they say so. But if they lead us to expect something, we know it will materialise. That Thompson was too tricky, and the new lot are not much better.' [46] On the other hand, 18 per cent of tradesmen interviewed remained in the ranks of the mother union. All of these expressed admiration for Bentum's leadership of the TUC, and scepticism as to the wisdom of 'moving so closely with the government as Quartey appears to be doing'.[47] Some tradesmen also followed J. K. Baaku in turning back from support of Quartey and taking a neutral stance when the latter proved ready to split the railway workers into two

Table 7.8. *Educational characteristics of Location labour force*

Job categories	% educated beyond 'elementary' level
Artisans	100%
Apprentices	100%
Tradesmen	59%
Labourers	27%

unions: 'There could be no reason for this except selfish political interest. I will not become a member of either until they come together, but attend the meetings of both and hit from outside.' [48]

The reunification of the railway workers

It is important to stress the fact that a certain community of political attitudes and perceived economic interest continued to characterise the railway workers in 1970–1, despite their division into competing camps. The large majority of supporters of both unions were extremely cynical about politicians as a class, and inclined to blame the management and government for low productivity and the need to resort to strike actions. They were also determined to assert the ethic of leadership accountability to the union rank and file (in distinction from the government view that the primary responsibility of union leaders was to 'explain' government policies to their rank and file). Admittedly, the splinter-union supporters displayed a somewhat more sympathetic attitude to the economic difficulties and policies of the PP regime, and proved ready, in their financial desperation, to connive at their leaders' cultivation of ties of friendship with Progress Party Ministers. But they immediately reacted, perhaps a little unrealistically, against any indication that the representative responsibilities of these leaders were being distorted or compromised by their party political loyalties. K. G. Quartey faced a crisis of credibility over this issue in his handling of rank-and-file opinion on the July 1971 budget.

At a Location mass meeting on 5 August, Quartey argued that, by seeking to relieve the unemployment problem and reduce food prices, the budget should bring substantial benefits to the workers. Several of his rank-and-file members, while not dissenting from this, insisted that the national development levy imposed an excessive burden on them, and should be modified to exempt the lower-paid (i.e. the skilled and unskilled manual workers). Quartey, in turn, agreed with this, but pointed out that the Campbell Wage Review Commission was due to release its report very soon, and might award them a more substantial wage increase than the amount due to be deducted by the levy. He promised to travel to Accra to request Minister Jatoe Kaleo for an assurance on this matter. If this was not forthcoming, then they would protest against the levy. 'No money come, no money go', he shouted, to enthusiastic applause. [49]

Just one week later, however, he reported back to the rank and file:

> The Minister has told me that there is no money in the country, and so there will be no increase for us. But he will be sending the Pay Research Unit very soon, so you must tell the workers to pay the

levy as requested. If you want promotions you should not follow the advice of people who say to go on strike.[50]

This was not at all well received. The first speaker from the floor expressed the widespread feeling of disenchantment:

> You have been to Accra just to see your girlfriends and have brought us back unwanted messages. You have not been able to do what we wanted. We are very fed up with your speech. It is making us very angry. I tell you, general secretary, if money is deducted from my pay next month, I will go on strike even if I have to do so on my own.[51]

Another rank-and-file member followed up with the charge that

> These politicians are asking us to tighten our belts while they are filling their own pockets. We all know the ins and outs of it. The same thing will happen to this regime as to the old one if they are not more careful. When will the Pay Research Unit come? We demand to know. If they do nothing for us, it will be the same as 1961.[52]

Quartey sought to pacify his followers by assuring them that if the Pay Research Unit had not arrived at Location within three weeks, then he would call them out on strike. Fortunately for him, and perhaps for the Progress Party regime, the PRU officials met with the leaders of the two unions within this time limit. Most of the splinter union's members were thereby persuaded to stay on duty during the September strike. They received their due reward with the announcement in November that the tradesmen's grievances would be redressed and that several categories of employee were to receive increases in their incremental scales. All the same, two or three hundred of the splinter-union members did join the strike, and approximately half of these 'crossed the carpet' back to the mother union, dismayed at the realisation that they were being used as a counter in the government's campaign against the TUC.

Others simply refused to reregister with the splinter union (the Industrial Relations Act of September 1971 required all unions to reregister their members) and, together with J. K. Baaku and others who had refused to join either union, set out to work for the reunification of the railway workers. The leadership of the splinter union refused to consider this prior to the military coup of January 1972. But, in March of that year, partly under pressure from the new regime, they agreed to form an Interim Management Committee, composed of representatives of both camps, and to participate in the election of officers for a reformed, reunified Railway Union. According to the admission of one of the former splinter-union leaders, 'There was much relief amongst our members at this news.'[53]

165

II CLASS, POWER AND IDEOLOGY

8

Class formation in Ghana

We now return to the general questions raised at the start of this study and consider them in a more systematic, theoretical manner than has been attempted hitherto. The foregoing chapters have demonstrated the importance of the railway workers as a group in the Ghanaian political arena. It is now appropriate to analyse the sources of this exceptional political strength and assess the significance of its being wielded with such relative consistency in opposition to post- as well as pre-Independence governments. One central question which must be considered here is how far a Marxist model of class conflict illuminates railway worker political behaviour. In more general (and less preconceived) terms, this section is primarily concerned with the interrelationship of socio-economic position, organisation, ideology and political action. What role, for example, should be attributed to ideological factors in determining railway worker political behaviour, and how does the railway workers' ideology (or 'political culture') reflect their socio-economic situation? It is clear that an assessment of the significance of railway worker political activity should in turn take into account its 'class' implications, though, as will be argued subsequently, this is not the only perspective from which it should be judged.

It is worth noting at the outset that a classical Marxist interpretation of the developing political role and orientation of industrial wage-earners in sub-Saharan Africa is far from generally accepted among latter-day Marxian theorists. This in itself is perhaps not entirely surprising (though it may well be short-sighted), given the behaviour until now characteristic of much of unionised labour in most of the African states – the general lack of sustained trade union radicalism, and the apparently passive incorporation of most unions into single-party systems or, more commonly now, their submission to the authoritarian control of military regimes. It is partly, no doubt, on account of its claim to explain these tendencies that the 'Fanonist' thesis of Giovanni Arrighi and John Saul has proved so widely influential.[1]

This thesis, in sharp deviation from the classical Marxist model, suggests that the economic interests and political affinities of the African proletariat on the one hand, and the post-Independence elites on the other, become increasingly complementary in the course of economic development. Both groups join, through the agency of government and overseas firms, in expropriating the economic surplus generated by the peasantry – the main (even the sole) productive force in most African societies, and the poorest, potentially most revolutionary class. The main domestic polarisation of interests occurs, to put it very simply, between two economic sectors, urban and rural, rather than within one mode of production.

Arrighi and Saul do, however, perceive one major source of differentiation within the urban wage-earner group. The mass of unskilled labourers are to be regarded as peasants temporarily engaged in wage employment, who derive the bulk of their subsistence from outside the wage economy, rather than as part of the urban proletariat proper. Together with the unemployed, they possess interests sharply antagonistic to the present order and might, as in Fanon's vision, come to act as the urban spearhead of a peasant-based revolutionary movement. As far as skilled and semi-skilled workers are concerned, on the other hand,

> Higher wages and salaries . . . foster the stabilization of the better-paid section of the labour force whose high incomes justify the severance of ties with the traditional economy. Stabilization, in turn, promotes specialization, greater bargaining power, and further increases in the incomes of this small section of the labour force, which represents the proletariat proper of tropical Africa. These workers enjoy incomes three or more times higher than those of unskilled labourers and, together with the elites and sub-elites in bureaucratic employment in the civil service, constitute what we call the labour aristocracy of tropical Africa. It is the discretionary consumption of this class which absorbs a significant proportion of the surplus produced in the money economy.[2]

Minor differences of interest might develop within this 'aristocracy', the imposition of wage restraint on unionised labour, for example, being made difficult by the unambiguously privileged position of the politicians and the salariat. Yet such differences are of slight consequence alongside the overriding consensus.

It is significant (though also somewhat ironical) that Elliot Berg and Jeffrey Butler resort to an essentially similar argument in their influential interpretation of trade union development in sub-Saharan Africa.[3] In their view, the large majority of unions are either apolitical by inclination or simply too weak to resist the government's attempt to control and incorporate them. The one group of workers possessing the organisational ability and collective strength necessary to play a significant political role – the skilled workers – has, they suggest, become relatively privileged since Independence and therefore disinclined to present any kind of radical opposition to the government or the established pattern of socio-economic development.

As a general statement, the 'labour aristocracy' thesis suffers from a number of serious failings and limitations, some the result of over-generalising from particular instances, others of a conceptual and theoretical nature. The most important of these can be stated quite simply and briefly. Conceptually, it is quite wrong to see the peasantry as a single class or as the sole productive, surplus-producing and exploited group in African societies. Empirically, Arrighi's and Saul's interpretation of the socio-economic position of unionised workers, whilst no doubt valid for many white-collar employees, and possibly for skilled workers in certain industries and countries, is quite misleading as to the relative real incomes of skilled and semi-skilled manual workers in the cities of Ghana – the 'backbone' of the trade union movement in that country. (One may suspect this is true of most other African countries, and that Arrighi's and Saul's presentation rests on an atypical, historically limited East African experience, though the full range of data required to substantiate this is not at present available.) [4] In any case, and this is the most important point, Arrighi and Saul operate theoretically with an over-simple conception of the relationship between objective economic position, 'class-consciousness' and radical political action.[5] The writings of Marx on this question, though admittedly susceptible to a degree of divergent interpretation, incorporate sophisticated sociological insights which the followers of Fanon ignore to their cost.

Surplus appropriation and income inequality

Arrighi and Saul focus on two main dimensions of class structure: the patterns of surplus appropriation and income distribution. Only implicitly does their analysis refer to the social and cultural relations of workers to each other or to other classes (as, for example, in its treatment of 'proletarianisation'). This latter dimension requires more explicit and extensive consideration. 'Class-consciousness' – without which classes can hardly be said to exist as political entities – is expressed in, and conditioned by, prevailing social and cultural formations. In each respect, it will be seen, the term 'labour aristocracy' seriously misrepresents the position of skilled manual workers in Ghana's developing social structure.

Firstly, it is far too simple to suggest that only the 'peasantry' produce any significant economic surplus, and that all urban wage-earners take part in expropriating this surplus. While it is undoubtedly true that the Ghanaian economy is highly dependent on the production and export of cocoa, the transport and service industries are hardly less important to cocoa's arrival on the international market than its actual cultivation. There is something to be said for Arrighi's and Saul's interpretation of the pattern of production and appropriation in African societies, recognising as it does the radically different politico-economic structures of industrialised and underdeveloped societies. But it is simply perverse to suggest that skilled manual workers, even if in government employment, are essentially non-productive, however much this may be true of many white-collar officials. A more balanced interpretation would recognise the existence of serious economic conflict *within* both urban and rural sectors of production as well as *between* them. The rural producers might most obviously be exploited by the buyers and distributors of agricultural produce – in the case of cocoa, foreign firms and government agencies. But Ghana's manual wage-earners, including the skilled workers, are in a similar and potentially no less serious position of conflict with the politico-administrative elite over the pattern of distribution of the national surplus, and over the failure to curb corrupt practices by state officials to the detriment of both rural producers and urban poor.

With what justification can the skilled workers be regarded as part of the urban poor? Saul and Arrighi include them in that class which enjoys incomes 'three or more times higher than those of unskilled labourers'.[6] The first point to be noted here is that this generalisation is based on East African experience. In Kenya in particular, the large majority of skilled workers are employed in capital-intensive, multi-national manufacturing enterprises, which, as Arrighi rightly points out, are so technologically structured as to permit a relative lack of emphasis on keeping wages as low as possible. The ability and willingness of these enterprises to pay high wages to attract and stabilise a skilled labour force results, he suggests, in a spiral process, with African governments becoming increasingly concerned to win over skilled workers from one sector to the other.[7]

In Ghana, however, a majority of the country's skilled workers have been employed in government industries or public corporations. In the absence of a serious labour shortage, private industries have tended to follow the government's lead in keeping wages down (though the wage rates for skilled workers in large-scale private enterprises have still been slightly higher than for government employees).[8] Consequently, the differential between skilled and unskilled workers' wage rates has not significantly widened since the 1920s and remains at something less than 2:1. In the Railway Administration, for example, the average earnings of skilled workers stood at N₵39 in 1970,[9] compared to the national minimum wage of N₵21 and the actual average earnings for unskilled railway workers of approximately N₵24 (see Table 8.1). Secondly, John Weeks' work suggests an important difference between East Africa and West Africa in the criteria used for assessing the minimum wage by both colonial and post-Independence administrations.[10] In East Africa, where the creation of a surplus wage labour force has proved a considerable problem for employers, and that of a stable, skilled labour force an even greater one, the minimum wage was calculated soon after the Second World War to take account of the costs for maintenance of workers' wives and children, and various other obligatory or socially desirable expenditures. By contrast, in Nigeria and Ghana, countries which have generally experienced little in the way of wage labour shortages, the minimum wage was calculated to cover no more than the basic subsistence costs of the individual worker. Successive wage commissions did no more than raise the minimum wage in correspondence with rises in the cost of living. Often, in fact, they did less than this on the grounds of preventing the emergence of significant urban–rural income differentials. Any suggestion by the more radical members of wage commissions that a more generous notion of 'need' should be utilised in making recommendations was invariably rejected by other members and by the administration of the day (with the partial exception of Biney's and Woode's influence on the relatively generous Lidbury–Gbedemah Award of 1952). The fact that the rates of pay for skilled workers in Ghana, unlike Kenya, have generally been kept down in steady relation to the minimum wage further helps to account for their lower relative incomes compared to those of skilled workers in East Africa.

Because of the reluctance of Ghanaian wage commissions to compensate workers fully for rises in the cost of living, the real wage levels

Table 8.1. *Rates of pay in the Railway Administration* (*per day*)

	1910	1930	1950	1970
Labourers	1*s*. 0*d*.	1*s*. 6*d*.	3*s*. 6*d*.	7*s*. 6*d*.[a]
Artisans	2*s*. 0*d*. to 3*s*. 0*d*.	2*s*. 6*d*. to 5*s*. 0*d*.	6*s*. 0*d*. to 10*s*. 0*d*.	12*s*. 0*d*. to £1

Source: *RAA*, Railway Administration Staff Lists.

[a] After 1968 many unskilled workers received considerably more than the national minimum wage of 7*s*. 6*d*., or 75 pesewas per day, in accordance with the Mills–Odoi Commission's recommendation that incremental scales be introduced for unskilled workers in government employment.

for both skilled and unskilled actually fell between 1939 and 1971 from an index point of 100 in the former year to one of 73 in the latter.[11] The 1950s provided a temporary exception to this tendency, with real wage rates rising back to the 1939 level, and reaching slightly above it by 1961. But a number of points need to be noted here. Firstly, the 1939 level was hardly considered 'aristocratic' for skilled workers, or even 'the bare minimum' for the unskilled, by those best qualified to judge. Captain J. Dickinson, the Colonial Government's first labour officer, estimated that the 1939 level 'is now on the level of 1914, and it is certain that the cost of living has risen since then'.[12] The wage rate for unskilled workers was, theoretically perhaps, the minimum required for an adequate diet, but 'since the labourer, like anyone else, spends a certain proportion of his wages on luxuries, cigarettes for example, or visits to a lover, he thereby does not reach the standard but lives in a sort of secondary poverty'.[13] Secondly (and this theoretically most crucial point will receive fuller consideration later), the increase in real incomes which the railway artisans enjoyed in 1950–61 did not prevent their becoming steadily more resentful of the growing self-enrichment and autocracy of the CPP leadership. Finally, the 1950s wage increases were largely the product of successful pressure by the unions on a relatively weak pre-Independence government. Once it was more firmly in the saddle, the CPP plutocracy proved unwilling to accept skilled labour as the most junior of financial partners.

The Mills–Odoi Commission estimated that between 1960 and 1966 the value of the minimum wage fell by some 45 per cent, and acknowledged that the living standards of unskilled labourers in the latter year were 'distressingly low'.[14] The commission considered it doubtful whether their real incomes compared favourably with those of hired farm labourers, the poorest section of the rural populace (at least in the southern half of Ghana). During 1968–71 the government's refusal to grant a wage increase in spite of continuing inflation meant a further deterioration in the real incomes of lower-paid wage-earners. While the precise extent of this is difficult to calculate, some indication is provided by the TUC's portrayal of the lower-paid worker's plight in its proposals to the Campbell Commission of 1971, as well as by the National Redemption Council Government's decision in September 1974 to double the minimum wage.[15]

Skilled manual workers have, of course, been consistently better paid than either unskilled workers or hired farm labourers, but it is, to say the least, highly debatable whether they have been (or are) 'privileged' compared to the mass of the 'peasantry'. It is extremely difficult to generalise about real rural incomes, partly because of the shortage of reliable data on the subject, partly because what data we do possess indicate immense differences in income between large and small farmers, and between average incomes in the different regions. In a recent article, Keith Hinchliffe exposed the unjustified assumptions underlying most estimates of the average urban–rural differential and, more particularly, their use to assess the position of the mass of lower-paid urban wage-earners.[16] Utilising exceptionally reliable and detailed statistics on the earnings of the main labouring groups in Northern Nigeria and a highly sophisticated comparative procedure, he concluded that, with the exception of those educated beyond secondary school level, 'Urban workers are very unlikely to be much better off than their farming brothers.' [17] It is not possible to attempt so sophisticated an analysis of the Ghanaian situation here, and the following assessment is based on rather rough approximations. The substantial applicability of Hinchliffe's conclusion to the case of Ghana is nevertheless clear.

Polly Hill's research has clearly illustrated the thoroughly capitalist structure of much Ghanaian cocoa production, and the early development of a large, imported, hired labour force to work on the cocoa farms.[18] In consequence, economic differentiation within the rural populace has already proceeded to a degree where the notion of a single peasant class is transparently inappropriate. Some indication of this is provided by Kodwo Ewusi's calculation of the distribution of income among cocoa farmers in 1963–4 (see Table 8.2). This clearly reveals the development of a class of large capitalist farmers, some of whom, according to Ewusi, earn as much as N₵12,000 per annum, while others might be categorised as 'middle' or 'poor' peasantry.

How then to generalise about rural–urban differentials? The difficulty is compounded by the tendency for different sizes and kinds of agricultural producer to be located in different parts of the country. (Most Ghanaian agriculturists are, of course, poorer than the majority of Ashanti/Brong-Ahafo cocoa farmers.) If, however, following Blair Rourke's observations, we take the Eastern Region as the median, information on

Table 8.2. *Distribution of income of cocoa farmers, 1963–4*

Income class, N₵	Percentage of farmers	Total income N₵ millions
1–60	18.0	1.7
60–120	20.0	4.2
120–240	22.0	9.1
240–600	25.0	22.2
600–1,200	10.0	19.1
1,200 and above	5.0	25.7

N.B. Not including imputed income from consumption of own food.
Source: Ewusi, *Distribution of Monetary Incomes*, p. 75.

the relative incomes of rural and urban households is provided by a survey conducted by Dutta-Roy.[19] This suggested an average imputed income for rural families of N₵33.08 per month, compared to one of N₵37.54 for urban families. This latter figure is marginally higher than the median monthly wage of skilled workers in Takoradi – N₵36.43 – calculated by Margaret Peil on the basis of a sample survey conducted in the same year (1967) as Dutta-Roy's.[20] When considering urban real incomes, moreover, one should take into account the higher costs incurred by many wage-earners in supporting dependants in the city. Some would also argue the need to adjust both rural and urban incomes for the effect of remittances from the urban to the rural areas, which, in the case of Ghana's skilled workers, certainly do remain sizeable.[21] It is debatable, however, to what degree this is a matter of unilateral or two-way transfer, and it is in any case unnecessary to take this into account to establish the main point: whatever difference does obtain between average rural incomes and those of skilled workers in Ghana's cities is clearly insufficient to justify depicting the latter as a privileged group.

Some indication of the factory workers' own perception of their economic position relative to that of the 'peasantry' is provided by Margaret Peil's survey of status perceptions.[22] The large majority of her interviewees, she points out, equated status ranking with relative income-levels. Factory workers placed 'farmers' 10th on the ladder of occupational prestige, 'fitters' (i.e. skilled workers) 21st, 'farm labourers' 33rd and 'building labourers' 34th, out of a total of 35 occupations. Of course, the perceptions of other groups might be expected to differ considerably from those of the factory workers themselves, and there are no grounds for thinking that the latter are any more objective than others. But none of the urban populace at all in touch with realities could imagine that skilled manual workers enjoy an 'aristocratic' standard of living. The most important sense in which they are better off than the unskilled and unemployed is that they enjoy relative security of employment. Very few of the unskilled workers I interviewed considered that the gap between skilled and unskilled workers' incomes was excessively great. Virtually all agreed that the greater training and skills of the artisans justified their being paid considerably higher wages.

Moreover, any such difference of income cannot but appear trivial in the light of the huge and growing gap between the mass of low–paid workers and the elite of politicians and senior civil servants. By 1968–71, as the Ghana TUC leadership frequently pointed out, the income differential between the lowest- and highest-paid employees in government service was in the proportion 1:39. In more concrete terms, the annual income of the general manager of the Railway Administration was

N₵6,972 and that of senior executive officers N₵1,608, whereas the skilled workers' starting rate was N₵402. The political elite were even more highly paid than the senior civil servants. At the end of the CPP period, Ministers received salaries of N₵9,000 per annum. The NLC regime awarded its civilian commissioners who were performing ministerial duties N₵6,000. The Progress Party Government decided to pay its Ministers N₵14,000 with additional allowances of N₵4,000. Workers in Sekondi-Takoradi often remarked, 'We workers in Ghana receive so much less than workers in Britain, yet our Ministers and judges receive so much more.'[23] Though inaccurate as regards the absolute salaries of British and Ghanaian Ministers, this view was at least correct in relative terms, and the bitterness with which it was expressed readily understandable.

Such statistics do not of course necessarily mean a great deal unless income tax rates are also taken into account. It is a commonly recognised fact of life in Ghana that members of the elite are normally able to avoid paying the full income tax for which they are liable. Yet, even at face value, Ghanaian income tax rates increase relatively slightly with income-levels. In 1970, a gross monthly emolument of N₵34 attracted a tax of 2 per cent of earnings, N₵100 attracted 6 per cent, N₵500 15 per cent and N₵1,000 27 per cent. There was no super tax.[24] This was a much lower rate of increase than that operative in the United Kingdom, for instance. The picture is further confirmed of a disproportionately rich Ghanaian elite.

Moreover, post-Independence development in Ghana has resulted in a large increase in the elite's proportionate share of national wealth. According to the estimates of Kodwo Ewusi, in 1956 the upper 6 per cent of wage- and salary-earners received 12.9 per cent of the total national income, in 1962 the upper 5.1 per cent received 20.3 per cent, and in 1968 the upper 4.6 per cent accounted for 24.7 per cent.[25] Ewusi concludes, 'The relative distribution of income in Ghana has radically deteriorated, resulting in the relative immiseration of the lower income groups.'[26]

Corruption

It is appropriate to remark briefly here on the position and attitudes of skilled industrial workers with regard to corruption. Corruption might most obviously be seen as a further mechanism of elite self-enrichment and, thereby, an additional source of mass–elite conflict. In certain instances, at least, this is probably too simple a view. As one writer has recently pointed out, 'corruption' and 'patronage' are closely related phenomena, and the apparent docility of the mass of the population in the face of their prevalence is to be explained, in part at least, by the fact that many do stand to benefit substantially from their operation.[27] This is less true of skilled industrial workers, however, than of almost any other group. These

177

workers generally enjoy relative security of employment but extremely limited mobility opportunities. Partly because of the strength of union organisation, their promotion is generally based on seniority rather than, as for clerical workers, on bosses' favouritism and examination qualifications. They consequently stand to gain little from patronage, which affects them mainly in the form of attempts by the government or, sometimes, TUC leaders to win over their union representatives, and is therefore sternly disapproved of as a threat to their corporate unity. Nor do they have the opportunity to benefit from the kind of corruption so widely practised by state officials who come into direct contact with the public. They do, on the other hand, suffer directly (and see themselves as so doing) from corrupt practices on the part of the politico-administrative elite. In the Ghana Railways, for example, the skilled workers frequently attribute the Administration's failure to make a profit, and their own consequent difficulty in justifying wage claims, to the corrupt practices of senior executives. It is widely suspected that railway finances are embezzled on a large scale, and that traffic is reduced by administrative staff demanding bribes from would-be buyers of freight space. Numerous other instances could be cited and their (at least partial) justification documented.

It might be argued that a considerable proportion of the money extracted in such ways is eventually redistributed back to the lower income group through elite hospitality, extended family obligations or other social networks. This question will be examined at greater length in the final section of this chapter. It is worth remarking here, however, that the skilled workers of Sekondi-Takoradi certainly do not think of corruption as operating in this way. It *is* sorely resented. Indeed, if corruption were not fairly widely resented in Ghana, it would be difficult to understand why newly ensconced regimes should attempt to court popular favour by initiating investigations into the corrupt practices of their predecessors. What distinguishes the unionised workers, and especially those of Sekondi-Takoradi, is perhaps less their resentment of corruption than their lack of resignation to it, their feeling that something can and should be done to check it. This feeling derives in part, no doubt, from their own relative success in checking corrupt practices within the political sub-community of the Railway Union. Hence their enthusiasm for Bentum's attempt to develop a similar role for the labour movement on a national scale, as the 'eyes and ears of society'.

Social status, mobility and patronage

The skilled workers of Ghana are most accurately categorised as a relatively secure section of the lower income group. Their depiction as a

178

labour aristocracy retains what little currency it still has in Ghana primarily as a stratagem of governing elites to foster division in the ranks of the poor and divert attention from the major discontinuities in the ladder of economic stratification. Nevertheless, one might properly ask: is not this picture of a society sharply divided into elite and masses quite as oversimplified as that presented by Arrighi and Saul? Surely, the pattern of stratification is more complex, the ladder of stratification more continuous than this suggests. To what degree does the existence of a sizeable middle stratum between elite and masses, and the persistence of a relatively open society with extended family and other ties between the different strata, inhibit the development of conscious class-antagonisms?

It is worth noting in this context that many of the Sekondi-Takoradi workers interviewed by the writer differentiated the social order in terms of 'those big men', 'comfortable people' and 'us poor', rather than a simple mass–elite division. The existence of a fairly distinct middle class was recognised, but the skilled workers did not consider themselves members of it. This is a different view from that generally taken by Ghanaian governments, which have persisted in including the skilled workers, though not the unskilled, in the middle-class category eligible for additional taxation in the form, for example, of the national development levy. Similarly, the 1960 *Survey of High-Level Manpower* distinguished three main strata in Ghanaian urban society: a top-level elite of professionals, senior civil servants and managers (and of course politicians) constituting some 4 per cent of the total urban labour force; a middle class of clerks, traders, miners, transport workers and other skilled workers constituting 16 per cent; and an unskilled category, including petty traders, accounting for 80 per cent.[28] But this categorisation is quite misleading as to the sharpest discontinuities in the prevailing wage and salary structure. The difference between skilled and unskilled workers' incomes is far smaller, in proportionate as well as absolute terms, than that between skilled workers and the middle strata of medium-scale businessmen and middle-ranking executives. Utilising statistics provided by Ewusi, one might rather arrive at the classification of main income groups shown in Table 8.3. This

Table 8.3. *Distribution of income by classes*

Class	% of employment
Lower (N₡1–800)	80.9
Middle (N₡800–2,400)	16.5
Upper (N₡2,400 and above)	2.3

Source: Ewusi, *Distribution of Incomes*, p. 55.

classification has the additional advantage that it corresponds as closely as any such generalisation can to the increasingly apparent differences in life-chances, consumption patterns and social habits between the various strata of Ghanaian urban society. Whereas the skilled worker's income, even if twice that of the unskilled worker, barely enables him to subsist on basic home-produced foodstuffs, the incomes of the middle and upper classes are sufficient to support a far more comfortable and Westernised style of living, entailing the regular consumption of certain imported foodstuffs and beer rather than akpeteshie (the locally produced gin), and the possibility of affording secondary school or even university education for one's children. The question of cultural differences and social distance between classes will receive more detailed consideration shortly. Here, it is important to emphasise the close relationship between education and mobility opportunities in Ghana, and the impact of differential access to educational opportunities on the formation of classes on an inter-generational basis.

While Ghana at Independence was a relatively open society, plentiful in opportunities for individual and inter-generational mobility, it has rapidly become more closed. Such opportunities as earlier existed lay mainly in the field of government employment, private business openings (on any large scale) being relatively limited. A declining economy, combined with the overstaffing of the bureaucracy and state enterprises under the CPP regime, has resulted in a sharp contraction of employment openings at all levels.[29] In this context, the introduction of higher and more rigid educational qualifications for employment in the clerical–executive branch of the civil service, together with the abolition of free secondary school education, might properly be interpreted as an attempt by the elite and middle class to consolidate their position on an inter-generational basis in the face of a serious decline in the number of higher positions available. Certainly, this has severely reduced the chances of sons of lower-paid workers entering the ranks of the elite or even the middle class. One indication that this reality is widely recognised is provided by a finding of Margaret Peil's survey.[30] Nearly all factory workers hoped that their children might in turn become factory workers, preferably in the skilled category. Very few could seriously entertain any hope of their children's becoming 'professionals' or even 'clerical staff'. Recognition of this reality was most pronounced, as one might expect, in Sekondi-Takoradi, the city which has experienced economic decline and the subsequent contraction of job openings in most acute form over the past decade. Only 3 per cent of Takoradi parents expressed the desire that their sons become professionals, compared to 22 per cent of Kumasi parents.

In Sekondi-Takoradi, at least, these three main income groups tend

180

increasingly to lead distinctive styles of social life and to mix predominantly with friends drawn from members of their own class. The elite generally keep 'closed' houses in secluded suburbs of the city, travel always by car rather than by public transport and consume imported European food-stuffs in the main. Their social life consists largely of having friends to dinner. If they go out to eat and drink, it is invariably to a club or to the local plush hotel, the Atlantic, inhabited almost entirely by white expatriates and members of the native elite. The middle class are more inclined to consume traditional foods and to maintain the traditional values of sociability and keeping an open house. They generally live in closer contact with the urban poor, in the smarter central residential areas. But they nevertheless lead distinctly more comfortable, indoor and Westernised lives than the mass of urban residents. If they go out drinking it is to a beer-bar, where the music is quiet and the atmosphere 'cool' (in the local parlance), and where most of the clientele are smartly dressed. Some do still drink akpeteshie occasionally, but this is very much 'on the quiet'. Very few would ever admit to frequenting akpeteshie bars, which they regard as rowdy and vulgar. For the urban poor, their house, or more commonly their single room, serves as little more than a bedroom. Life is led almost entirely out of doors, strolling the streets or sitting and talking with friends on street corners. They generally drink in the akpeteshie bars, which consist of little more than a small shack, or occasionally in one of the dancing bars where both beer and local gin are sold.

This differentiation of various types of hostelry, catering for different social classes, is a far more significant phenomenon than the work of most sociologists suggests. Drinking with friends is a major social activity in Ghana, and the different types of bar present a highly visible indication of social class barriers. The position of the skilled workers in this class structure is vividly illustrated by their social drinking habits. Unless they are single men, the skilled workers cannot possibly afford to drink in beer-bars regularly. On most evenings, therefore, the skilled workers meet friends in akpeteshie bars, where the conversation often turns to the great drinking exploits of Pobee Biney and other cultural heroes. Yet many of these same workers do attempt to save a couple of cedis a month in order to spend at least one evening in a beer-bar with the more esteemed amongst their friends or possibly with middle-class relatives. There is a certain ambivalence, therefore, in the skilled workers' cultural orientation, corresponding to their socio-economic position on the extreme threshold of the middle-class world.

It has become a commonplace of the literature on social stratification in Africa that the persistence of the extended family and its network of obligations has inhibited the process of class formation by maintaining regular contact and patronage ties between members of the elite and relatives among the lower social strata.[31] In the case of Sekondi-Takoradi, at least, such a formulation is quite misleading as to the nature and regularity of contact between the majority of workers and members of the elite. It is certainly true that most workers still attribute great importance to extended family ties and to participation in family events, especially funerals. But such family activities take up only a very small proportion of their leisure time, most of which is spent with friends of roughly similar socio-economic position. In any case, very few workers are at all closely related to members of the elite, and those extended family ties which are most regularly maintained tend to be those between members of similar educational and socio-economic status. The principle of reciprocity, of being able (or expecting one day to be able) to return equivalent favours to those received, operates as a restricting factor on both Ghanaian friendships and, increasingly, extended family relationships. Most of those workers I interviewed who claimed to be related to 'big men' said that they would be far too embarrassed ever to ask such a relative to lend them money or find them a job because they knew they could do no similar favour in return. Some said they could not even consider visiting such relatives since they knew the relatives would be thinking that the purpose of the visit was to beg a favour. It is a commonplace of akpeteshie-bar conversation, as distinct from the sociological literature, that members of the elite display unmistakable snobbery and annoyance with the theoretical obligations of the extended family when visited by lower-strata relatives. As one railway worker put it:

> What? A rich man give money to his poor relatives? A rich man only knows his parents. It makes little difference whether they are relatives or not, he soon forgets his poor cousins and friends. They do not even give 20 pesewas to the very poor. Have you ever seen a wealthy man stop his Mercedes to get out and dash [give money to] a poor man? Not at all. It is rather we workers who have to look after our jobless brothers and friends. The rich men are too selfish.[32]

Participation in voluntary associations is of interest here as they provide, in theory at least, arenas of regular mass–elite contact and communication. More particularly, ethnic associations might be seen as fostering the perpetuation of tribal divisions which cross-cut, and thereby inhibit awareness of, class-type divisions. Yet associational life in Sekondi-Takoradi is extremely sparse. At one time, apparently, it was more vigorous. Busia informs us of the popularity of tribal associations in the city in 1949–50, and emphasises their importance in providing mutual assistance and arbitration in disputes.[33] But, by 1971, only one ethnic association was found to be in active existence, that of the Ashantis, the Asante Mmoa Kuo. It seems probable that those described by Busia collapsed during the two intervening decades owing to problems of efficient administration and financial trustworthiness (and, in particular, to the tendency of treasurers to run off with the subscriptions).[34] Common tribal origin has proved no reliable basis for mutual trust. A few small, multi-tribal mutual-help associations, generally organised on a neighbourhood basis, are still in operation. But most inhabitants of Sekondi-Takoradi now prefer to participate in very small, informal mutual-aid groups, consisting of no more than ten members, who are usually from the same home town or village and know each other extremely well. They are also usually of similar class position.[35]

The only form of associational life in which any substantial proportion of the Sekondi-Takoradi populace participates is provided by the various churches. These are certainly classless in the sense that people from all social strata are to be found amongst their membership. The older 'historic' churches, such as the Roman Catholic, Methodist and Presbyterian Churches, tend rather to be differentiated along ethnic lines, having originally established themselves in different regional areas. But even here the growth of class-consciousness is to be observed as contributing to the drift of many lower-strata members away from the 'historic' to the 'spiritualist' churches. The Apostolic Church and the Musama Disco Christo Church, in particular, have large and rapidly expanding congregations in Sekondi-Takoradi.[36] A large part of their appeal would seem to lie in the 'healing' services they claim to provide, and in the preference of many lower-strata Ghanaians, especially women, for their more traditional musical style. But, in addition, there is a clear difference in the social composition and ethos of the two types of church. The more brotherly, less status-conscious atmosphere of the spiritualist churches is an important attraction for many new recruits. A railway worker who had recently joined the Apostolic Church put it this way:

> The most obvious difference between us and the Methodist Church is that they don't do the clapping and joyful singing the way we do. There's a difference in ways of worshipping God. We observe God's instruction in the Bible, that if you want to worship Him, it's best to do so by clapping of hands and joining together in brotherly, happy singing. But also we don't believe in looking up to rich men. I mean, in the Methodist Church, all the men wear suits to services and all the women kente cloth. They'll tell you to go home if you go in wearing clothes like these [working clothes]. Well, if I don't own a suit, how can I go to worship there? And they're really very pompous,

183

those people. The wealthiest or most important amongst them expect to be given the official positions in the church. And when they're collecting money for Thanksgiving or at harvest time, for instance, they say, 'You should pay so much because you're a lawyer, and you should pay so much because you're a worker.' And you have to pay even if you can't afford it. And then the wealthy ones will embarrass you by shouting, 'I can afford to pay more than the 5 cedis you said, here's 10 cedis.' And then another one shouts, 'Here's 15 cedis.'

It's not that we don't have wealthy men in our church. We have an army officer at our church in Accra, I'm told. And we have some very big collections. Two months ago, we collected N₵260 for an out-dooring. But we just pay how much we want to. It all comes from the heart. It's voluntary and therefore better in the sight of God. And wealthy people are not the officials in our church, rather the older, wiser men. We all mix together, and your dress doesn't make any difference. That's why a lot of people are coming to join our church from the Methodists and Presbyterians.[37]

Conclusion

Post-Independence development in Ghana has resulted in a large pro-portionate increase in the share of national wealth going to the top-level elite, and a considerable expansion in size of the 'comfortable' middle class of medium-scale businessmen, large cocoa farmers and middle-ranking civil servants; but the skilled and unskilled manual workers have suffered relative impoverishment of a degree which has wiped out any significant difference between their own and average rural incomes. These three income groups increasingly approximate to classes in the sociological sense. Children of the lower income group are severely disadvantaged in terms of life chances, or mobility opportunities, relative to those of the elite and middle class. Each class tends to lead a distinct style of life and to mix (at all regularly) only with people of roughly similar economic and educational status. The theoretical obligations of the extended family are increasingly ineffective in serving to maintain regular contact between members of different classes.

Of course, this class differentiation is not complete or absolute. It would also appear to be much less pronounced in Kumasi, where commerce provides the main form of employment and the gradation of income levels is far more continuous, than in Sekondi-Takoradi or Tema, where a majority of the population is in wage and salary employment in industry and the state bureaucracy. But in Sekondi-Takoradi, at least, class differences and barriers have developed in a highly visible form and

184

they are not significantly cross-cut by ethnic or other types of division. If social barriers are less rigid than in England, for instance, they are all the more resented for being of recent origin and of little traditional legitimacy. Also, the difference in living standards between the elite and the lower class is even more extreme.

The level of urban unemployment has risen rapidly since 1966. Official figures are notoriously inaccurate, but most observers estimate that something like 20 per cent of the adult male labour force is unemployed or seriously underemployed.[38] The skilled workers are, of course, relatively privileged compared to this group, but only in this sense are they a labour aristocracy, and even this is the aristocracy of 'noblesse oblige' to care for dependants rather than of luxurious consumption. Their economic and social distance from the middle class is considerable; they are able to afford only occasional forays into the 'smart clothes, beer-bar' world of the latter. If their position on the extreme threshold of the middle class induces a certain ambivalence in their aspirations and cultural orientation, this only serves to increase the militancy of their pressure for a radical redistribution of national wealth. Glimpses of a more comfortable world exacerbate their discontent at being forced ever further down into the ranks of the urban poor.

9

Power and organisation

One of the most striking aspects of post-Independence politics in the African states is the relative ease with which the 'masses', at one time seen as involved in a populist surge toward greater participation, have in fact been effectively excluded from active political involvement. The chief exception to this tendency, in many states, has consisted in the continuing strength of workers' organisation (whether official or unofficial) and their ability to stage major political strikes in protest at government policies. Elliot Berg and Jeffrey Butler might well be correct in suggesting that 'political' strikes have been the exception rather than the rule in both pre- and post-Independence Africa.[1] Infrequent as they may have been, such political strikes as have occurred nevertheless appear significant enough within this general context of popular passivity to merit serious consideration. Arrighi and Saul, however, viewing such strikes as instances of mere 'reformist opportunism' and considering rural passivity to be a temporary phenomenon, insist that 'considerable attention must continue to be paid to the emphasis of Frantz Fanon who placed his hopes for significant transformation in post-colonial Africa upon the peasantry's outrage at widening economic and social differentials'.[2]

There are a number of reasons for considering this formulation seriously misjudged. It is hardly necessary to concur entirely with Marx's more extreme castigations of peasant passivity in order to recognise the difficulties confronting the peasantry's development of a shared consciousness, of a unifying radical ideology, or of the autonomous political organisation necessary to concerted political action. As Saul has himself acknowledged,

> Parochialism cuts deep in the rural areas; the outlines of the broader exploitative environment, world-wide and territorial, which oppresses him, are not easily perceived by the peasant . . . Even if peasant political action (rather than apathetic resignation and/or preoccupation with quasi-traditional involvements closer to home) is forthcoming

186

it may still prove either to be quite localised and isolated in its spontaneous expression, or else forced too easily into channels of mere regional and ethnic self-assertiveness by a territorial leadership which divides in order that it may continue to rule.[3]

This necessarily leads to a recognition of the importance of political work (organisational and ideological) performed by 'outsiders' for the 'peasant' revolutions which have occurred in the twentieth century and for any which might conceivably emerge in the future. Yet professional revolutionaries, it would seem, need more than a sense of injustice to work with, more even than impressive moral stature, if they are to persuade the peasantry that the risks of rebellion are worth taking. Colin Leys has aptly summarised the work of Barrington Moore, Hamza Alavi aud Eric Wolf as showing that 'It generally requires a rare combination of tyranny and misery to produce a peasant revolt, let alone a peasant revolution; short of which the clientilist political structures characteristic of peasant society have a resilience that can easily be underestimated'.[4]

Even if such a rare combination should come to characterise the African countryside, and even if 'independent' African societies should prove more productive of committed revolutionaries than at present, one further observation must induce doubts as to the likelihood of outsiders and peasants linking up in an effective revolutionary movement. The present revolutions of the twentieth century have all been in an important sense, 'nationalist' in character (even if they have also been more than purely nationalist), some form of anti-colonial ideology serving to provide, initially at least, the requisite ideational rapport between peasant communities and 'intellectual' outsiders. It is, as President Nyerere of Tanzania has observed, 'another thing when you have to remove your own people from the position of exploiters'.[5] And the intricate mechanisms of neo-colonialism are likely to present a more elusive target than the notably direct dependencies of colonial rule. Given Saul's recognition of most of these obstacles, his continuing belief in the revolutionary potential of the peasantry must appear as essentially wilful optimism.

The politics of the Ghanaian peasantry

One danger of a 'revolutionary' perspective is that it tends to divert attention from a more immediate, less heady, but nonetheless important question. What ability have the peasantry (or peasantries) displayed in a country such as Ghana to unite in resisting economic exploitation and abuses of power by the politico-administrative class? Note the reference to 'peasantries'. The notion of a single peasant class, we have already observed,

187

is transparently inappropriate in the case of Ghana. Agricultural producers vary greatly in the nature and extent of their involvement in the market-economy, as well as in the directness of their economic exploitation by the state. Evidence was also presented in the previous chapter to indicate the very considerable differences in size and wealth of agricultural cultivators both within the main cocoa-growing areas and between the different regions. Of these two dimensions of differentiation, the first is probably less important as an obstacle to concerted rural opposition. Research in at least one locality suggests that the poorer, indebted cocoa farmers were far more enamoured of the CPP Government and the loans it distributed through the Cocoa Purchasing Company than their more secure counterparts, and were consequently a source of some weakness in the attempt to present a united front against the regime's pricing policies.[6] Generally, however, both wealthy farmers and relatively poor peasants within a particular locality have tended to unite in defence of communal (and common occupational) interests.

Communal and regional cleavages amongst Ghana's agricultural producers are partly a reflection of differing modes and items of production. In consequence of the uneven spread of cocoa production the majority of peasants in the Western Region, for example, do not share the dominant economic interest of the Ashanti producers in the level of the cocoa price. Their primary relationship is one of conflict over the regional distribution of rural development finance. Such regional jealousies and communal sentiments can, moreover (as the past has clearly shown), undermine the solidarity of cocoa producers located in different areas of the country.

Before turning to a consideration of cocoa-farmer politics, it is worth remarking on the marked political passivity displayed by the generally poor, small-scale cultivators of the non-cocoa-growing areas. With the partial exception of essentially communalistic movements, such as the support given to the Northern People's Party in 1954–6, and the secessionist movement among the Ewe of the Volta Region, these small peasants have presented no overt or organised opposition to post-Independence ruling elites. Part of the explanation for this is perhaps that, being relatively poor and lying outside the aegis of state or state-sponsored buying organisations, they have suffered less in the way of direct governmental exploitation. In addition, Marx's comment is certainly relevant here: 'In so far as there is merely a loose inter-connection among these small peasants, and the identity of their interests begets no unity and no political organisation, they do not form a class.'[7]

This is, however, too simple an assessment for unqualified application to the Ghanaian cocoa farmers.[8] In spite of the very considerable income differences between them, the cocoa farmers do constitute a form of class, in the sense that they occupy essentially the same position in the structures of economic production and appropriation. On occasion, moreover, they have proved themselves capable of creating autonomous political organisation for the protection of their (keenly appreciated) common interests. The contemporary weakness of such organisation relative to that of the railway workers is nevertheless strikingly apparent.

The cocoa hold-ups of the 1930s well illustrate the requisites and limits of concerted protest on the part of Ghana's cocoa farmers.[9] Small, middle and large producers all participated (most voluntarily, some through coercion), but the hold-ups were organised and led by the wealthier farmers in conjunction with the chiefs (themselves often wealthy farmers). The chiefs were clearly in an extremely delicate political position, and generally avoided any open display of support for the hold-ups, projecting themselves (to the colonial authorities at least) as mediators between the farmers on the one hand, and the expatriate companies and the government on the other. But, secretly, they lent their full support to the hold-ups in those areas where they were effective, delegating their power to swear fetish oaths and arraign defaulters to the head farmers in their districts in order to enforce general compliance. That the support and solidarity of the chiefs was crucial to united action was clearly revealed by the relative degrees of success of the various hold-ups. Those of 1931–2, and 1933–4 were effective only in a minority of localities. It was only with the restoration of the Ashanti Confederacy Council in 1935, and the forging of an alliance between this body and the Provincial Councils of the Colony, that it proved possible to enforce a nation-wide hold-up – that of 1937–8.

The alliance of middle and wealthy cocoa farmers persisted into the early years of the CPP regime, and became more overtly political. But it also began to split along regional lines. Under the CPP regime no more than under the colonial regime did the large-scale farmers necessarily see themselves as allied with the governing elite. On the contrary, they, as much as the middle peasantry, had serious cause for grievance at the extortion of state officials and the level of taxation imposed on them in order to finance urban development projects. However, under the CPP regime, those who would engage in oppositional activity had more reason to fear subsequent government reprisals. In 1954–6 there appeared to be a good chance of displacing the CPP regime and replacing it with a government less inimical to their (and Ashanti) interests. This discontent (and optimism) furnished the main material basis of mass support for the National Liberation Movement (1954–6), which succeeded in presenting a serious challenge to the CPP's continuation in power.[10] Yet the majority of cocoa farmers in the colony ultimately determined not to support it in

189

the 1956 general elections, thereby illustrating the persisting strength of communal divisions. According to Dennis Austin, 'As they [the southern farmers] listened to the propaganda coming out of the Ashanti capital, and saw the preparations being made for the extension of the party into the Colony, they saw the NLM not as the farmer's friend but as the spearhead of a new Ashanti invasion of the south.'[11]

With the failure of the NLM, the cocoa farmers appear to have become more wary of engaging in oppositional activity. Certainly, the United Party's attempt to resuscitate the movement in 1958–60 met with a far more limited response, and the understandable caution of chiefs and wealthy farmers may well have been crucial here.[12] With the subsequent detention of the United Party leadership, and the smashing of its organisation, the cocoa farmers proved unable to maintain or create any independent organisation, however informal, to assert their interests in concerted fashion. Essentially, this was due to the tightness and ruthlessness of CPP control, which involved suppressing or co-opting any elements which might have been able to organise and lead opposition – most notably, the farmer–chiefs.[13] The period of CPP tyranny had relatively permanent effects on the power of chieftaincy (which, having once been so thoroughly undermined, could not be expected ever to recover fully) and consequently on the ability of the cocoa farmers to organise in protection of their interests. One should also note here the role of the United Ghana Farmers' Council in suppressing independent cocoa-trading organisations which might have provided leadership and lines of communication for oppositional politics.[14]

Admittedly, this hypothesis concerning the obstacles to peasant organisation was not seriously tested under the NLC and Progress Party regimes, since relations between the peasantry and the governing elite markedly improved. It is over-simple to imagine that peasantry (rich, middle or poor) conceive of their interests as being consistently at odds with those of the politico-administrative elite. Under the NLC and Progress Party regimes many peasants, especially those in the Ashanti and Brong/Ahafo Regions, benefited substantially from the rural development programme. Unlike the urban lower class, these rural producers remained enthusiastic supporters of the PP Government to the end (though large-scale fraud on the part of government-sponsored cocoa-buying agents gave rise to rumblings of disillusionment even among the Ashanti cocoa farmers late in 1971).

In September 1971, the Sekondi-Takoradi strikers found that there was conflict between their own perceived interests and those of the cocoa farmers. It would be absurd to suggest that the cocoa farmers thereby showed themselves to be fundamentally allied with the politico-administrative elite while the railway workers represented the forces of radicalism. It is unnecessary to reverse Arrighi's and Saul's formulation in order to refute it. Both sides to this conflict consisted of mass groupings defined partly along class and partly along communal lines. Instances of conflict between them can be expected to recur, since it is an obvious (though not necessarily wise) political strategy for ruling regimes to play off the most highly politicised section of the peasantry – the farmers of Ashanti and Brong/Ahafo – against the workers and urban masses of the southern coastal towns. One might simply point out that the Sekondi-Takoradi workers represent (in a Burkean sense at least) a mass grouping, most of whose members are, if anything, poorer than the majority of the Ashanti and Brong/Ahafo farmers; that they would appear to have a broader and more coherent conception of their reformist aims; and that they retain a strength of independent organisation (if not of electoral influence) which it is doubtful that the cocoa farmers now possess.

What of the political potential of the unskilled urban workers and the unemployed? In Ghana, as in other societies, the unskilled have generally depended on the skilled workers for organisation and leadership. The unemployed have proved unable to unite on any large scale in pursuit of the most basic of common interests.[15] Lacking a common meeting–ground (apart, possibly, from the employment exchange), and character-ised by intense competition among themselves for any source of sus-tenance, they have rather proved, as Adrian Peace has described them, 'the most politically promiscuous of all socio-economic strata, in the African or any other political arena, constantly at the beck and call of the highest bidder'.[16] Those few instances of their incorporation as active participants in revolutionary movements (e.g. in 'Frelimo') have been made possible by precisely the depth of organisation forged by others.

Conversely, it is the railway workers' strength of organisation, indepen-dent and democratic, and their ability to resist suppression, division or control by ruling regimes, which accounts for their singular significance in the Ghanaian political arena. What are the main sources of this excep-tional political strength?

The sources of railway worker political strength

Corporate solidarity The power of the railway workers derives essentially from the strength of their corporate solidarity. Through united strike action they are able to exploit their strategic position in the national economy, disrupting the flow of imports and exports along the national transport system. This is an especially powerful weapon in a country such as Ghana, where a temporary halt in the flow of exports, and the

191

consequent loss of much-needed foreign exchange, can have disastrous repercussions for the economy as a whole. The power of the Sekondi-Takoradi workers has declined in this respect with the construction of a new and larger harbour at Accra-Tema and the failure, thus far, to co-ordinate collective action between workers in the two cities, but it remains very considerable.

Corporate solidarity tends to be self-reinforcing. So long as they maintain their solidarity, the rank and file know that they are relatively secure from threats of victimisation or dismissal for participation in strike actions, and their leaders from intolerable periods of detention. (Strike leaders frequently have been detained, but they have always been able to rely on their successors in union office to exert pressure for their early release.) In turn, this knowledge makes junior officials the more ready to step into the positions of leadership vacated by those arrested and so maintain the organisation essential to unity in the course of major strike actions.

This sense of corporate solidarity further enables the railway workers to maintain an exceptional degree of control over the election and behaviour of their officials. When regimes have sought to impose officials on the union, or to induce them to co-operate with the government against the wishes of the rank and file, they have generally succeeded only in the case of top-level officials, whose control over the membership and their middle-level representatives has consequently been tenous in the extreme. Owing largely to the (traditional) strength of the ethic of solidarity and accountability, and the vigour (and occasional violence) with which the rank and file have been accustomed to assert it, these middle-level representatives have proved remarkably resistant to 'buying off' strategies on the part of the government and top-level union officialdom.[17]

The railway workers' success in maintaining their unity has not been absolute. In 1970–1 in particular, they were deeply and critically divided. Amongst other factors, the very power which the railway workers possess through their solidarity has led ruling regimes to make especially vigorous attempts to undermine it. Nevertheless, it is the relative strength of their sense of solidarity exerting a strong pressure to reunification even in 1970–1 which deserves emphasis and causal analysis here.

Common class interest The railway workers have long possessed a keen awareness of common class interest. In the narrower sense with which this subsection is concerned, this class-consciousness derives from three main considerations. Firstly, all manual workers have shared a common interest in struggling to obtain concessions from the government, since wage increases for unskilled workers have generally been accompanied by similar proportionate increases for skilled workers, and vice versa.

Secondly, such concessions have generally had to be forced from the government by direct action, or the threat thereof, since successive regimes, both colonial and independent, have refused to institute regular arrangements for collective bargaining with Railway Administration employees. Thirdly, a general and notorious shortage of promotion opportunities for manual employees in the Railway Administration has inclined them to concentrate on securing collective benefits rather than individual advancement.

The skilled workers, although earning twice as much on average as unskilled workers, have generally been equally dissatisfied with their real wage-level. This is related to the question of relative job stability and commitment, but in a less simple manner than most writers suggest. Most of the skilled railway workers are almost totally dependent on their wages to maintain a living, have wives and children to support in the city, and expect to continue in their occupation for some considerable time. But few consider wage employment a permanent career. Most rather aspire eventually to save enough to set up in business, to 'become independent'. Even small businesses generally bring better returns than a skilled worker's wage, and involve less work. Moreover, a private business involves work for oneself rather than an employer, and it is considered undignified for an old man to be in wage employment. However, this aspiration requires considerable capital savings for its fulfilment. Consequently, as Adrian Peace has pointed out for the similar case of the Lagos proletariat, the desire of workers to leave industrial employment and enter the informal economy paradoxically increases the pressure for higher wages and thereby workers' willingness to engage in collective action.[18]

Cultural community The development of class-consciousness in the fuller sense of the term nevertheless involves, as both Marx and Weber recognised, rather more than this awareness of common interest: it involves a certain ideational unity and the creation of a common culture or sense of 'belonging together'. As the 'alternation' theorists have shown, a keen and actively displayed sense of common class interest is far from incompatible with the urban African's tendency to continue to identify with his tribe, village or other 'traditional' community; the different identifications are rather 'compartmentalised' and expressed in different contexts.[19] Robin Cohen has argued that this approach needs to be supplemented by an examination of the way in which the circumstances of urban life are tendentially, if unevenly, eroding the relative importance of traditional links over time.[20] Other writers, focusing on the abundant evidence of the continuing, even increasing, political salience of (suitably modified) communal identities in the developing world, see the real problem as one of designating

193

those situational contexts in which one form of identification is likely to take precedence over another.[21]

These two approaches need not ultimately, perhaps, be considered mutually exclusive; but, for anything other than the most long-term of perspectives, the latter would seem to be of greater (initial) analytical utility. The conclusion to be drawn from several studies of intra-union conflict, for instance, would appear to be that such conflict is especially likely to take place along tribal lines where particular categories of worker are predominantly recruited from particular tribal groups (and, more especially, where there is growing competition from previously disqualified groups for access to valued occupational positions), or where competition for control of the union is intensified by the intervention of 'outside' politicians.[22] In the case of the Ghanaian railway labour force, we have seen, the majority of unskilled and semi-skilled workers on the permanent way have been recruited from the Northern and Upper Regions, whilst nearly all the skilled and semi-skilled workshop employees have come from the southern part of the country and, more particularly, the Fanti tribal grouping. Three main reasons may be advanced as to why this coincidence of ethnic/cultural and occupational lines of division has not thus far constituted a source of serious political disunity within the Railway Union. In the first place, southern Ghanaians have, until recently at least, been happy to allow the northerners a virtual monopoly of permanent way positions, regarding such work as beneath them. The second reason may be illuminated by a comparison of the position of northerners in the mining industry and in the railways. The northerner mineworkers' geographical concentration in the main mining townships, and their strategically central position in the operation of their industry, have together provided the basis for occasional eruptions of conflict with their fellow miners from the south – a basis assiduously cultivated by colonial district officers, for example, during the militant phase of the nationalist movement. In the railways, by contrast, the majority of northerner employees have been stationed not in the main railway worker conglomerations at Sekondi-Takoradi, but in small gangs situated every five or six miles along the railway track. By virtue of their geographical situation, they have not been in a position to present any threat to the internal solidarity of the Sekondi-Takoradi concentration, while the strategic power of this latter, politically most active of groups, its ability to bring the national railway and harbour system to a halt, has operated independently of the support of up-country workers. One possible source of 'tribalistic' conflict has thus been notably absent – dependence on each other's support for the successful pursuit of strike actions and the mutual recriminations which might follow from a failure to unite. This negative explanation might be

194

supplemented by a more positive one. The northerner permanent waymen have in fact lent their support to the Sekondi-Takoradi railway workers in strikes such as that of 1961 when their own financial interests were not directly at stake. A great deal of the credit for such unity, and for the generally close co-operation between the two groups, must be accorded to the intelligence of the permanent waymen's leaders in recognising their ultimate correspondence of interests – a correspondence deriving, of course, from the skilled workers' consistent drive to achieve a general increase in the wage-levels of all lower-paid workers.

It nevertheless remains the case that the relationship between northerners and southerners in the union is more accurately described as one of tactical alliance than as one of any deeply imbued sense of solidarity. Recent developments, moreover, suggest that this might prove an increasingly fragile alliance. As the growing level of unemployment has forced more southerners to seek unskilled jobs, southerner and northerner permanent waymen have come into conflict over such issues as the necessity of possessing educational qualifications for promotion to supervisory positions. This particular issue has been at least temporarily resolved through compromise formulae; and the union leaders' support for the exemption of all railway workers from the 1971 Aliens' Compliance Order (which would have compelled many permanent waymen to leave the country) indicated the continuing influence of a protectively paternalistic attitude toward their non-southerner members. Future conflicts of serious proportions between the two groups must nevertheless be considered likely.

There can be no doubt, however, of the deep sense of corporate identity displayed by the skilled and semi-skilled railway workers of Sekondi-Takoradi. This has obviously been facilitated by their common ethnic origin and by their sharing the same (or similar) 'traditional' culture: the majority are Fanti and nearly all members of the larger Akan cultural grouping. But, on this initial basis, there has developed a corporate 'proletarian' culture which is a distinctive product of their urban and industrial experience.

A situation such as that at the Location workshops, where three or four thousand workers are concentrated in approximately four square miles, most of them working at machines just a few yards from each other, makes for regular and easy communication between them, and a strong awareness of common interest. Union mass meetings are easy to arrange and assemble. The workers sit together at lunchtime, discussing personal problems, union affairs and national politics. Union officials are easily contacted, and they and other 'articulates' enlighten the less informed workers as to the implications of new government policies and developments (or non-developments) in other parts of the country.

This close contact and regular communication extends beyond the bounds of the work-place to the residential situation and leisure pastimes of the railway workers. In each of their main residential areas – the Administration-owned estates in Takoradi and Ketan, and the private accommodation at Esikado (the so-called 'home of railway unionism') – the railway workers are neighbours and regular drinking companions as well as workmates. Those who live in other parts of the twin-city frequently patronise the bars of Esikado at weekends. The Railway Club at Sekondi provides a social centre for some, catering for both sporting and drinking activities. The skilled railway workers of Sekondi-Takoradi therefore constitute a close-knit and relatively stable social and cultural community. Within this community, the ideas of such men as Pobee Biney have been the more easily communicated and developed as the basis of a shared ideology or political culture.

10

The political culture of the railway workers

The regrettably small body of literature on African labour concerning the issue of 'consciousness' has mostly focused on the particular issue of 'class-consciousness' in so preconceived a manner as to obscure a more basic and more open question. Have African workers (or particular groups) developed a distinct, radical political sub-culture (relative, that is, to the dominant culture of the national political elite), and, if so, what is its nature? By 'radical political sub-culture' I wish to denote a set of inter-dependent attitudes, norms and conceptions in which grievances giving rise to (or considered as justification for) protest action are intimately related to a view of elitist and authoritarian tendencies in the surrounding society as substantially illegitimate; in which, quite commonly at least, the aims and propellants of protest extend beyond narrow occupational grievances to a desire to effect radical alterations in the prevailing political and socio-economic order. On a loose usage of the term, any such culture which is the common property of a class-grouping might, of course, be considered a form of class-consciousness. It is suggested here, however, that it is important to ask just how any particular example approximates to (or deviates from) the model Marx envisaged as characterising the proletariat of developing capitalist societies.

It is clear from the foregoing historical analysis that the Sekondi-Takoradi railway strikes of 1950, 1961 and 1971 were all highly political in conception. That is to say, they were consciously directed against the government rather than the management, and were expressions of protest at general policies and characteristics of the regimes in question rather than narrowly occupational grievances. It would further appear that they exhibited a certain ideological consistency or continuity. The 1950 strike, though openly staged in support of Nkrumah's 'Positive Action' campaign, was designed to articulate a particular radical form of nationalism, rather than to indicate anything but the most conditional support for the Convention People's Party as such. The strike of 1961 expressed the railway

197

workers' disillusionment with the CPP regime, and, more particularly, its failure to live up to the radical expectations and promises of the early nationalist campaign. That of 1971 was a further protest against the elitist and authoritarian conduct of government, in this instance by the Progress Party regime of Dr Busia. In retrospect, Pobee Biney's exhortation to beware too close an association with ruling parties, and to prepare to struggle for a minimal realisation of original nationalist aims, appears as a continuous thread linking all these strike actions. While such an interpretation might exaggerate Biney's personal influence, it is nevertheless clear that the railway workers have developed a distinctive anti-elitist political sub-culture which must be considered an important intervening variable in the translation of their economic interests into political action.

In beginning to describe this sub-culture, it is important to stress the mutual interrelation of the various constituent elements – in brief, militancy, the norms of collective solidarity and independence of government, radical discontent with the prevailing socio-economic order, and a strong impulse to political participation. This interdependence might be held to reinforce the strength of each constituent element, especially since it is quite consciously perceived by at least the more articulate and influential members of the rank and file. (In reality, the political culture of the railway workers, as of any group, is differentially determined by individuals according to their political weight, the intensity of their views and their relative articulateness.) This is not to say that any one element necessarily produces or presupposes all the others. As Eric Hobsbawm remarks with his customary lucidity, 'A willingness to raise barricades does not necessarily indicate an extremist programme.'[1] In the particular case of the Sekondi-Takoradi railway workers, militancy might be held to result in part from specific characteristics of the labour force (discussed below) and from a lack of adequate institutionalised channels for negotiating wage demands. But the exceptional strength of the railway workers' militancy can only be fully understood in relation to their concern with general issues of government – in particular, their radically critical attitudes toward the existing socio-economic order – and the role conceived for the strike weapon within the context of a wide-fronted political struggle.

In terms of Almond's and Verba's simplistic typology of political cultures – 'participant', 'subject' and 'parochial'[2] – the railway workers possess a highly participant culture. Opinions on the government's policy decisions and general performance are openly expressed and discussed at mass meetings of the union, and frequently conclude with the phrase 'We must make our voice heard on this matter.'[3]

The tenor of such discussions is generally critical and non-deferential. The reverse side of the railway workers' high opinion of their own rightful political status is a corresponding irreverence and suspicion toward the government. Governments are expected to misrule in the interests of a select elite. But, rather than accepting this, the railwaymen seek to criticise the government whenever possible and express scorn for those who resign themselves to such misrule: 'The trouble with most of our workers here in Ghana is that they are too timid. They are too frightened to speak up.'[4] The ideal political system should be open and responsive. The automatic tendency of the ruling class to seek to close up the system has to be checked by the forceful assertion of the popular will – most notably, by the use of the strike weapon. The workers have to act as 'the eyes and ears of society' – and also its arm.

But while the railway workers' culture is highly political in this sense, it is at the same time determinedly non-partisan, or, to be more accurate, supra-partisan. The union is not to be bound by too close an association with a political party. A temporary, informal alliance with a political party might be accepted, by some members at least, for the purpose of helping finance a major strike action, though even this is likely to attract the disapproval of most members as undermining the credibility of their claim to speak simply for 'the people'. Alternatively, union leaders might seek to cultivate their ties with government leaders in order to gain concessions. But the railway workers have too clear a sense of their own political goals, and of the distance between these and those of any party bandwagon, to compromise their independence willingly. The working assumption of Railway Union political culture is that untrustworthiness and oligarchic self-interest are to be expected of all party politicians and of any union leader who associates too closely with them: 'There are two things the railway workers will not stand for. An untruthful leader, someone who changes his mind to suit his interest. And a leader who sides too strongly with a political party. They know he will sell them out.'[5]

What are the railway workers' political goals? One is certainly the liberal-reformist ideal of an open and responsive political system, and it can be argued that this ideal derives partly from socialisation in the processes and ethics of internal Railway Union politics (even though the theory of small-group socialisation operates, generally, on somewhat unsure foundations). But the railway workers clearly have more specific, socio-economic goals which inform their striving to participate as an effective independent force in national politics. While the discussions of political issues at union mass meetings cover a wide range of areas, they have one consistent theme: the desirability and urgency of a more equitable distribution of the national income.

Since the railway workers have generally been in a defensive position, both politically and economically, since Independence, they often express this social ideal in a somewhat defensive manner: for example, 'We are telling all those big men that they should shoulder their fair share of the national burden.'[6] However, it is clear from the applause accorded the more positive and aggressive statements of reformist aims by Pobee Biney in 1947–56, and by rank-and-file leaders in the course of the 1961 and 1971 strikes, that a more radical ideal is implicit in such negative formulations. This is also demonstrated by the explicit manner in which, in the summer of 1971, many railway workers talked privately of 'wanting to make all those big men to leave the country alone', and 'taking away half their salaries so that we poor can eat and live like men'.[7]

It is in any case clear that far from according legitimacy to the existing pattern of socio-economic stratification, the railway workers deeply resent the failure to reform the pattern inherited at Independence, and the development since then of an ever-widening elite–mass gap. It is important, however, to be more precise as to just which forms and degrees of socio-economic differentiation are especially resented. The railway workers are not, strictly speaking, social egalitarians. They are generally prepared to acknowledge the legitimacy of considerable differences in income-levels so long as these correspond in some reasonable way – it is impossible to be very precise about this – to differences in skill-level, initiative and contribution to the community. More particularly (and very significantly from the perspective of class-consciousness), they do not generally condemn the wealth of self-made businessmen – largely, no doubt, because this is what they aspire ideally to become. Hoping one day to save enough capital to start up in business themselves, the skilled workers tend to emphasise the hard work and intelligence required for entrepreneurial success. Many successful businessmen are held in high esteem, particularly those (a fair number) who continue to live in the poorer quarters of town, displaying generosity to those with some claim on their assistance or hospitality. Only those wealthy capitalists are seriously criticised who are believed to be ungenerous, who are suspected of gaining the capital for the establishment of their businesses through embezzlement of public funds, or (which is not very different) whose business success appears to stem primarily from their political contacts.

The principal objects of the railway workers' resentment, the foci of their sense of social injustice, are twofold. First is the fact that middle- and senior-level clerical and executive staff receive so much higher salaries than skilled or unskilled manual workers. Such income disparities (where the ratio between the lowest and highest salaries of government employees had reached 1:39 by 1971) do not appear to be justified by the criteria of training, experience or responsibility for the efficient operation of the public service. The second and most acute source of grievance is the wealth, high living and indifference to socio-economic reform of the political class itself. It is considered quite intolerable that those who owe their positions, in theory at least, to the votes and/or confidence of 'the people', should proceed to 'sell them out', award themselves vast salaries, treat public property as though it were their own and rush with such offensive haste to sever their social ties with those they claim to represent. The railway workers clearly feel they have especial cause for indignation in this respect, since they played so prominent a role in achieving Independence. This focusing of resentment on the expropriation of public as private wealth helps to explain what might otherwise appear as an inconsistency. Although the Progress Party elite were, if anything, more wealthy, more obviously wealthy and more detached than the leaders of the CPP regime, they were regarded more tolerantly than the latter by many railway workers. It was possible to argue that the majority of Progress Party leaders were wealthy men before they came to power, and could therefore less readily be suspected of having enriched themselves through the abuse of political office. On the other hand, some railway workers were far more concerned with the fact that the introduction of fee-paying for post-primary education, together with the PP regime's award of such high salaries to MPs and pensions to judges, was tending to make the social structure more closed and inegalitarian than ever before.

Class, mass, community and political consciousness

In so far as the railway workers' political culture is hostile to the inequities of the prevailing socio-economic order, and stresses their distinctive political role in striving to change this pattern, it might perhaps be described as a form of class-consciousness. In at least four major respects it deviates, however, from the classical Marxist model of proletarian class-consciousness. In the first place, it is liberal-reformist in orientation rather than truly revolutionary. The idea of forming a Labour Party, or seeking to take over control of the state in some other manner, though occasionally voiced, has never been taken very seriously.[8] The legend of Pobee Biney certainly endows railway worker political culture with an aggressive strain and rhetoric; and there can be no doubting the radicalism of the changes the railway workers would (ideally) like to see in Ghanaian society. But this revolutionary impulse has, until now at least, been firmly held in check by a keen sense of political realism involving, most importantly, a pessimistic assessment of the support likely to be forthcoming from other groups. Accordingly, the railway workers have come to resign themselves, with growing defensiveness, to exerting restraint or pressure within a political system controlled by others.

201

Secondly, the 'exploiting' class is identified not as the indigenous capitalist class, nor clearly even as foreign capitalist interests, but rather as the domestic class of politicians and senior civil servants. Given business' high degree of dependence on the politics of access to state machinery, the failure to develop a strong independent capitalist class and the predominance of public over private employment, such an emphasis is readily understandable. The distinctive characteristic of railway worker culture lies in the deep conviction of the essentially exploitative character of all regimes. Different as these regimes might be in ideology, in the particular clientele networks they seek to benefit, or even, within a certain range, in general policies, they all become (and are expected to become), from the railway workers' point of view, mere variants or sections of a single political class.

In the third place, the railway workers do not conceive of their oppositional activity simply as that of a section of the national working class (i.e. unionised labour). They rather project themselves as the spokesmen of the people. This is perhaps more appropriately described as mass- than as class-consciousness. During Bentum's leadership of the TUC, considerable progress was made in the development of a nationwide sense of working-class identity; but here, too, there was a tendency to justify the TUC's political self-assertion in terms of acting as 'the eyes and ears of society'. The cynical observer might view this as an obvious device to rationalise the union leadership's political ambitions, and the rank and file's economic demands, by laying claim to the representation of a wider constituency than the unionised workers alone, themselves very much a minority group within the national society. There is undoubtedly something to this, and the claim to mass representation is, of course, strictly speaking, illusory. Nevertheless, the important point is that the railway workers do believe in the idea of an essential unity of interest of the common people vis-à-vis the political class. In their view, it is lent credibility by the supporting activity of other sections of the urban masses in such major strikes as those of 1961 and 1971. It should also be recognised that there is some truth to the railway workers' self-image, that other groups clearly do look on occasion to the more articulate and organised railway workers for the expression of a generalised sense of social injustice, and that this sense of identity and responsibility imbues the railway workers' political culture with a very real element of idealism.

Finally, it has seemed justified, till now, to emphasise the generalised nature of railway worker attitudes, and so highlight their distinctiveness. Generally speaking, political attitudes and behaviour in Ghana are more realistically described in terms of identification with the people of particular localities or particular personalities and patrons. The contrast in the case of the railway workers is indeed striking. Nevertheless, the relatively principled nature of railway worker political attitudes is in practice qualified by the influence of local identifications. One important element in the popularity of Biney, Woode and Ocran, for instance, was undoubtedly the fact that they were local men as well as radicals. More important from the point of view of our concern here, it seems clear that when the railway workers talk of acting as the spokesmen of the people, they have primarily in mind the people of the Central and Western Regions of Ghana, and, even more particularly, the people of Sekondi-Takoradi. These are the people by whose welfare the performance of the government tends to be judged, and to whom the railway workers look for moral and material support in times of confrontation with the government.

It is of course far from unusual, in the 'advanced' countries as well as the underdeveloped, to find a pronounced communal dimension and sense of identity informing militant forms of working-class action: forms which some historians, at least, would classify as manifestations of class-consciousness. The Marxist notion of a self-conscious national working class, if not entirely mythical, needs always in historical reality to be qualified by recognition of the uneven development and, indeed, qualitative differences of consciousness as between particular groups. Even so, this term does not seem properly applicable to an instance in which the notion of (national) class identification is so weakly developed relative to that of mass spokesmanship, and the communal element in this 'mass-consciousness' is so salient. If one seeks a single term to depict the distinctive nature of railway worker political culture as a reformist and communally refined form of mass-ism, then the most appropriate would appear to be 'radical populism'.

The roots of railway worker radicalism

The depiction of railway worker political culture in so general, bloodless a manner involves one major element of distortion. In reality, such attitudes are frequently expressed through the more colourful medium of historical legends to which the railway workers look for guidance at times of critical decision-making. Indeed, one of the major conclusions of this study as to the sources of labour radicalism consists in recognising the partially independent influence of a group's historical tradition, selectively glorified and institutionalised as 'myths', upon subsequent attitudes and behaviour. The subjective moral impetus provided for the 1961 strike by the nature of the railway workers' 'Positive Action' involvement under Pobee Biney has already been noted. Similarly in the summer of 1971, when discussing union–government relations and the legitimacy of alternative courses of action, the railway workers frequently referred back to the experience and aims of the 1961 strike. No observer could doubt that they were highly aware, and equally proud, of the lead they had given in the early development of Ghanaian trade unionism and in resistance against governmental oppression ever since. Admittedly, this tradition was amenable to various, selective interpretations and contemporary applications. But it was not merely a lump of clay, capable of being moulded to fit any temporarily desired course of action.

On one common interpretation of Marxian theory (supported, most notably, by Lenin),[9] the growth of class-consciousness is not a spontaneous or automatic corollary of developing socio-economic conditions, but rather requires some sort of ideological break-through. The highly uneven development of class-consciousness amongst workers is largely to be explained by the more or less successful educative activity of Marxist intellectuals, or by a particular group's possession of historical 'myths' supporting a revolutionary stance. The consciousness of the Sekondi-Takoradi railway workers is not, perhaps, 'revolutionary'. They do, however, exhibit an intense anti-elitism and a readiness for radical political action which, perhaps somewhat surprisingly given the nature of socio-economic change in post-Independence Ghana, are far from universal amongst Ghanaian workers. One important reason for this is clearly the belief in the legitimacy (under certain conditions) of political strikes lent them by Biney's ideological influence and their historical tradition.

At the same time, certain special characteristics of the Sekondi-Takoradi railway workers help to account for their receptivity to Biney's views. Unlike the mineworkers, for instance, who are relatively isolated in the up-country mining townships, they live at the geographical, social and cultural centre of Ghana's third-largest city. Here, the conduct of the national political elite is highly visible. The railway workers are in close touch both with national political developments and with other discontented, disadvantaged groups. Since, moreover, they identify with Sekondi-Takoradi as a relatively permanent 'second home', they share the general disillusionment of the 'common people' of that city with the conduct of government officials and the lack of benefits accruing to the city from the attainment of Independence. One thus finds a sense of shared deprivation, of belonging and suffering together, which helps to account for the railway workers' conviction of acting as 'spokesmen of the people' and for the fairly strong communalistic element we have noted as characterising their political culture.

Such factors might be expected to influence the attitudes of other groups of Sekondi-Takoradi wage-earners, and the political culture described

204

above is indeed substantially characteristic of the Sekondi-Takoradi proletariat as a whole. It is nevertheless significant that, in the strikes of 1950, 1961 and 1971, these other local groups all looked to the railway and harbour workers to provide the lead. They were (and still are) commonly regarded as the most politically conscious and assertive, as well as the most powerful, section within the Sekondi-Takoradi proletariat. In this respect, it is worth ᾳoting that railway workers were among the first groups to unionise in virtually all of the African territories, developing a militant style of unionism which frequently brought them into sharp confrontation with the colonial authorities, and, in many instances, with the new regimes soon after Independence.[10] It would therefore appear that African railway workers in general, or, to be more precise, the skilled workers who provide the main driving force and source of leadership in railway unionism, possess characteristics which mark them out as an exceptionally militant and politically conscious group. These are not difficult to discern.

In the first place, a relatively high proportion of skilled railway workers possess at least some education, which provides them with requisite organisational skills and access to political news and ideas, as communicated through newspapers and pamphlets.[11] This, however, is equally true of skilled workers in other industries. What is particularly distinctive about skilled railway workers is their very high skill-level, their intimate association with the pioneering technological force in underdeveloped societies. Many so-called 'skilled' workers in Africa are, in reality, only semi-skilled by international standards. The railway artisans and enginemen, however, are a genuinely skilled group who have undergone many years of training, and who, as is obvious to any observer of a railway workshop, take a great deal of pride in their work and abilities. They are, in consequence, extremely sensitive to disrespectful treatment on the part of the management or government, and especially inclined to resent the low economic status accorded them relative to clerical and executive staff of no greater training or practical responsibility for the efficient operation of the railway system. It was this sense of status incongruity, and accompanying resentment, which, as we have seen, originally led to the formation of the Ghanaian Railway Union, and which might still be held to lie at the root of the railway workers' generalised sense of social injustice.

The railway system is the arterial system of the underdeveloped economy. The strategic economic importance of the railway engine, together with its technological qualities, tend to imbue those working with it with a corresponding sense of their own importance and power. A steam engine in motion is an impressive sight for the most detached observer. For the engine-driver, or those artisans responsible for keeping it in running order, it reflects strength and glory on themselves. Through their initimate association with the railway engine, skilled railway workers come to see themselves as the powerful motor and driving force of national economic development, the harbingers of technological, and, in turn, of political modernisation. They are not alone in seeing themselves thus. In the eyes of the local populace more generally, the railwaymen possess something of heroic status as pioneering masters of the 'magical' modern technology. Herein lie significant psychological bases of railway workers' militancy, solidarity and political self-assertion.

Thirdly, the development of a shared political culture clearly requires some formal or informal organised network of communication. The railway workers possess such a network in the engine-drivers travelling up and down the railway system. On the most superficial level, their mobility would appear to facilitate the co-ordination of strike action (though, as we have seen, up-country railway workers have not always been ready to support the Sekondi-Takoradi workers). More important, the geographical mobility of the enginemen serves to engender a highly concrete sense of the nation, and a keen awareness of economic and political developments. This awareness is in turn easily, and almost inevitably, transmitted to the close-knit concentration of artisans at the Sekondi workshops and Takoradi harbour. The potential significance of this network is vividly summed up in the image of Pobee Biney arriving in Sekondi, standing on the foot-plate of his engine surrounded by workshop artisans, to whom he imparts the latest news of nationalist awakening up-country.

Finally, the railway workers' network of communication is at its most dense within Sekondi-Takoradi. As we have seen, the skilled railway workers of that city constitute a close-knit, relatively stable, social and cultural community (though one, it is important to emphasise, that is not sharply cut off from the surrounding urban community). This community's keen sense of its own history has ensured that the stories and ideas of Pobee Biney and other radical leaders have been passed on from one generation to another and thus preserved as a living cultural influence.

Conclusion

The railway workers of Sekondi have a quite exceptional history of political activity. Partly because of this legacy, they are markedly more assertive than other groups of Ghanaian workers. In spite of my presentation of one clearly deviant case, Elliot Berg's and Jeffrey Butler's early characterisation of African trade unions as generally displaying little political strength or inclination might still appear substantially accurate.[1] Yet I would strongly suggest that, in so far as they were correct in this view, it was for very largely the wrong reasons. They accordingly misconstrued the dymanics and direction of union development. By focusing on the behaviour of the majority of workers (or unions), they also overlooked the significance of particular, more radical groups.

Berg and Butler correctly identified the skilled workers as the real force to be reckoned with in African unions. They were mistaken not only in predicting their development as an increasingly privileged group, but in suggesting that any economic gains they did make would necessarily disincline them from radical political activity. The Sekondi railwaymen have consistently assessed the legitimacy of Ghanaian regimes by wider (and more radical) criteria than immediate wage benefits. It really would seem to matter not only who the workers are (in economic terms), but how they see themselves, their social role and their rightful status within a just society. It will not do to dismiss the role of ideology in African trade unionism simply because it is not specifically Marxist or revolutionary ideology, or some preconceived model of class-consciousness, which is involved.

Both ideological communication and the power to oppose the government require an efficient (and relatively autonomous) organisational network. Berg and Butler attributed the weakness of African unions in large part to organisational problems, and in this they were surely correct. But the sources of weakness which they emphasised – financial difficulties and ethnic heterogeneity of membership – have been among the least

207

important in Ghana. The main problem for Ghanaian workers has been that of gaining control of their own union, or of developing an informal corporate solidarity within it. The opportunistic initiation and control of embryonic unions by CPP 'apparatchiks' represented, in part, a pre-empting of their development as genuine workers' organisations. But the CPP legacy was double-edged. It also provided the organisational machinery which could later be taken over and moulded by workers to give expression to their own interests and opinions. Within the independent TUC that developed in 1966–71 one could perceive a widespread movement to adopt, and a growing organisational ability to assert, the social-democratic values and militant style of unionism long advocated by the Sekondi railway workers.

The trade union movements of Ghana and several other African states have in fact developed an organisational and political strength which their counterparts transparently lacked at a comparable stage in the historical evolution of European industrialism. The civilian administrative structures of these states, by contrast, though superficially powerful, constitute ineffective systems for the maintenance of public order or political stability in the face of any major popular upheaval. Hence labour protest activity has already, in several instances, ushered in military regimes to cope with a situation of political crisis. And, confronted with successive governments' refusals to check the process of increasing (and hardening) mass–elite differentiation, the reformism at present characteristic of unionised labour may give way to a more explicitly revolutionary orientation and potential.

Certainly, if a broadly based radical movement is to emerge, then those groups which lack the organisational mechanisms for concerted political action are likely to look for a lead to those which do and are prepared to use them, and, in Ghana, this would appear to apply to the proletariat alone. Yet, in all realism, such a prospect must be considered extremely distant. By attracting the longing gaze of Marxist observers, it may also serve to divert attention from the more modest, but real political achievements of organised labour to date, and its more immediate potential contributions.

It is not entirely accurate, after all, to suggest that the regimes of Ghana and most other African states have been (or are) totally insensitive to popular pressure and expressions of protest. Unionised labour and other interest-groups are sometimes able to wield considerable negative influence over the conduct of government, and thus over their own destinies. African governments do vary substantially, within the external constraints imposed on them, in the relative probity, beneficence and civility of their rule, and this variation is not entirely independent of the attitudes and

208

influence of local interest-groups, even if the exact connection is sometimes impossible to trace with any precision.

The point about such protests as the 1961 Sekondi-Takoradi strike is not that a segment of labour, such as the railway workers, can (or cannot) hope to displace a regime on their own account. It is simply that they (and they virtually alone) can at least resist the forces of government control, and, on occasion, articulate widespread popular discontent. Under more favourable circumstances, they might (as in 1966–71) provide the main power-base for a national trade union movement, capable of articulating reformist demands on a wider platform and more regular basis. Little in the way of immediate or tangible reforms might materialise. But at least such challenges might restrain the rapacious self-interest of ruling elites, encourage the development of a more conciliar style of rule, and serve to uphold some semblance of the ethic of popular accountability in Ghanaian political life.

Appendix

Survey questionnaire administered to a sample of railway workers at Sekondi Location.

Face-sheet

Age
Tribe and place of origin
Job category
Family size (and number of non-nuclear dependants)
Length of time resident in Sekondi-Takoradi
Length of time working in the railways
Future intentions and aspirations
Father's occupation
Educational level

Questions

1   Which union do you belong to? Why do you prefer this to the other union?
2   What do you consider to be the most important qualities of a good trade union leader?
3   Have you ever been, or would you like to be, a union official? Why, or why not?
4   Do you think the present TUC leadership is doing a good job?
5   When do you think it is legitimate for workers to strike? What do you think is the main cause of the large number of strikes in Ghana?
6   Do you think Ghana's politicians and senior civil servants are (a) mostly fairly honest, (b) setting an example of making sacrifice, (c) capable of improving the country's economic situation?
7   Do you generally approve of the recent budget? Why, or why not?
8   Do you agree that the government's first priority should be rural development?
9   Are you hopeful of gaining any wage increase from the Campbell Commission or the Pay Research Unit?
10   Thinking of the next few years, which three of the following goals do you think the unions should concentrate on achieving:
    a   Obtaining improved conditions of service and promotion opportunities.
    b   Bridging the wages gap between the lower- and higher-paid.
    c   Obtaining more influence in the administration of the industry.

210

d   Developing more union spirit and solidarity among workers.
e   Improving the education and discipline of the workers.
f   Making workers more politically conscious.
g   Establishing a fuller programme of social activities and facilities.
h   Helping to provide employment for the jobless.

Method of administration

The survey was administered to a random sample (using this term in a rather loose sense) of 90 workers at Sekondi Location. The original intention was to interview 1 in 12 of the Location labour force, the highest proportion which could be attempted given the limited resources of finance and personnel (the writer and a research assistant). The procedure adopted for the selection of interviewees was simply to map out a set course of the Location workshops, and then to walk along this course interviewing every twelfth individual at work along it. Obviously, this was not so strictly random as other possible techniques (selecting names on a statistical basis from the labour-force roll, for instance), but it was felt that the attendant advantages of this approach outweighed technical considerations of reduced representative validity. If respondents were able to observe for themselves that their selection was random, and that their names were unknown to the interviewer, they would, it was felt, be more at ease in answering the questionnaire, more inclined to be honest and outspoken. (In fact, many insisted that their names be noted, and cited if quoted.) The noisy and familiar atmosphere of the shop-floor was also likely to be more congenial in this respect than that of an office in the executive buildings. It was partly with the aim of establishing a relationship of openness and trust between interviewer and respondents that the writer had previously spent a great deal of time wandering around the workshops in conversation with the leaders of both unions, thereby establishing himself as a familiar and non-partisan figure. Moreover, the leaders of both unions requested their members at mass meetings to lend their full co-operation to the research project. The vast majority of respondents did in fact prove willing to talk frankly, and at considerable length. It was therefore possible to develop some understanding of how the respondents themselves formulated the topics being investigated.

Clearly, however, the resultant sample was not 'random' or representative in any strict sense, most importantly because the percentage of workers in each job category actually interviewed was far too small. Unfortunately, it proved necessary to bring the survey to a premature close before certain sections of the workshops had been fully covered. By the first week of September, it was apparent that a major confrontation between the government and the TUC was looming near, probably to be supported by strike action on the part of RPWU members. In this situation of mounting tension, the writer accepted the Railway Management's advice that the survey be discontinued. In consequence, only 4.7 per cent instead of the proposed 8 per cent of Location workers were in fact interviewed (see Table A.1). The representative status of the survey was obviously impaired thereby, and in consequence it is not possible to claim validity for the findings to any great degree of statistical precision. For the purposes of this analysis, however, no great degree of precision seemed necessary. Certain general patterns were clearly indicated by the high degree of correlation between variables (a minimum score of 0.5 by Yule's Q measurement of association being considered clearly indicative). Beyond this, the strength and significance of these patterns could be assessed by reference to other sources of information, especially the actors' own expressed perceptions of the situation.

Table A.1. *Representative status of sample survey of Location workers*

Job category	Number in labour force	Numbers interviewed	Percentage
Artisans	630	30	4.8
Tradesmen[a]	890	34	4.0
Apprentices	270	15	5.5
Labourers	250	11	4.4
Total	2,040	90	4.7

[a] For the criterion and significance of the distinction between 'artisans' and 'tradesmen', see pp. 160–1 above.

Notes

Abbreviations

ADM   Administrative Files
CSO   Colonial Secretary's Office
GNA   Ghana National Archives
GTUCA   Ghana TUC Archives
MEUA   Mines Employees' Union Archives [In 1961 the official title of the Mines Employees' Union was changed to the Mineworkers' Union]
RAA   Railway Administration Archives
RUA   Railway Union Archives

Introduction

1 See, for example, Bruce Millen, *The Political Role of Labour in Developing Countries* (Washington, 1963), J. Meynaud and A. Salah-Bey, *Trade Unionism in Africa* (London, 1967), and M. Neufeld, 'The Inevitability of Political Unionism in Under-developed Countries', *Industrial and Labour Relations Review*, 13 (April 1960), pp. 363–86.
2 See, for example, L. Trachtman, 'The Labour Movement of Ghana: A Study of Political Unionism', *Economic Development and Cultural Change*, 10 (January 1962), pp. 190–9, and R. Gerritsen, 'The Evolution of the Ghana Trade Union Congress under the Convention People's Party: Towards a Re-Interpretation', *Transactions of the Historical Society of Ghana*, 13 (1974), pp. 229–44.
3 Two recently published exceptions to this generalisation are Peter C. Lloyd, *Power and Independence: Urban Africans' Perception of Social Inequality* (London, 1974), and Adrian Peace, 'The Lagos Proletariat: Labour Aristocrats or Populist Militants', in R. Sandbrook and R. Cohen (eds.), *The Development of an African Working Class* (London, 1975), pp. 281–302.

Chapter 1. The railway and harbour workers of Sekondi-Takoradi: a sociological profile

1 Throughout most of this book I refer simply to the 'Railway Union' since changes of official title have been so numerous. Exceptions occur only in the

213

case of historically and analytically significant divisions into more than one union.

2 *Gold Coast Handbook* (London, 1928), pp. 113–14.

3 On 'forced' labour recruitment in the Northern Territories, see R. Thomas, 'Forced Labour in British West Africa: The Case of the Northern Territories of the Gold Coast 1906–27', *Journal of African History*, 14 (1973), pp. 79–103.

4 Statistics provided by the Personnel Department of the Ghana Railways and Harbour Administration.

5 Gold Coast, *Census of the Population, 1948* (London, 1950), p. 97. Sekondi-Takoradi was officially designated a twin city in 1954.

6 In 1971 there were about fifteen large or medium-sized firms in Sekondi-Takoradi, manufacturing cigarettes, cocoa-butter, paper products, minerals, furniture, household utensils, cement blocks and boats.

7 The term 'lower-paid workers' is used throughout this study to refer to those earning less than N₵50 per month in 1971 – i.e. all unskilled workers, skilled workers (with the exception of their foreman and a few of the most senior amongst them) and junior clerical workers. This categorisation clearly comprises nearly all those who, in Britain, would normally be termed simply 'workers' or 'the working class', but, in view of the more vague and ambiguous usage of these terms in Ghanaian discourse, it was considered necessary to be more explicit. It is worth noting, however, that virtually all the railway unionists interviewed in 1971 agreed in identifying 'the workers' in accordance with this categorisation.

8 For the definition of the 'informal sector' and its alleged absorption of many of those officially classified as unemployed, see Keith Hart, 'Informal Income Opportunities and Urban Employment in Ghana', *Journal of Modern African Studies*, 2, 1 (1973), pp. 61–89.

9 Margaret Peil, *The Ghanaian Factory Worker: Industrial Man in Africa* (Cambridge, 1972), pp. 101–3.

10 Interviews with five ex-councillors.

11 D. Kimble, *A Political History of Ghana, 1850–1928* (Oxford, 1963), p. 44.

12 Interview with J. Y. Abdulai, 20 September 1971.

13 Margaret Peil provides evidence to suggest that the rate of inter-ethnic marriage is considerably higher in Sekondi-Takoradi than in other Ghanaian cities (*op. cit.* p. 192).

14 *Ibid.* p. 9.

Chapter 2. The origins and dynamics of Railway Union development

1 The earliest recorded strike would seem to be that of the Cape Coast canoemen in 1896. And, in 1898, the first commissioner for the Northern Territories was deploring the formation of 'a trade union of a most pernicious kind' among the carriers from the coast. See Kimble, *op. cit.* p. 44.

2 The 1921 Census recorded 37,450 urban wage-employees, though this did not include the mineworkers, estimated at 10,000 in 1921. Cited in Kimble, *op. cit.* p. 40.

3 J. I. Roper, *Labour Problems in West Africa* (Harmondsworth, 1958), p. 35.

4 A. J. Murray and J. A. Crocket, *Report on the Prevalence of Silicosis and Tuberculosis among Mineworkers in the Gold Coast* (Accra, 1941), p. 13.

5 Richard Wright, *Black Power* (London, 1956), p. 304.

6 Interviews with officials and ex-officials of the Mines Employees' Union, August 1974.
7 For a fascinating account of how the founders of the Zambian Mineworkers' Union overcame just this problem, see A. L. Epstein, *Politics in an African Urban Community* (Manchester, 1958), pp. 48–101.
8 For example, in 1936, the Secretary of Mines wrote that 'Serious consideration must be given to the possible formation of Trade or similar Unions. At least one body has been formed to interest itself in labour matters, and there are other signs that attempts are being made to induce workers to form themselves into trade or occupational groups.' *GNA* Accra, CSO 716/33, Secretary for Mines to Colonial Secretary, 5 March 1936.
9 A. B. Holmes, 'Economic and Political Organisations in the Gold Coast: 1920–45' (PhD thesis, University of Chicago, 1972), p. 358.
10 Guggisberg's initiative should probably be seen as an attempt to restore the government's competitive position as an employer of labour, rather than simple capitulation to the railway workers' demands.
11 Roper, *op. cit.* p. 30.
12 *Ibid.* pp. 52–4.
13 *RAA*, Brown, chief mechanical officer, to general manager, 5 October 1923.
14 Kimble, *op. cit.* p. 44.
15 Interview with H. B. Cofie, retired railway artisan, 5 June 1971.
16 According to one of the founders of the association, 'We did not know much about trade unionism in those days. We moved by experimenting. Whatever we felt was needed by our fellow workers we tried to provide. We interested ourselves in everything: sports, entertainment, even disputes among our members.' (*Ibid.*)
17 *Ibid.*
18 *RAA*, general manager to Colonial Secretary, 9 November 1938.
19 Report of the Labour Department, 1939–40. Cited in E. A. Cowan, *Evolution of Trade Unionism in Ghana* (Accra, 1961), p. 12.
20 *Ibid.*
21 *Ibid.*
22 *RAA*, Vandyck to general manager, 15 May 1939.
23 Cowan, *op. cit.* p. 13.
24 *GNA* Accra, ADM 5/1/76, Macdonald to Colonial Secretary, 16 January 1940.
25 In addition to the restoration of the 1929 rates of pay, the railway workers won an increase in annual leave and in the number of pensionable posts. Only their request for pay on public holidays was turned down.
26 Interviews with H. B. Cofie and J. C. Vandyck, retired railway artisans, 5 June 1971.
27 Quoted by R. B. Davison, 'The Story of the Gold Coast Railway', *West Africa*, 11 August 1956, p. 587.
28 Ansu Datta, 'The Fante Asafo: A Re-Examination,' *Africa*, 42, 4 (October 1972), pp. 305–15.
29 Alan Cawson, 'Traditional Organisation and Urban Politics: Political Parties and the Cape Coast Asafo' (paper presented to the African Urban Politics Seminar of the Institute of Commonwealth Studies, London, 1973).
30 Datta, *op. cit.*
31 *GNA* Accra, CSO 1481/30, report of Western Province commissioner, 'Labour Conditions in the Gold Coast,' 1936.

Chapter 3. The railway workers in the nationalist movement – the meaning of political commitment

1 See, for example, Ioan Davies, *African Trade Unions* (London, 1966), and Meynaud and Salah-Bey, *Trade Unionism in Africa*.
2 Elliot Berg and Jeffrey Butler, 'Trade Unions', in J. S. Coleman and C. S. Rosberg (eds.), *Political Parties and National Integration in Tropical Africa* (Berkeley, 1964), pp. 340–81.
3 *GNA* Accra, CSO 716/33, Colonial Secretary to Secretary for Native Affairs, 2 October 1937.
4 *GNA* Sekondi, Acc 351/15, governor's telegram to commissioner for the Western Province, 26 November 1941.
5 *GNA* Sekondi, Acc 357/17, commissioner for the Western Province to Colonial Secretary, 3 December 1941.
6 *GNA* Sekondi, Acc 357/21, prison superintendent, Sekondi, to director of prisons, Accra, 27 December 1941.
7 *RUA*, Railway Union Executive Council Minutes, 28 January 1942.
8 *RUA*, Railway Union Executive Council Minutes, 7 January 1942.
9 The most important of these measures were: the Conspiracy and Protection of Property (Trade Disputes) Ordinance, 1941, which incidentally did not cover civil servants; the Trades Dispute (Arbitration and Inquiry) Ordinance, 1941; and the Defence (Settlement of Labour Disputes) Order, 1941. An important measure with specific reference to the Railway Union was the Trade Union (Gold Coast Railway African Employees' Union) Order in Council, 1943, which authorised civil servants – i.e. the permanent staff – to join the union, and therefore made possible incorporation of the clerical staff. For fuller details of this legislation, see Cowan, *Evolution of Trade Unionism*, pp. 15–19.
10 Interview with H. B. Cofie, 5 June 1971.
11 J. S. Patrick, *What is a Trade Union?* (Nairobi, 1951), p. 1.
12 Ghana, Labour Department, *Annual Report, 1942* (Accra). Cited in Cowan, *op. cit.* p. 13.
13 Interview with H. B. Cofie, 5 June 1971.
14 Frank Wudu, *A Fallen Labour Hero of Ghana* (Accra, 1968), p. 3. Frank Wudu (or Woode) was general secretary of both the Railway Union and the Gold Coast TUC, 1947–9.
15 Interview with David Sam, former clerical officer, Ghana Railways, 5 March 1971.
16 J. B. Blay, *The Gold Coast Mines Employees' Union* (Devon, 1950), pp. 11–12.
17 As late as 1957, the MEU general secretary, D. K. Foevie, was complaining of the reactionary attitude of the northern tribal headmen, but warned: 'This situation, although very deplorable, cannot be rectified overnight, since they are likely to cause a split in the branches by their influence.' MEUA, National Executive Council Minutes, 28 February 1957.
18 Wudu, *op. cit.* p. 8.
19 Dennis Austin, *Politics in Ghana, 1946–60* (London, 1964), pp. 49–103.
20 Birmingham's index can be accepted as providing a fairly accurate indication of fluctuations in the real wage-levels of both skilled and unskilled workers in government employment, since these maintained a steady relation to each other throughout the period in question. See W. B. Birmingham, 'An Index

of Real Wages of the Unskilled Labourer in Accra', *Economic Bulletin of Ghana*, 4, 3 (1960), pp. 2–6.

21 David Apter, *The Gold Coast in Transition* (Princeton, 1955), p. 69.

22 The 'pilot-boys' were so termed because they earned a living from acting as guides to sightseers, and directing visiting sailors and soldiers to prostitutes. Many of them had 'no settled place of abode', and also engaged in petty theft. Their numbers swelled during the war, when there were many sailors and soldiers about in Takoradi, but there were still quite a number there in 1949: Busia and his assistants came into contact with 150 in the course of a social survey. See K. A. Busia, *Report on a Social Survey of Sekondi-Takoradi* (Accra, 1950), pp. 96–100.

23 Meyer Fortes, 'The Impact of the War on British West Africa', *International Affairs*, 21, 2 (April 1945), pp. 206–20.

24 See, for example, Austin, *op. cit.* p.74.

25 Richard Rathbone, 'Businessmen in Ghanaian Politics', *Journal of Development Studies*, 9, 3 (April 1973), pp. 391–402.

26 Interview with J. Piadoo, railway artisan, 6 June 1971.

27 Interview with Kofi Imbeah, railway artisan and union official, 10 June 1971.

28 *RUA*, J. S. Annan's report to the Railway Union Working Committee, 27 October 1945.

29 All details on Wallace-Johnson and the West African Youth League are taken from Holmes, *Economic and Political Organizations*, pp. 670–732.

30 Holmes quotes a report in the *African Morning Post* of 28 April 1938 on a meeting of the WAYL at which 'Comrade Pobee Biney was charged with having misappropriated the funds of his branch. He appeared to be guilty'. Holmes, *op. cit.* p. 720.

31 Interviews with R. S. Blay, ex-Sekondi Branch chairman of the United Gold Coast Convention, 2 July 1971; and with H. B. Cofie and J. C. Vandyck, ex-Railway Union officials, 5 June 1971.

32 Interview with J. C. Vandyck, 5 June 1971.

33 For instance, in a statement to the press, F. Awonowoor Williams expressed his view that 'true aristocracy after true religion is the greatest blessing a nation can enjoy – of the old school of politics were men of education and substance, and merchant princes, working in the interests of the country. Apart from one or two members of the Convention People's Party, their leaders and supporters are the flotsam and jetsam and popinjays of the country. It is therefore the bounden duty of every informed citizen to unite to save the social and political order'. Cited in Cowan, *op. cit.* p. 102.

34 Interviews with Kofi Imbeah, 10 June 1971, and J. Piadoo, 6 June 1971.

35 Ayi Kwei Armah, *The Beautyful Ones Are Not Yet Born* (London, 1969), p. 101. A. Y. Ankomah, a prominent organiser of the 1961 strike against the Nkrumah Government, admitted that 'He [Nkrumah] had even me captured with his sugar-coated words in those days, and I've always been a straightforward man. There were no exceptions. It was irrational. He just swept you along with his determination. It was only later we discovered he wanted to be a dictator.' (Interview with A. Y. Ankomah, 3 August 1971).

36 The following account of Biney's career and ideology is based on Wudu, *Fallen Labour Hero*, and interviews with many of the older railway workers in June–August 1971.

37 Interview with Kofi Imbeah, 10 June 1971.

38 Wudu, *op. cit.* p. 5.

39 *Ibid.* p. 6.
40 *RAA*, G. N. Burden to Korsah Committee, 20 February 1947.
41 Interview with Kofi Imbeah, 10 June 1971.
42 The Korsah Committee eventually awarded wage increases of some 50 per cent to Government manual workers. (See Table 3.1).
43 Interview with J. K. Baaku, railway worker, 21 July 1971.
44 Interview with Kofi Imbeah, 10 June 1971.
45 Interview with Isaac Adjey, railway artisan, 14 July 1971.
46 For several months in 1949–50 Nkrumah advocated a political strategy known as 'Positive Action' in support of his demand for 'Self-government now'. This meant resort to boycotts, strikes and other forms of civil disobedience on the pattern of Gandhi's politics of non-violent protest.
47 *RUA*, Railway Union Working Committee Minutes, 3 February 1949, and interview with Kofi Imbeah, 17 July 1971.
48 *RUA*, Railway Union Executive Council Resolutions, 23 April 1919.
49 For further details, see Cowan, *Evolution of Trade Unionism*, p. 25.
50 Interview with Kofi Imbeah, 17 July 1971.
51 Cited in Cowan, *op. cit.* p. 48.
52 Charles Arden-Clarke, 'Eight Years of Transition in Ghana', *African Affairs*, 57, 226 (January, 1958), p. 32.
53 R. Saloway, 'The New Gold Coast', *International Affairs*, 32, 4 (October 1955), p. 471.
54 Peter Worsley, ' The Concept of Populism', in G. Ionescu and E. Gellner (eds.), *Populism, Its Meaning and National Characteristics* (London, 1970), pp. 212–50.
55 *Ibid.* pp. 243–4.

Chapter 4. The politics of TUC reorganisation under the CPP regime

1 Chamber of Mines Report, June 1952 (mimeo).
2 *RUA*, Executive Council Minutes, 10 March 1952.
3 Tettegah's practical trade union experience consisted of acting as secretary to the small G. B. Ollivant Employees' Union in 1951–3. Meyer had even less practical experience or rank-and-file support when he entered the service of the Gold Coast TUC in 1953. Indeed he took this step in his own words 'only because my friend John Tettegah, whom I knew from the Accra CPP meetings, asked me to help in the reorganisation. This was really a very difficult decision because I already had a good career in view in my company, but I agreed when Tettegah assured me that Nkrumah had promised his full financial and moral support for our efforts'. Interview with Joe-fio N. Meyer, 9 October 1971.
4 Personal communication with Richard Rathbone. According to one of the few railway worker informants who could recall anything about the Ghana Calling Association, 'We knew it was just the akpeteshie talking: Pobee went crazy for a while when he came out of prison.' Interview with F. Piadoo, 23 June 1971. Those who took it seriously certainly numbered no more than twenty or thirty.
5 The total dues-paying membership of the Railway Union in March 1952 was 2,050 – less than a third of its membership in December 1949. *RUA*, Delegates' Conference Minutes, 25 March 1952.

6 *Daily Graphic*, 22 October 1951, p. 1.
7 *Daily Graphic*, 24 October 1951, p. 1.
8 *Daily Graphic*, 27 October 1951, p. 8.
9 *Daily Graphic*, 17 November 1951, p. 1.
10 Wudu, *Fallen Labour Hero*, p. 3.
11 *Gold Coast TUC Policy Statement*, July 1953 (mimeo).
12 For evidence of close financial links between the AATUF and the Soviet trade union centre, see Benjamin Bentum, *Trade Unions in Chains* (Accra, 1967).
13 The 1953 TUC Constitution stated that the headquarters should be located in the town of residence of the TUC general secretary. It is difficult not to believe that Tettegah's replacement of Turkson-Ocran was already envisaged in senior CPP circles.
14 *Report of the Committee on Trade Union Organisation to 11th Annual Congress of the Gold Coast TUC, September 1954*. Cited in J. K. Tettegah, *A New Chapter for Ghana Labour* (Accra, 1958), p. 13.
15 By 1957, only 26 per cent of urban wage-earners were unionised, almost exactly the same percentage as ten years before. The number of unions, however, had increased from 56 to 95.
16 Interview with G. A. Balogun, administrative secretary of the Ghana TUC 1958–66, 3 August 1974.
17 See *The Pioneer*, 12 August 1955, p. 1.
18 Representation of national unions in the Supreme Congress was proportional as follows: up to 500 members – 1 delegate; 500 to 1,000 – 2 delegates; 1,000 to 5,000 – 3 delegates; 5,000 to 10,000 – 4 delegates; 10,000 to 20,000 – 6 delegates; over 20,000 – 8 delegates.
19 For an elaboration of this point, see J. Kautsky, *The Political Consequences of Modernisation* (New York, 1972), p. 116.
20 Resolution adopted by the 13th Annual Congress of Gold Coast TUC, October 1956. Cited in Tettegah, *op. cit.* p. 14.
21 Gerritsen, 'Evolution of the Ghana TUC'.
22 I. Davies, *African Trade Unions* (Harmondsworth, 1966), p. 175.
23 Interviews with various mineworkers, including M. B. Rockson, MEU chairman, 26 August 1974.
24 Kojo Botsio, secretary of Central Committee of CPP to Committee on Workers' Organisation, 11 January 1959. Cited in Cowan, *Evolution of Trade Unionism*, p. 105.
25 Tettegah, *op. cit.* p. 28. The TUC's 45 per cent share was to be allocated as follows: 25 per cent to general administration and regional organisation, 5 per cent to strike solidarity fund, 10 per cent to social welfare and insurance, 5 per cent to business enterprises. In practice, the TUC was not adequately financed by members' dues and received various government subsidies. For details, see the *Report of the Commission of Enquiry into the Funds of the Ghana TUC* (Accra, 1968).
26 *RUA*, Working Committee Minutes, 20 June 1958.
27 See *The Report of the [Mills–Odoi] Commission on the Structure and Remuneration of the Public Services in Ghana* (Accra, 1967), p. 31.
28 Kwaw Ampah, secretary-general to the TUC in 1964–6, was to recognise the importance of this private/public sector distinction: 'Quite contrary to what is happening in some of the state corporations there is to some extent

respect for trade union organisation in the private industries. This may be due to the fact that, unlike in the state enterprises, there are collective agreements between our unions and the respective employers.' *GTUCA*, Executive Board Minutes, 25 January 1966.

29 J. K. Tettegah, *Towards Nkrumaism: The Role and Tasks of the Trade Unions* (Accra, 1962), p. 14.

30 Ghana, Labour Department, *Annual Report, 1955–6* (Accra), p. 8.

31 Gold Coast, *Legislative Assembly Debates*, issue no. 3 (Accra, November 1955), col. 661.

32 Oral testimony strongly suggests that Tettegah did harbour ambitions of displacing Nkrumah with his own union-based machine, and that suspicions to this effect motivated Nkrumah's removal of Tettegah to the Workers' Brigade and, later, to the All-African Trade Union Federation. Interview with G. A. Balogun, 4 September 1974.

Chapter 5. The railway workers' response to CPP socialism: the strike of 1961

1 St Clair Drake and L. A. Lacy, 'Government versus the Unions: The Sekondi-Takoradi Strike, 1961', in G. Carter (ed.), *Politics in Africa: 7 Cases* (New York, 1966), pp. 67–118 (p.115).

2 Davies, *African Trade Unions*, p. 109.

3 Drake and Lacy, *op. cit.*

4 Interview with Maxwell Annobil, harbour worker, 19 October 1971.

5 Interview with F. Awortwi, railway artisan, 29 August 1971.

6 Keith Hart and John Weeks have rightly pointed to factors making for exaggeration in most estimates of the level of unemployment in West African cities. It would nevertheless be wrong, I believe, to deny that the level of genuine unemployment is high, or that many of those working in the informal sector make so precarious an existence as to be forced to look to more securely employed relatives for financial assistance. See K. Hart, 'Informal Income Opportunities', and J. Weeks, 'An Exploration into the Problem of Urban Imbalance in Africa', *Manpower and Unemployment Research in Africa*, 6, 2 (1973), pp. 9–37.

7 Interview with J. Dadson, railway artisan, 19 September 1971.

8 Interview with A. Y. Ankomah, 15 August 1971.

9 Quoted by Davison, 'Story of the Gold Coast Railway', p. 587.

10 Busia, *Social Survey*, pp. 31–50.

11 *Sekondi-Takoradi Survey of Population and Household Budgets, 1955* (Accra, 1956), p. 16.

12 *Ashanti Pioneer*, 26 July 1952, p. 6.

13 *Daily Graphic*, 5 March 1954, p. 3.

14 *Report of the Commission of Enquiry into the Affairs of the National Housing Corporation* (Accra, 1967).

15 *GNA* Sekondi, Acc 158/6, Ministry of Local Government Report for quarter ended 31 December 1956, according to which, 'The Council has as much faith in the Ministry's promises as the Ministry has in the Council's accounting.'

16 Interviews with J. Flynn (Sekondi businessman), Atta Hussaini (municipal councillor for Ward 5, 1954–60) and T. N. Kankam (municipal councillor for Ward 7, 1954–60).

17 The regional commissioner for the Western Region was J. K. Arthur, whose main claim to high status in the party was the part he had played in 'capturing' the Mineworkers' and UAC Employees' Unions in 1950–8.
18 Interview with S. Smith, railway artisan, 7 August 1971.
19 These were Grace Ayensu, wife of the vice-chairman of Sekondi-Takoradi Council, J. W. Acquah; and Christina Wilmot, a telephonist in the Public Works Department.
20 *RUA*, Delegates' Conference Minutes, 5 August 1950.
21 *RUA*, Working Committee Minutes, 19 August 1950.
22 *RUA*, Working Committee Minutes, 1 September 1950.
23 The Lidbury–Gbedemah Commission awarded an increase of 38 per cent to unskilled labourers, 25 per cent to skilled workers, and progressively smaller proportionate increases to higher-paid government employees. This was obviously well received by many of the lower-paid workers. But, since this was intended to be the permanent post-war settlement, Biney and Woode were dissatisfied with both the size of the increase for the lower-paid, which barely covered the rise in the cost of living since 1950, and with the failure to make more radically egalitarian changes in the overall wage structure.
24 Interview with Isaac Adjey, railway artisan, 14 July 1971.
25 *RUA*, Delegates' Conference Minutes, 25 March 1951.
26 Formerly, each of the eight union branches had two representatives on the Working Committee, while each of the ten departmental associations, (e.g. electrical, marine, clerical) had one only. Since the up-country branches, together with the Clerical and Stores Associations, generally elected clerical staff as their representatives, this meant that clerical unionists normally outnumbered technical unionists on the Working Committee. The reform of 1952 provided for two delegates from each association, most of which were based in Sekondi-Takoradi and generally elected technical men as their representatives.
27 Interview with A. Y. Ankomah, 23 August 1971.
28 Interview with Albert Johnson, Railway Union clerk (1954–69), 5 October 1971.
29 See above, pp. 63–4.
30 *Daily Graphic*, 17 October 1955, p. 12.
31 For example, Davies, *African Trade Unions*, p. 109.
32 Interviews with Kofi Imbeah, railway unionist, 12 June 1971, and A. Y. Ankomah, 23 August 1971. For details of the NLM, its programme and sources of support, see Austin, *Politics in Ghana*, pp. 253–81.
33 *RUA*, Delegates' Conference Minutes, 5 May 1956.
34 Numerous stories were recounted to the author in 1971 of Nkrumah's unsuccessful attempts to bribe Biney into toeing the party line. Eventually, in 1963, Nkrumah offered the destitute Biney a job as a government security agent which the latter accepted, but – the legend insists – 'only to keep body and soul together' and without any intention of performing the functions of the appointment.
35 Interview with Albert Johnson, 5 October 1971.
36 Interview with J. Apprey, railway artisan, 23 August 1971.
37 *RAA*, Railway Administration Staff List, 1970.
38 Interview with Kofi Imbeah, 22 August 1971.
39 *RUA*, Working Committee Minutes, 13 February 1958.

40 *RUA*, Working Committee Minutes, 24 July 1958.
41 Interview with A. B. Essuman, railway artisan and Location Branch secretary (1962–70), 14 October 1971.
42 *RUA*, Working Committee Minutes, 14 August 1958.
43 *RUA*, Working Committee Minutes, 24 July 1958.
44 *Ibid.*
45 *Ibid.*
46 *Ibid.*
47 Such cultivation of up-country officials often takes the form of promising to arrange their transfer to Sekondi-Takoradi in return for 'loyal' service.
48 Interview with A. K. A. Bello, secretary of the Traffic Association (1956–61) and later Accra branch secretary, 5 November 1971.
49 *RUA*, Misc/32, Joint Council of Railway Unions Bulletin, no. 1. Grammatical errors in text uncorrected.
50 *RUA*, Misc/32, Prime Minister to JCRU general secretary.
51 *RUA*, Executive Council Minutes, 3 March 1960.
52 *RUA*, Working Committee Minutes, 2 May 1960.
53 In this new 'model' constitution, the president of the union gained the right to appoint all ad hoc committees, to fill all temporary vacancies at the level of national officers with his own nominees, and 'to suspend individual members or officers of the Branch Unions or Departmental Associations where, in his judgment, their activities are in violation of the declared policies of the National Union'. *RUA*, Executive Council Minutes, 8 February 1960.
54 When questioned in July–August 1971 as to the most important qualities of a good trade unionist, 93 per cent of railway worker interviewees immediately responded, 'He should be straightforward', or 'He should be plain-talking'. Questionnaire survey conducted by the writer.
55 Interview with A. B. Essuman, 18 July 1971.
56 J. D. Holm, 'Ideology and Socio-Political Development in Nkrumah's Ghana' (PhD thesis, University of Chicago, 1966), p. 311.
57 Nicholas Kaldor, 'Taxation for Economic Development', *Journal of Modern African Studies*, 1, 1 (March 1963), p. 22.
58 For fuller details of the budget, and the general economic background, see Drake and Lacy, 'Government versus the Unions', on which this brief account is based.
59 Ghana, *Parliamentary Debates*: *Official Reports*, 24 (7 July 1961), col. 133.
60 The average expenditure pattern in Sekondi-Takoradi was as follows: food, 57.0 per cent (local foods, 52.3 per cent); clothing, 14.8 per cent; drink and tobacco, 5.1 per cent; fuel and light, 6.0 per cent; services, 4.9 per cent; rent and rates, 6.0 per cent; durable goods, 2.5 per cent; miscellaneous, 3.0 per cent. *Sekondi-Takoradi Survey of Population and Household Budgets* (*1955*), p. 14.
61 *Ashanti Pioneer*, 5 September 1961, p. 8.
62 Interview with W. N. Grant, 20 October 1971.
63 *RUA*, Working Committee Minutes, 20 July 1961.
64 *RUA*, Working Committee Minutes, 31 August 1961.
65 *RUA*, Working Committee Minutes, 31 August 1961.
66 *Daily Graphic*, 8 September 1961, p. 1.
67 *RUA*, Working Committee Minutes, Tettegah to Railway Union general secretary, 12 September 1961.
68 Interview with Kofi Imbeah, 4 June 1971.

69 Interview with Moses Braimah, secretary of Permanent Waymen's Association, 3 October 1971.
70 Interview with T. B. Ward, railway unionist, 6 June 1971.
71 *Ibid.*
72 Interview with Alice Koomson, 15 August 1971.
73 Interview with Kofi Imbeah, 4 June 1971.
74 Drake and Lacy, *op. cit.* p. 93.
75 *Evening News*, 1 May 1961, p. 4.
76 For fuller details of the United Party, see Austin, *Politics in Ghana*, pp. 384–94.
77 Of the 32 opposition MPs at Independence, 3 were being held in detention, 1 was in exile and 12 had crossed to the government side by 1960. It is difficult to assess the true extent of the UP's electoral support, since malpractices in the conduct of the 1960 plebiscite appear to have been widespread. See Austin, *op. cit.* p. 393.
78 Interview with A. B. Essuman, 14 August 1971.
79 Interview with A. Y. Ankomah and Alice Koomson, 15 August 1971.
80 Interviews with Kofi Imbeah, 12 June 1971, and J. K. Baaku, 7 October 1971.
81 Ghana, Office of the President, *Statement by the Government on the Recent Conspiracy* (Accra, 1961).
82 *Evening News*, 8 April 1961, p. 1.
83 The limits which Nkrumah tried to impose on his followers' accumulation of wealth were in themselves an indication of the fortunes already amassed. It was ruled from the president's office that party members should not own (a) more than two houses of a combined value of £20,000; (b) more than two motor cars; (c) plots of land (other than those covered by (a) above) with the present total value greater than £500. Austin, *op. cit.* p. 405.

Chapter 6. The development of an independent and democratic trade union movement

1 *Ghanaian Times*, 27 February 1966, p. 1.
2 *Report of the Commission on the Structure and Remuneration of the Public Services in Ghana* (Accra, 1967), p. 29. Hereafter cited as the *Mills–Odoi Report*.
3 *Report of the Commission of Enquiry into the Funds of the Ghana TUC* (Accra, 1968).
4 Interview with Joe-fio N. Meyer, 15 November 1971. Also see Bentum, *Trade Unions in Chains*, pp. 9–16.
5 Editorial, *The Worker*, 5 July 1965.
6 *Ibid.*
7 Ghana, *Parliamentary Debates: Official Reports*, 39 (25 May 1965), col. 189.
8 Interview with John Abakah, secretary of the Compagnie Française Afrique Occidentale Branch of the Industrial and Commercial Workers' Union, 3 September 1971.
9 See ch. 7, p. 150.
10 Interview with Joe-fio N. Meyer, 15 November 1971.
11 Interview with Kofi Imbeah, 17 July 1971.
12 Interview with Dr W. G. Bruce-Konuah, 11 November 1971.
13 Personal details provided by Benjamin Bentum in private correspondence, 14 August 1973.

14 Nkrumah's continuing respect for Bentum's abilities was reflected in his appointment as Minister of Forestries in September of the same year.
15 Interview with G. A. Balogun, Administrative secretary of the TUC (1958–66), 4 August 1974.
16 *Report of the First Biennial Congress of the TUC of Ghana*, 5–7 June 1966 (mimeo, Accra, 1966), p. 3.
17 This phrase was frequently used by speakers at Sekondi-Takoradi District Labour Council meetings which the writer attended in June–August 1971, and by workers in interviews conducted during the same period.
18 See ch. 8, p. 174.
19 *Ghanaian Times*, 27 February 1966, p. 1.
20 This fact gave rise to the common belief that Bentum had been secretly working against the CPP regime from within. Though far from conclusive, some evidence in support of this view is provided by an interview with Police-Inspector Harlley, according to which 'Mr Harlley had briefed Bentum on the coup some time in advance and had advised him to gather support in the unions'. R. Pratt, 'Political Opposition in Ghana, 1966–72' (MA thesis, SOAS, University of London, 1973), p. 16.
21 *RUA*, Railway Union Working Committee Minutes, 4 March 1966.
22 For a fuller description of the character and style of government of the NLC regime, see Robert Pinkney, *Ghana under Military Rule, 1966–69* (London, 1972), and Robert Dowse, 'Military and Police Rule', in D. Austin and R. Luckham (eds.), *Politicians and Soldiers in Ghana* (London, 1975), pp. 16–37.
23 *Ghanaian Times*, 8 March 1966, p. 6.
24 TUC Executive Board Resolutions, article VI, 2 (7 October 1966), published in *Ghana Workers' Bulletin*, 1, 4 (October 1966), p. 4.
25 *Ibid.* Article XII, 2 (b).
26 *Ghana Workers' Bulletin*, 1, 9 (August 1968), p. 3.
27 'Statement issued by the Ghana TUC on the "Report of the Commission on the Structure and Remuneration of the Public Services in Ghana"', Annexure 1, *Report of the Committee on Review of Salaries and Pensions in the Public Services of Ghana* (Accra, 1969) (hereafter cited as *Mensah Report*), p. 64.
28 Speech reported in the *Ghanaian Times*, 19 September 1968, p. 1.
29 *Ibid.*
30 For instance, in an article in *The Pioneer* on 16 July 1969, Bentum argued that three main factors were responsible for the high incidence of strikes in Ghana: '(a) Management and Government's lack of understanding of industrial relations and of the value of the work done by the TUC... (b) There will be no industrial peace without a bridging of the wages gap . . . (c) The high cost of food.'
31 Annexure 1, *Mensah Report*, p. 28.
32 Annexure 1, *Mensah Report*, p. 65.
33 Article in *The Pioneer*, 5 April 1969, p. 7.
34 For details, see the *Report of the Commission of Enquiry into Obuasi Disturbances* (Accra, 1970).
35 *West Africa*, 7 June 1969, p. 653.
36 Out of 90 workers interviewed, 44 per cent claimed to have voted for the Progress Party, 20 per cent for one of the other parties, and 36 per cent not to have voted in the elections. It is possible that a number of those who claimed not to have voted were simply reluctant to reveal their party affiliation.

37 For penetrating analyses of the determination of allegiances in four predominantly 'rural' constituencies, see the essays by Joseph Peasah, Maxwell Owusu, Mark Graesser, and especially John Dunn, in Austin and Luckham (eds.), *Politicians and Soldiers.*

38 *Report of the (Jiagge) Commission to Enquire into the Assets of Specified Persons* (Accra, 1969).

39 Interview with Samuel Essien, Takoradi correspondent of the *Ghanaian Times*, 7 September 1971.

40 Anon., *The Birth of the Second Republic* (Accra, 1970). p. 82.

41 *The Pioneer*, 5 July 1969, p. 3.

42 *The Spokesman*, 22 May 1970, p. 1.

43 *Ghanaian Times*, 19 June 1969, p. 1.

44 *RUA*, Railway Union Working Committee Minutes, 14 September 1969.

45 Dr Fynn, a university history lecturer and a Progress Party candidate in the elections, explained that 'Many university graduates have decided to do politics because it is irritating to see incompetent and dishonest men running the affairs of the nation.' *The Pioneer*, 13 August 1969, p. 3.

46 Quoted in *The Birth of the Second Republic*, p. 34.

47 This account is based on structured interviews with 90 railway workers in Sekondi-Takoradi during August 1971, the results of which, though they cannot be assumed to be typical of the views of other groups of workers in any strict sense, are certainly indicative of labour reactions more generally. For further details of the questionnaire and its administration see the Appendix.

48 J. H. Mensah's budget statement was reproduced in full in the *Daily Graphic* and *Ghanaian Times*, 27–30 July 1971. In addition, both of these newspapers published special supplements on 17 August, explaining its rationale in somewhat simpler terms for the benefit of the mass audience.

49 The peculiar combination of elitist and populist ideological tendencies which characterised the Progress Party leadership was well illustrated by a remark of Dr Busia's reported in the *Daily Graphic* on 31 August 1971. Dr Busia explained his decision to cut his own and other Cabinet Ministers' salaries as a result of a trip he made to a village where the drinking water was visibly filthy. On returning to his home, he apparently thought to himself, 'I can sit in Accra and the water I use in my toilet is cleaner than the water my fellow-countrymen are drinking.'

50 Budget statement, *Ghanaian Times*, 30 July 1971, p. 6.

51 *Ibid.*

52 *Daily Graphic*, 10 May 1971, p. 4.

53 Budget statement, *Ghanaian Times*, 30 July 1971, p. 6.

54 Budget supplement, *Ghanaian Times*, 17 August 1971, p. 6.

55 *Ibid*, p. 7.

56 Interview with railway worker, 23 August 1971.

57 Interview with railway worker, 21 August 1971.

58 See ch. 7, Table 7.4.

59 *The Pioneer*, 21 November 1969, p. 1.

60 This, at least, was the impression of the senior community development officer for the Western Region. Interview with H. Bossman, 2 August 1971.

61 Interview with railway worker, 28 August 1971.

62 *Ghanaian Times*, 17 September 1971, p. 1.

63 This (admittedly very rough) estimate of the increase in price of local

foodstuffs is based on conversations with market-women and customers in Sekondi market on 13 August 1971.

64 Interview with Joseph Ansah, 8 July 1971. It is worth quoting in full the remark of this 75-year-old Sekondi inhabitant, who was private secretary to the famous pan-Africanist J. Caseley Hayford in the 1930s, the uncle of the PP Minister J. Kwesi Lamptey, and in no sense a radical: 'Our workers are now having to eat food, this gari, formerly considered fit only for pigs in the old days, food not fit for Ghanaians. And meanwhile the government carries on playing "moneytics". I really would not wish to live much longer to see my beloved Ghana in the days of bloody revolution that are coming.'

65 Speaker at a Railway Union mass meeting on 26 August 1971 at which the writer was present.

66 Interview with railway worker, 17 August 1971.

67 *Ghanaian Times*, 28 August 1971, p. 1.

68 At the end of the CPP period, Ministers received salaries of N₵9,000 per annum.

69 *The Spokesman*, 18 May 1970, p. 1.

70 J. H. Mensah, quoted in the *Ghanaian Times*, 11 September 1971, p. 2.

71 *The Star*, 18 December 1970, p. 1.

72 *The Spokesman*, 5 January 1971, p. 1.

73 *The Spokesman*, 25 May 1971, p. 1.

74 *Daily Graphic*, 3 December 1969, p. 3.

75 Dr Busia's speech to the TUC Congress of August 1970, reported in the *Ghanaian Times*, 1 August 1970, p. 3.

76 *The Spokesman*, 30 June 1970, p. 1.

77 *Ghanaian Times*, 10 May 1971, p. 5.

78 The sanitary workers went on strike 10–15 June, the dockworkers 20–24 June and the railway enginemen 3–13 July.

79 See, for example, reports of speeches by Victor Owusu and Stephen Krakue in *The Spokesman*, 11 May and 22 June 1971.

80 *Daily Graphic*, 28 June 1971, p. 5.

81 *Daily Graphic*, 28 June 1971, p. 5.

82 *Ghanaian Times*, 9 July 1971, p. 8.

83 *Ghanaian Times*, 14 July 1971, p. 1.

84 *Ghana Workers' Bulletin*, 3, 9 (September 1970), p. 2.

85 The Ghana Confederation of Labour required the government's special assistance even to exist, since, according to the Industrial Relations Act of 1958 (still in force, though amended in 1965), only one trade union centre, the TUC, was permitted legal identity in Ghana. Similarly, the main force behind the GCL, the splinter Railway and Harbour Employees' Union, had required the government's special intervention to gain registration, since it did not possess the membership – 40 per cent of the total labour force in an industry – legally required for the establishment of a second union within that industry. In addition, overt support was provided for the new centre by ministerial statements in the national press. See, for example, the statement of the Minister of Labour in the *Daily Graphic*, 28 August 1971, p. 3.

86 For example, see the speeches reported in the *Ghanaian Times*, 4 August 1971, p. 1, and *Daily Graphic*, 28 August 1971, p. 5.

87 *The Spokesman*, 28 July 1970, p. 1.

88 *Proposals Submitted by the TUC (Ghana) to the Salary Review Commission* (Accra, 1971).

89 See, for example, Baiden's speech reported in the *Daily Graphic*, 28 June 1971, p. 3.
90 In fact, Dr Busia dismissed 608 civil servants within one month of taking office, but he was apparently under pressure to go further than this in sacking 'suspects' and replacing them with party loyalists. See *The Times* (of London), supplement on Ghana, 30 September 1971.
91 If the local organisation of the Progress Party was somewhat skeletal by 1971, that of the Justice Party was non-existent. The J.P's leading representatives in Sekondi-Takoradi consisted of a young lawyer, of absolutely no local standing or renown, who spent most of his time in the expatriate-dominated Golf Club and confessed that he wasn't much interested in politics; and a building contractor, former CPP chairman of the City Council, who was totally discredited politically as a result of his reputation for fraudulent practice.

It was significant that, shortly after the military coup of 13 January 1971, several Justice Party leaders were detained along with Progress Party officials, and the new government leader, Colonel Acheampong, 'blamed some members of the former opposition for compromising their position by obtaining big government loans, thus laying themselves open to political blackmail'. *West Africa*, 25 February 1972, p. 12.
92 TUC Secretariat statement in *The Spokesman*, 24 July 1970.
93 Speech delivered by Richard Baiden to a meeting of the Sekondi-Takoradi District Labour Council on 7 July 1971 at which the writer was present.
94 Out of 24 local officials of the Railway Union who attended a TUC course on industrial relations in June 1971, 16 were under thirty-five years of age, 22 were educated to middle-school level and 9 had taken further courses of some kind to improve their education (i.e. not including apprenticeship or specifically trade union courses).
95 *The Pioneer*, 17 November 1969, p. 3.
96 *Ghanaian Times*, 3 September 1971, p. 5.
97 Interview with Dr W. G. Bruce-Konuah, 11 October 1971.
98 *Daily Graphic*, 7 September 1971, p. 2.
99 *Ghanaian Times*, 27 August 1971, p. 1.
100 Interview with J. K. Baaku, railway worker, 4 September 1971.
101 *Daily Graphic*, 17 August 1971, p. 4.
102 *Ghanaian Times*, 17 August 1971, p. 1.
103 *Ibid.*
104 *Ghanaian Times*, 4 August 1971, p. 1.
105 *Ghanaian Times*, 21 August 1971, p. 5.
106 *Ghanaian Times*, 1 September 1971, p. 5.
107 *Ghanaian Times*, 27 August 1971, p. 1.
108 *Ibid.*
109 *Ghanaian Times*, 8 September 1971, p. 1.
110 *Daily Graphic*, 10 September 1971, p. 1.
111 *Ghanaian Times*, 15 September 1971, p. 1.
112 Private communication with Jon Kraus, who interviewed five general secretaries of the national unions in the summer of 1972.
113 Private communication with Jon Kraus.
114 This resolution did not in fact materialise in a new TUC, owing largely to the organisational chaos into which the unions were thrown by the Industrial Relations (Amendment) Act of 9 September 1971.

115 *Daily Graphic*, 17 September 1971, p. 4.
116 The writer was present at the strikers' demonstrations.
117 Interview with B. T. Nahr, railway unionist, 13 September 1971.
118 Conversation overheard in Sekondi bar, 15 September 1971.
119 Interview with Robert Mensah, 15 September 1971.
120 Speech delivered by R. Mensah to a meeting of strikers on 16 September 1971 at which the writer was present.
121 For statistics on the pattern of income distribution in Ghana, see above, pp. 175–7.

Chapter 7. The railway workers divided: the sources and structure of political conflict in the Railway Union

1 *Ghanaian Times*, 23 January 1970, p. 3.
2 *Ghanaian Times*, 22 June 1970, p.3.
3 *Ghanaian Times*, 24 August 1971, p. 8.
4 The following analysis of the Railway Union division is based on several sources of data: official records of the mother union for 1961–71, direct observation of union mass meetings and of day-to-day interaction between union officials and rank and file, interviews with officials of both unions and a questionnaire survey of the workers employed at the Sekondi-Location workshops. For details of the questionnaire and the method of its administration, see the Appendix.
5 Interview with W. N. Grant, 20 October 1971.
6 Interview with Dr W. G. Bruce-Konauh, 11 November 1971.
7 The general manager of the Railway Administration in 1971, P. O. Aggrey, had been Clerical Association secretary of the Railway Union in the late 40s, and his principal secretary, J. S. Appiah, had been vice-chairman of the union in 1958–61: but, as far as the author could discover, these instances were unique.
8 Nearly all of the union officials at Location in 1961–71 were junior foremen, but instances of officials being appointed foremen were extremely rare. Out of the 36 foremen at Location in 1970–1, only 2, John Eshun and E. Class-Peters, had ever been prominent officials (i.e. national officers, or branch or association secretaries or chairman).
9 For comparative purposes, see the lucid analysis of the effect of alternative mobility opportunities on union leaders' attitudes and behaviour presented by Robert Bates in his study of the Zambian mineworkers, *Unions, Parties and Political Development* (New Haven and London, 1971), pp. 91–7.
10 Of the other Sekondi-Takoradi railway unionists, T. B. Ward was appointed a member of the City Council Management Committee, and J. K. Baaku and T. C. Bentil served as local ward officials for the Progress Party in 1969–71.
11 In 1971, Railway Union officials received the following monthly salaries or honoraria: (N₵=£0.42) general secretary, N₵170; national chairman, N₵16; deputy general secretary, N₵18; national vice-chairman, N₵12; trustees, N₵10; branch secretaries, N₵5; and branch chairmen, N₵4.
12 *RUA*, Railway Union Executive Council Minutes, 13 August 1952 and 23 March 1966.
13 Sample survey interviews, August 1971.
14 Maxwell Owusu, for example, argues that 'Both wealth and power are

related means to the supreme social value – high status, social recognition and social dignity.' Maxwell Owusu, *Uses and Abuses of Political Power* (Chicago, 1970), p. 5.
15 Interviews with A. B. Essuman, 15 July 1971, and A. E. Forson, 17 June 1971.
16 *RUA*, Railway Union Executive Council Minutes, 20 November 1962.
17 *RUA*, Railway Union Delegates' Conference Minutes, 24 February 1963.
18 See above, p. 160.
19 *RUA*, Railway Union Executive Council Minutes, 17 October 1963.
20 *Ibid*.
21 *RUA*, Railway Union Executive Council Minutes, 15 June 1965.
22 *RUA*, Railway Union Executive Council Minutes, 8 March 1966.
23 *RUA*, Railway Union Executive Council Minutes, 30 April 1966.
24 *RUA*, Railway Union Delegates' Conference Minutes, 5 July 1966.
25 Interview with K. G. Quartey, 30 June 1971.
26 Interview with Kofi Imbeah, 14 June 1971.
27 *RUA*, Railway Union Delegates' Conference Minutes, 13 October 1968.
28 *Mills–Odoi Report*, para. 168. For details of the 'tradesmen's case' see above, p. 160.
29 *RUA*, Railway Union Executive Council Minutes, 6 August 1969.
30 *RUA*, Railway Union Executive Council Minutes, 6 January 1970.
31 Careerist motivations possibly influenced these unionists' behaviour. Ward had been advised by Bentum that he was in line for the post of TUC regional secretary, and clearly did not want to prejudice his chances by associating with the splinter unionists. Forson and Bello were perhaps playing for time to discredit the Quartey faction and mount their own campaigns for election as general secretary. But it was certainly also the case that Forson, Bello and Imbeah were acting in line with the stance they had consistently taken since 1967.
32 *RUA*, Railway Union Executive Council Minutes, 13 March 1970.
33 *RUA*, Railway Union Delegates' Conference Minutes, 15 June 1970.
34 Interview with J. K. Baaku, 28 August 1971.
35 *Ghanaian Times*, 7 May 1970, p. 3.
36 Interview with A. E. Forson, 2 October 1971.
37 K. G. Quartey's speech to a mass meeting of the RHEU on 5 August 1971 at which the writer was present.
38 The source for this table, and for all subsequent tables in this chapter, is the questionnaire survey of workers at the Sekondi Location workshops which the writer conducted in July–August 1971. For details, see the Appendix.
39 This questionnaire was modelled on one administered to a sample of Chilean unionists by Henry A. Landsberger. See H. A. Landsberger, 'The Labour Elite: Is It Revolutionary?', in S. M. Lipset and A. Solari (eds.), *Elites in Latin America* (New York, 1967), p. 275. The results are very similar for the Chilean and Ghanaian samples. I would wish to dissent from Landsberger's interpretation of these results, however. A predominant concern with gaining economic concessions rather than 'making workers more politically conscious' is not necessarily a non-ideological orientation as Landsberger suggests. Among other considerations, it is likely that many interviewees interpreted 'political consciousness' as meaning 'party political involvement'.
40 Interview with B. Maurice, apprentice, 7 August 1971.
41 *RUA*, Railway Union Executive Council Minutes, 18 February 1963.

42 Interview with U. I. Viala, Apprentices' Association secretary, 15 August 1971.
43 Interviews with K. Oforri (RHEU Marine Association secretary), 9 September 1971, and B. T. Nahr (RPWU Takoradi Branch chairman and formerly Marine Association secretary), 12 September 1971.
44 Interview with K. Mensah, crane driver, 28 August 1971.
45 Interview with J. E. Annan, RPWU Marine Association Secretary, 18 July 1971.
46 Interview with F. K. Awortwi, artisan, 7 August 1971.
47 Interview with J. H. Amissah, tradesman, 24 August 1971.
48 Interview with A. J. Odonkor, railway tradesman, 14 August 1971.
49 K. G. Quartey's speech to a mass meeting of the RHEU on 5 August 1971, at which the writer was present.
50 K. G. Quartey's speech to a mass meeting of the RHEU on 12 August 1971, at which the writer was present.
51 Unidentified speaker at the RHEU mass meeting on 12 August 1971.
52 A. Rockson, tradesman, speaking at the RHEU mass meeting on 12 August 1971.
53 Private correspondence with A. B. Essuman, 10 April 1972.

Chapter 8. Class formation in Ghana

1 See G. Arrighi and J. Saul, 'Socialism and Economic Development in Tropical Africa', *Journal of Modern African Studies*, 6, 2 (1968), pp. 141–69, and 'Nationalism and Revolution in Sub-Saharan Africa', in R. Miliband and J. Saville (eds.), *The Socialist Register 1969* (New York and London, 1969), pp. 137–88.
2 Arrighi and Saul, 'Socialism and Economic Development', p. 149.
3 Berg and Butler, 'Trade Unions'.
4 For the case of Nigeria, see Adrian Peace, 'Industrial Protest in Nigeria', in E. de Kadt and G. P. Williams (eds.), *Sociology of Development* (London, 1973), pp. 141–67.
5 John Saul has recently attempted to remedy this defect and to outline the difficulties and preconditions of eliciting 'a shared consciousness and joint political action' on the part of the peasantry. See John Saul, 'African Peasants and Revolution', *Review of African Political Economy*, 1 (1974), pp. 41–68.
6 Arrighi and Saul, *op. cit.* p. 149.
7 G. Arrighi, 'International Corporations, Labour Aristocracies and Economic Development in Tropical Africa', in R. I. Rhodes (ed.), *Imperialism and Underdevelopment: A Reader* (New York, 1970), pp. 220–67.
8 According to the 1967 Mills–Odoi Commission, the average earnings of skilled and unskilled workers in the private sector 'appeared to be between 20 per cent and 25 per cent above those in the public sector'. *Mills–Odoi Report*, para. 184.
9 Calculated from data on incomes provided in *RAA*, Railway Administration Staff List (1970).
10 See John F. Weeks, 'Wage Policy and the Colonial Legacy – A Comparative Study', *Journal of Modern African Studies*, 9, 3 (1971), pp. 361–87.
11 For details see above, Tables 3.1, 5.2 and 6.1.
12 Quoted in Birmingham, 'Index of Real Wages', p. 16.

13 *Ibid.*
14 *Mills–Odoi Report*, para. 186.
15 Employing statistics on basic nutritional requirements provided by the Ghana Ministry of Health, together with a list of food item prices drawn up by TUC officials from observation of market prices in Accra, the TUC estimated that the cost of a balanced diet for a single worker would be N₵1.05 per day. The minimum wage of N₵0.75 would not cover the worker's basic food costs, and the skilled worker's average income of N₵1.30 would barely suffice, without even considering additional obligatory expenditures on food, housing, clothing, etc., for the upkeep of a family in the city. *Proposals Submitted by the TUC Executive Board to the Campbell Salary Review Commission* (Accra, 1971, mimeo), pp. 18–20.
16 Keith Hinchcliffe, 'Labour Aristocracy – A Northern Nigerian Case Study', *Journal of Modern African Studies*, 12, 1 (1974), pp. 57–67.
17 *Ibid.* p. 66.
18 P. Hill, *The Migrant Cocoa Farmers of Southern Ghana* (Cambridge, 1963), pp. 178–92.
19 Blair Rourke, *Wages and Incomes of Agricultural Workers in Ghana* (Legon, 1970), p. 82, and D. K. Dutta-Roy, *The Eastern Region Household Budget Survey* (Legon, 1968).
20 Peil, *The Ghanaian Factory Worker*, p. 76.
21 According to Peil's survey, 72 per cent of skilled workers regularly remitted part of their wages to relatives in the countryside, the average amount sent being N₵36.64 per year or N₵3.05 per month. *Ibid.* p. 210.
22 *Ibid.* p. 118.
23 Interview with B. T. Nahr, 8 July 1971.
24 Ghana, *Central Revenue Department's General Information on Taxation in Ghana* (Accra, 1970).
25 Ewusi, *op. cit.* p. 96.
26 *Ibid.* p. 95.
27 Donal B. Cruise O'Brien, *Saints and Politicians* (Cambridge, 1975), p. 151.
28 Ghana, *Survey of High-Level Manpower in Ghana, 1960* (Accra, 1961).
29 On the subject of overstaffing under the CPP regime, see Douglas Rimmer, 'The Crisis in the Ghanaian Economy', *Journal of Modern African Studies*, 4, 1 (1966), pp. 17–32.
30 Peil, *op. cit.* p. 111.
31 See, for example, P. C. Lloyd, *Classes, Crises and Coups* (London, 1971), pp. 101 and 135, W. A. Schwab, 'Social Stratification in Gwelo', in A. Southall (ed.), *Social Change in Modern Africa* (London, 1961), pp. 126–44, and, in the same volume, J. E. Goldthorpe, 'Educated Africans', pp. 145–58.
32 Interview with B. Maurice, 13 August 1971.
33 Busia, *Social Survey*, pp. 74–5.
34 Interview with S. Biney, community development officer for Sekondi-Takoradi District, 10 June 1971.
35 For example, the three groups with which the writer became familiar consisted of (a) a bank manager, a car importer, an assistant headmaster, a police lawyer and two sisters who owned a bar and lodging house (Ga); (b) two school teachers, a naval officer, a cloth seller and two clerks (Ashanti); and (c) three skilled workers, a taxi driver, a technical school teacher and two seamstresses (Fanti).

231

36 This assertion is based on interviews with church leaders, and the (perhaps more reliable) evidence that both of these sects were in the process of constructing large new churches in Sekondi in 1971. Information on the origins and beliefs of these churches is provided in C. G. Baeta, *Prophetism in Ghana* (London, 1962), pp. 9–27, 28–67.

37 Interview with J. Blankson, 3 July 1971.

38 See Keith Hart, 'Informal Income Opportunities', pp. 61–89, and Weeks, 'Urban Imbalance in Africa', pp. 9–32. Although Weeks and Hart are concerned in these articles to emphasise that many of the officially unemployed are in fact productively employed in the informal sector, the essentially bulk-breaking or criminal nature of much of this informal activity suggests a situation of extensive underemployment.

Chapter 9. Power and organisation

1 Berg and Butler, 'Trade Unions', p. 350.

2 Arrighi and Saul, 'Nationalism and Revolution', p. 175.

3 Saul, 'African Peasants', pp. 42–3.

4 Colin Leys, 'Politics in Kenya: The Development of Peasant Society', *British Journal of Political Science*, 1 (1971), p. 337.

5 Julius K. Nyerere quoted in *The Nationalist*, Dar es Salaam, 5 September 1967, and cited in Saul, *op. cit.* p. 51.

6 See Maxwell Owusu, 'Politics in Swedru', in Dennis Austin and Robin Luckham (eds.), *Politicians and Soldiers in Ghana* (London, 1975), pp. 233–63, esp. p. 234.

7 Karl Marx, *The Eighteenth Brumaire of Louis Bonaparte* (New York, 1932), p. 19.

8 Technically speaking, most Ghanaian cocoa producers are perhaps most accurately described as 'peasants', whilst that sizeable minority who employ considerable numbers of hired labourers might be termed 'capitalist farmers'. In the interests of simplicity however, it is intended in the following section to use the collective term 'cocoa farmers'.

9 This analysis is based on evidence presented in Holmes, 'Economic and Political Organizations', pp. 264–5.

10 For further details, see Austin, *Politics in Ghana*, pp. 250–316.

11 *Ibid.* p. 344.

12 *Ibid.* p. 384–95.

13 This assertion is based on evidence presented in Owusu, *Uses and Abuses*, pp. 195–241; and by Richard Crook in 'The CPP in Ashanti, 1959–66', paper delivered to a seminar on 'The CPP in Retrospect' at the Institute of Commonwealth Studies, University of Oxford, 26 May 1973.

14 See Bjorn Beckman, *Organising the Farmers: Cocoa Politics and National Development in Ghana* (Uppsala, 1976), pp. 229–47.

15 This is not of course to deny that many unemployed display impressive skill and initiative in organising themselves on a small scale for criminal or semi-criminal activities; or that such activities might be seen as carrying political implications.

16 Peace, 'Lagos Proletariat', p. 284.

17 Behind the moral sanctions operating to maintain the principle of leadership accountability lies ultimately, of course, the threat of physical force. Instances

of individual officials' being actually beaten up appear to have been extremely rare in the union's history. But there have been numerous occasions on which a 'mob' from Location has surrounded the union headquarters threatening physical violence if their demands were not adopted as official union policy.

18 Peace, *op. cit.*
19 See, for example, J. C. Mitchell, *The Kalela Dance*, Rhodes-Livingstone Paper, 27 (Manchester, 1957), and Epstein, *Politics in an Urban African Community.*
20 Robin Cohen, *Labour and Politics in Nigeria* (London, 1974), p. 24.
21 See, for example, Howard Wolpe, *Urban Politics in Nigeria* (Berkeley, 1974), pp. 7–8.
22 See, for example, Billy J. Dudley, *Parties and Politics in Northern Nigeria* (London, 1968), pp. 238–41, and Dorothy Remy, 'Economic Security and Industrial Unionism: A Nigerian Case Study', in R. Sandbrook and R. Cohen (eds.), *The Development of an African Working Class* (London, 1975), pp. 161–77.

Chapter 10. The political culture of the railway workers

1 E. J. Hobsbawm, *Labouring Men* (London, 1968), p. 374.
2 Gabriel Almond and Sidney Verba, *The Civic Culture* (Princeton, 1963), p. 17.
3 This was perhaps the most commonly used phrase at mass meetings of the two Railway Unions which the writer attended in June–September 1971.
4 Interview with A. E. Forson, 3 September 1971.
5 Interview with J. K. Baaku, 12 September 1971.
6 Speech by Kofi Imbeah at a union mass meeting, 14 August 1971.
7 Interviews with Isaac Aygepong and Francis Dadzie, 26 August 1971.
8 The idea of forming a Labour Party was briefly discussed by the railway workers in 1949, 1969 and November 1971. *RUA*, Railway Union Executive Council Minutes, 3 April 1949 and 7 March 1969.
9 V. I. Lenin, *What Is to be done?*, ed. S. V. Utechin (Oxford, 1963), pp. 68–81.
10 See, for example, the references to railway unionism in Davies, *African Trade Unions*, esp. pp. 141–2, and R. D. Grillo, *African Railwaymen: Solidarity and Opposition in an East African Labour Force* (Cambridge, 1973). Also, for interesting accounts of particular railway strikes, see H. E. Conway, 'Labour Protest Activity in Sierra Leone', *Labour History*, 15 (1968), pp. 49–63, and C. Allen, 'Union–Party Relationships in Francophone West Africa: A Critique of "Teleguidage" Interpretations', in R. Sandbrook and R. Cohen (eds.) *The Development of an African Working Class* (London, 1975), pp. 99–125. A most moving account of the 1947–8 French West African rail strike is provided in Sembene Ousmane's novel, *God's Bits of Wood* (London, 1970).
11 Such literature includes Marxist pamphlets, of course, but these do not seem to have had much impact on the African rank and file, except perhaps in the Sudan. For information on the Sudanese labour movement I am indebted to conversations with Bill Warren.

CONCLUSION

1 Berg and Butler, '*Trade Unions*'.

Bibliography of sources cited

ARCHIVES

Ghana National Archives, Accra and Sekondi (*GNA*)
Ghana TUC Archives, Accra (*GTUCA*)
Railway Administration Archives, Takoradi (*RAA*)
Railway Union Archives, Sekondi (*RUA*)
Mines Employees' Union Archives, Tarkwa (*MEUA*) [In 1961 the official title of
   the Mines Employees' Union was changed to the Mineworkers' Union]

OFFICIAL

(a) *Reports of Committees and Commissions* (published by the Ministry of
       Information, Accra)
     *Report of the Commission of Enquiry into the Affairs of the National Housing
       Corporation*, 1967.
     *Report of the Commission on the Structure and Remuneration of the Public
       Services in Ghana*, 1967. [*Mills–Odoi Report*]
     Report of the Commission of Enquiry into the Funds of the Ghana TUC, 1968.
     *Report of the (Jiagge) Commission to Enquire into the Assets of Specified
       Persons*, 1969.
     *Report of the Committee on Review of Salaries and Pensions in the Public
       Services of Ghana*, 1969. [*Mensah Report*]
     Report of the Commission of Enquiry into Obuasi Disturbances, 1970.

(b) *Gold Coast/Ghana Government*
     Gold Coast Handbook, London, 1928.
     Gold Coast, *Census of the Population, 1948*, Crown Agents for the Colonies,
       London, 1950.
     Gold Coast, *Legislative Assembly Debates, 1955*, Accra.
     Gold Coast, Office of the Government Statistician, *Sekondi-Takoradi
       Survey of Population and Household Budgets, 1955*, Statistical and Eco-
       nomic Papers, no. 4, Accra, 1956.
     Ghana, Census Office, *1960 Population Census of Ghana*, Accra, 1961.
     Ghana, *Central Revenue Department's General Information on Taxation in
       Ghana*, Accra, 1970.
     Ghana, Labour Department, *Annual Reports, 1951–67*, Accra.

234

Ghana, Office of the Planning Commission, *Seven Year Development Plan* Accra, 1964.
Ghana, Office of the President, *Statement by the Government on the Recent Conspiracy*, Accra, 1961.
Ghana, *Parliamentary Debates: Official Reports, 1957– *, Accra.
Ghana, *Survey of High-Level Manpower in Ghana, 1960*, Accra, 1961.

(c) *Ghana TUC*

Gold Coast TUC Policy Statement, Accra, 1953 (mimeo).
In the Cause of Ghana Workers, Accra, 1962.
Proposals Submitted by the TUC (Ghana) to the Salary Review Commission, Accra, 1971 (mimeo).
Report of the First Biennial Congress of the TUC of Ghana, Accra, 1966.
Report on the Activities of the TUC, Third Biennial Congress, Accra, 1970.

NEWSPAPERS

Ashanti Pioneer (formerly *The Pioneer*), independent, Kumasi.
Daily Graphic, independent, Accra.
Evening News, organ of the Convention People's Party, Accra.
Ghanaian Times, independent, Accra.
Ghana Workers' Bulletin, organ of the TUC, Accra.
The Light, organ of the TUC, Accra.
The Spectator, independent, Accra.
The Spokesman, independent, Accra.
The Star, organ of the Progress Party, Accra.
The Worker, organ of the TUC, Accra.
West Africa, independent, London.

PUBLISHED (BOOKS AND ARTICLES)]

Allen, C., 'Union–Party Relationships in Francophone West Africa: A Critique of "Teleguidage" Interpretations', in R. Sandbrook and R. Cohen (eds.), *The Development of an African Working Class*, London, Longman, 1975, pp. 99–125.
Almond, G. and S. Verba, *The Civic Culture*, Princeton, Princeton University Press, 1963.
Anon., *The Birth of the Second Republic*, Accra, Editorial and Publishing Services, 1970.
Apter, D., *The Gold Coast in Transition*, Princeton, Princeton University Press, 1955.
Arden-Clarke, Sir C., 'Eight Years of Transition in Ghana', *African Affairs*, 57, 226, January 1958, pp. 29–37.
Armah, A. K., *The Beautyful Ones Are not yet Born*, London, Heinemann, 1969.
Arrighi, G., 'International Corporations, Labour Aristocracies and Economic Development in Tropical Africa', in R. I. Rhodes (ed.), *Imperialism and Underdevelopment: A Reader*, New York, Monthly Review Press, 1970, pp. 220–67.

235

Bibliography

Arrighi, G. and J. Saul, 'Socialism and Economic Development in Tropical Africa', *Journal of Modern African Studies*, 6, 2, 1968, pp. 141–69.

Arrighi, G. and J. Saul, 'Nationalism and Revolution in Sub-Saharan Africa', in R. Miliband and J. Saville (eds.), *The Socialist Register 1969*, New York and London, 1969, pp. 137–88.

Austin, D., *Politics in Ghana, 1946–60*, London, Oxford University Press, 1964.

Baeta, C. G., *Prophetism in Ghana*, London, SCM Press, 1962.

Bates, R., *Unions, Parties and Political Development*, New Haven and London, Yale University Press, 1971.

Beckman, B., *Organising the Farmers: Cocoa Politics and National Development in Ghana*, Uppsala, Scandinavian Institute of African Studies, 1976.

Bentum, B., *Trade Unions in Chains*, Accra, TUC, 1967.

Berg, E., 'The Development of a Labour Force in Sub-Saharan Africa', *Economic Development and Cultural Change*, 13, 1965, pp. 394–412.

Berg, E. and J. Butler, 'Trade Unions', in J. S. Coleman and C. S. Rosberg (eds.), *Political Parties and National Integration in Tropical Africa*, Berkeley, University of California Press, 1964, pp. 340–81.

Birmingham, W. B., 'An Index of Real Wages of the Unskilled Labourer in Accra', *Economic Bulletin of Ghana*, 4, 3, 1960, pp. 2–6.

Blay, J. B., *The Gold Coast Mines Employees' Union*, Devon, A. H. Stockwell, 1950.

Busia, K. A., *Report on a Social Survey of Sekondi-Takoradi*, Accra, Government Printer, 1950.

Cohen, R., *Labour and Politics in Nigeria*, London, Heinemann, 1974.

Conway, H. E., 'Labour Protest Activity in Sierra Leone', *Labour History*, 15, 1968, pp. 49–63.

Cowan, E. A., *Evolution of Trade Unionism in Ghana*, Accra, TUC, 1961.

Datta, A., 'The Fante Asafo: A Re-Examination', *Africa*, 42, 4, October 1972, pp. 305–15.

Davies, L., *African Trade Unions*, Harmondsworth, Penguin, 1966.

Davison, R. B., 'The Story of the Gold Coast Railway', *West Africa*, 11 August 1956, p. 587.

Dowse, R., 'Military and Police Rule', in D. Austin and R. Luckham (eds.), *Politicians and Soldiers in Ghana*, London, Frank Cass, 1975, pp. 16–37.

Drake, St Clair and L. A. Lacy, 'Government versus the Unions: The Sekondi-Takoradi Strike, 1961', in G. Carter (ed.), *Politics in Africa: 7 Cases*, New York, Harcourt, Brace and World Inc., 1966, pp. 67–118.

Dudley, B. J., *Parties and Politics in Northern Nigeria*, London, Frank Cass, 1968.

Dunn, J., 'Politics in Asunafo', in D. Austin and R. Luckham (eds.), *Politicians and Soldiers in Ghana*, London, Frank Cass, 1975, pp. 164–213.

Dutta-Roy, D. K., *The Eastern Region Household Budget Survey*, Legon, Institute of Statistical Social and Economic Research, 1968.

Epstein, A. L., *Politics in an African Urban Community*, Manchester, Manchester University Press, 1958.

Ewusi, K., *The Distribution of Monetary Incomes in Ghana*, Legon, Institute of Statistical Social and Economic Research, 1971.

Fanon, F., *The Wretched of the Earth*, London, Macgibbon and Kee, 1965.

Fortes, M., 'The Impact of the War on British West Africa', *International Affairs*, 21, 2, April 1945, pp. 206–20.

236

Gerritsen, R., 'The Evolution of the Ghana Trade Union Congress under the Convention People's Party: Towards a Re-Interpretation', *Transactions of the Historical Society of Ghana*, 13, 1974, pp. 229–44.

Goldthorpe, J. E., 'Educated Africans', in A. Southall (ed.), *Social Change in Modern Africa*, London, Oxford University Press, 1961, pp. 145–58.

Gould, P., *The Development of the Transportation Pattern in Ghana*, Northwestern University Studies in Geography, 5, 1960.

Graesser, M., 'Politics in Sekyere', in D. Austin and R. Luckham (eds.), *Politicians and Soldiers in Ghana*, London, Frank Cass, 1975, pp. 264–99.

Grillo, R., *African Railwaymen: Solidarity and Opposition in an East African Labour Force*, Cambridge, Cambridge University Press, 1973.

Hart, K., 'Informal Income Opportunities and Urban Employment in Ghana', *Journal of Modern African Studies*, 2, 1, 1973, pp. 141–69.

Hill, P., *The Migrant Cocoa Farmers of Southern Ghana*, Cambridge, Cambridge University Press, 1963.

Hinchcliffe, K., 'Labour Aristocracy – a Northern Nigerian Case Study', *Journal of Modern African Studies*, 12, 1, 1974, pp. 57–67.

Hobsbawm, E., *Labouring Men*, London, Weidenfeld and Nicholson, 1968.

Kaldor, N., 'Taxation for Economic Development', *Journal of Modern African Studies*, 1, 1, March 1963, pp. 7–23.

Kautsky, J., *The Political Consequences of Modernisation*, New York, John Wiley, 1972.

Kimble, D., *A Political History of Ghana, 1850–1928*, Oxford, Oxford University Press, 1963.

Landsberger, H., 'The Labour Elite: Is It Revolutionary?', in S. M. Lipset and A. Solari (eds.), *Elites in Latin America*, New York, Oxford University Press, 1967, pp. 267–90.

Lenin, V., *What is to be Done?*, ed. S. V. Utechin, Oxford, Clarendon Press, 1963.

Leys, C., 'Politics in Kenya: The Development of Peasant Society', *British Journal of Political Science*, 1, 1971, pp. 307–38.

Lloyd, P. C., *Classes, Crises and Coups*, London, Macgibbon and Kee, 1971.

Lloyd, P. C., *Power and Independence: Urban Africans' Perception of Social Inequality*, London, Routledge and Kegan Paul, 1974.

Marx, K., *The Eighteenth Brumaire of Louis Bonaparte*, New York International Publishers, 1932.

Meynaud, J. and A. Salah-Bey, *Trade Unionism in Africa*, London, Methuen, 1967.

Millen, B., *The Political Role of Labor in Developing Countries*, Washington, Brookings Institution, 1963.

Mitchell, J. C., *The Kalela Dance*, Rhodes-Livingstone Paper, 27, Manchester, Manchester University Press, 1957.

Murray, A. J. and J. A. Crocket, *Report on the Prevalence of Silicosis and Tuberculosis among Mineworkers in the Gold Coast*, Accra, Government Printing Office, 1941.

Neufeld, M., 'The Inevitability of Political Unionism in Underdeveloped Countries', *Industrial and Labour Relations Review*, 13, April 1960, pp. 363–86.

O'Brien, D. B. Cruise, *Saints and Politicians*, Cambridge, Cambridge University Press, 1975.

Ousmane, S., *God's Bits of Wood*, London, Heinemann, 1970.

Owusu, M., *Uses and Abuses of Political Power*, Chicago, University of Chicago Press, 1970.

Owusu, M., 'Politics in Swedru', in D. Austin and R. Luckham (eds.), *Politicians and Soldiers in Ghana*, London, Frank Cass, 1975, pp. 253–6.

Patrick, J., *What Is a Trade Union?*, Nairobi, Kenya Labour Department, 1951.

Peace, A., 'Industrial Protest in Nigeria', in E. de Kadt and G. P. Williams (eds.), *Sociology of Development*, London, Tavistock Press, 1973, pp. 141–67.

Peace, A., 'The Lagos Proletariat: Labour Aristocrats or Popular Militants', in R. Sandbrook and R. Cohen (eds.), *The Development of an African Working Class*, London, Longman, 1975, pp. 281–302.

Peasah, J., 'Politics in Abuakwa', in D. Austin and R. Luckham (eds.), *Politicians and Soldiers in Ghana*, London, Frank Cass, 1975, pp. 214–32.

Peil, M., *The Ghanaian Factory Worker: Industrial Man in Africa*, Cambridge, Cambridge University Press, 1972.

Pinkney, R., *Ghana under Military Rule, 1966–69*, London, Methuen, 1972.

Rathbone, R., 'Businessmen in Ghanaian Politics', *Journal of Development Studies*, 9, 3, April 1973, pp. 391–402.

Remy, D., 'Economic Security and Industrial Unionism: A Nigerian Case Study', in R. Sandbrook and R. Cohen (eds.), *The Development of an African Working Class*, London, Longman, 1975, pp. 161–77.

Rimmer, D., 'The Crisis in the Ghanaian Economy', *Journal of Modern African Studies*, 4, 1, 1966, pp. 17–32.

Roper, J. I., *Labour Problems in West Africa*, Harmondsworth, Penguin, 1958.

Rourke, B., *Wages and Incomes of Agricultural Workers in Ghana*, Legon, Institute of Statistical, Social and Economic Research, 1970.

Saloway, Sir R., 'The New Gold Coast', *International Affairs*, 32, 4, October 1955, pp. 469–76.

Saul, J., 'African Peasants and Revolution', *Review of African Political Economy*, 1, 1974, pp. 41–68.

Schwab, W., 'Social Stratification in Gwelo', in A. Southall (ed.), *Social Change in Modern Africa*, London, Oxford University Press, 1961, pp. 126–44.

Tettegah, J., *A New Chapter for Ghana Labour*, Accra, TUC, 1958.

Tettegah, J., *Towards Nkrumaism: The Role and Tasks of the Trade Unions*, Accra, TUC, 1962.

Thomas, R., 'Forced Labour in British West Africa: The Case of the Northern Territories of the Gold Coast 1906–27', *Journal of African History*, 14, 1973, pp. 79–103.

Trachtman, L., 'The Labour Movement of Ghana: A Study of Political Unionism', *Economic Development and Cultural Change*, 10, January 1962, pp. 190–9.

Uphoff, N., 'The Expansion of Employment Associated with Growth of GNP: A Projective Model and Its Implications for Ghana', *Economic Bulletin of Ghana*, 2, 4, 1972, pp. 3–16.

Weeks, J., 'Wage Policy and the Colonial Legacy – A Comparative Study', *Journal of Modern African Studies*, 9, 3, 1971, pp. 361–87.

238

Weeks, J., 'An Exploration into the Problem of Urban Imbalance in Africa', *Manpower and Unemployment Research in Africa*, 6, 2, 1973, pp. 9–37.

Wolpe, H., *Urban Politics in Nigeria*, Berkeley, University of California Press, 1974.

Worsley, P., 'The Concept of Populism', in G. Ionescu and E. Gellner (eds.), *Populism, Its Meaning and National Characteristics*, London, Weidenfeld and Nicolson, 1970, pp. 212–50.

Wright, R., *Black Power*, London, Dobson, 1956.

Wudu, F., *A Fallen Labour Hero of Ghana*, Accra, State Publishing Corporation, 1968.

UNPUBLISHED

Cawson, A., 'Traditional Organisation and Urban Politics: Political Parties and the Cape Coast Asafo', paper delivered to the Institute of Commonwealth Studies Seminar on African Urban Politics, London, 1973.

Crook, R., 'The CPP in Ashanti, 1959–66', paper delivered to the Institute of Commonwealth Studies Seminar on the CPP in Retrospect, University of Oxford, 26 May 1973.

Holm, J., 'Ideology and Socio-Political Development in Nkrumah's Ghana', PhD thesis, University of Chicago, 1966.

Holmes, A. B., 'Economic and Political Organisations in the Gold Coast: 1920–45', PhD thesis, University of Chicago, 1972.

Lacy, L. A., 'A History of Railway Unionism in Ghana', MA thesis, University of Legon, 1965.

Pratt, R., 'Political Opposition in Ghana, 1966–72', MA thesis, SOAS, University of London, 1973.

Roberts, B., 'Labour in the Tropical Territories of the Commonwealth', PhD thesis, London School of Economics, 1964.

Index

240

242